SOLDIERS OF FREEDOM

SOLDIERS OF FREEDOM

*An
Illustrated
History of
African Americans
in the Armed
Forces*

KAI WRIGHT

BLACK DOG
& LEVENTHAL
PUBLISHERS
NEW YORK

Published by
Black Dog & Leventhal Publishers, Inc.
151 West 19th Street
New York, NY 10011

Distributed by
Workman Publishing Company
708 Broadway
New York, NY 10003

Manufactured in Spain

Cover and design by Liz Driesbach

ISBN: 1-57912-253-1

h g f e d c b a

Library of Congress Cataloging-in-Publication Data

Wright, Kai.
Soldiers of freedom : an illustrated history of African Americans in
the Armed Forces / Kai Wright.
p. cm.
Includes bibliographical references and index.
ISBN 1-57912-253-1
1. United States--Armed Forces--African Americans--History. 2. United
States--Armed Forces--African Americans--Biography. I. Title.
UB418.A47 W75 2002
355'.008996'073--dc21
2002008000

CONTENTS

ACKNOWLEDGMENTS

Over the years of our nation's history, research librarians working in the people's employ have collected, catalogued and maintained millions of images such as those presented in this book, ensuring their availability to the American public. It is to this cadre of civil servant scholars, the keepers of our history, that we all owe a great debt. For this book, I am particularly grateful for the patient guidance offered to me by the research staffs of the Library of Congress's Prints and Photographs Division, the National Archives and Records Administration's Still Picture Unit, and the Defense Visual Information Center. The Library of Congress and the National Archives, often taken for granted by policy makers and overlooked by citizens, house some of the country's most valuable resources. No visit to Washington, D.C. is complete without touring these institutions, both to witness their beautiful architecture and to learn about the wealth of resources that they offer. And we must all insist that our leaders continue to use our tax dollars in support of these institutions, making the treasures they store accessible to generations of Americans to come.

In addition to the scores of historians whose work I have drawn upon in putting together Soldiers of Freedom, a number of individuals have assisted in helping me wade through the history and navigate the logistics of publishing this book. I thank Dr. Frank Smith, founder of the African American Civil War Memorial Museum in Washington, D.C. and the research staff of Howard University's Moorland-Springarn Research Center for their help with the Civil War era. Thanks to Aimee Lessard, a proud Marine, for allowing me to crib off of her in familiarizing myself with military protocols and ranks. And thanks to Barbara Oliver and her colleagues at the Library of Congress's photoduplication service center for shepherding my large and always incorrectly submitted requests.

The book is another amazing brainchild of my publisher, J.P. Leventhal, and I thank him and Michael Driscoll for recruiting me to work on it. Thanks to my editor Rebecca Koh, who gracefully guided the project from an idea to a finished product. Thanks also to Liz Driesbach whose design has brought both words and images to life.

Finally, as with everything, my work on this project was made possible by the love and support of my friends and family. From my parents and grandparents to my partner Mark Bailey, thanks to all of you who have always provided the immovable foundation I need to strike out on one exciting adventure after another.

INTRODUCTION

The truism "war is hell" did not begin with Vietnam. It was the first war in which the gruesome details came streaming into American living rooms every evening via the media, but it was not the first to be a nightmarish affair. At points during the Revolutionary War, many of General George Washington's troops fought clothed only in old blankets. They went days without food and water, drinking from streams filthy with both human and animal feces. They worked day and night, seven days a week, and were rarely paid a cent of their promised salaries. Their most mortal threats came not from British troops but from starvation and disease; during the dreadful winter of 1777 at Valley Forge, some 2,500 American rebels died largely from exposure to the unforgiving elements.

These horrors did not end with the Revolution. In Korea, troops shipped in from the Pacific fought through the war's first bitter winter with nothing but warm weather supplies, sometimes marching barefoot through snow and ice. Throughout American history, warfare has proved a painful and ugly business, robbing society of vibrant young men and women in the prime of their lives—too often for purposes far less noble than our nation's leaders have professed. War is not something to glorify, but rather to disdain.

Why, then, this book? Because in post-Vietnam America, where citizens have more willingly and openly condemned the act of war than in previous eras, our society has too often also condemned those charged, usually by force of law, with carrying it out. So this book honors the deeds of men and women of any race who have sacrificed their lives in battles not of their own making.

As a volume of black history, however, this book has another purpose. Throughout time, the African American soldiers who have participated in this country's wars have done so not merely in defense of the nation. America's longevity, frankly, has often been but a tangential result of service in the minds of black soldiers. From the Revolution through the Civil War, blacks fought primarily in an effort to secure their collective freedom. Each conflict brought a renewed debate within the community about whether and how African Americans should participate, a discussion that always turned on what strategy and which combatant was most likely to hasten emancipation. Following the Civil War and throughout most of the 20th century, blacks by and large fought in a two-pronged effort to earn their birthright of full American citizenship and assert their humanity in the face of charges that African

Americans were too cowardly, stupid, and treacherous to be trusted on the battlefield. And in more recent years, many African Americans have chosen careers in the armed forces largely because they provide greater opportunities than any available in the civilian workforce. This is not to say that the African American service member's patriotism is less profound than his or her white colleague's, but rather that it is more nuanced. So this book chronicles the paradoxical struggle of the black soldier throughout history; the simultaneous fight on behalf of and in opposition to America.

This odd balance has been made even more precarious by the fact that the military has always stood at the front line of our nation's race war. From the days of slavery to the civil rights movement, black political leaders believed the military's unjust racial policies to be the most vulnerable to attack, and thus targeted considerable resources at changing them. And indeed, time and again, the necessities of battle trumped those of segregation, causing the military to moderate its institutional racism. African American leaders have also repeatedly gambled that changes in military race relations would spark similar reassessments in society at large. This is why Frederick Douglass so insistently pushed Abraham Lincoln to allow blacks to fight and then, once the president conceded, tirelessly recruited young freemen to enlist. His sons were among the first to sign up for the historic Massachusetts 54th Regiment, made famous by the Academy Award–winning movie *Glory*. During World War I, W.E.B. DuBois spearheaded a similarly relentless campaign for more and better assignments for black troops and led recruiting efforts to enlist them. During the buildup to World War II, Asa Philip Randolph considered integrating the ranks so important a goal that he risked all of his hard-fought political capital in a dangerous stand-off with the White House while trying to end military segregation.

In the short term, few of those leaders' gambles paid off, as liberalized military policies made no immediate impact on the nation's racial caste system as a whole. Moreover, it seemed that for every inch of progress they eked out of the armed forces, black leaders lost a foot in the subsequent backlash within the institution. But in the process they forced the services to confront some of America's most volatile racial fault lines long before the rest of the nation.

Ironically, today's military finds itself wading through America's social quagmires once again. Debates range from whether gay men and women should be allowed to serve openly to questions about affirmative action and its effectiveness in creating leadership opportunities for women and minorities. Those who wish to block progress offer the same argument as their predecessors who stood against moderating racial policies as far back as the Civil War: that the military cannot outpace the society it protects. On the contrary, the armed forces has a legacy of being a pioneer in American social change. When President Harry Truman kicked Jim Crow out of the armed forces in 1948, most of the country was still years, arguably decades, from doing the same. And today, Colin Powell's unparalleled place in American history stands as the payoff for the army's unprecedented efforts to advance African Americans to leadership positions during the 1970s. The only question is whether the military will continue with its tradition, by dealing with hot-button issues such as those surrounding gay and female service members, as well as by tackling the lingering racial disparities in its upper ranks.

The photos presented here are primarily the work of military photographers, and almost all are in the public domain. They are an example of the incredible treasures tucked away in two of our country's most important institutions: the National Archives and Records Administration and the Library of Congress. From the Civil War forward, remarkable military photographers have trudged across battlefields around the world to document the experiences of their fellow service members. Their work is often overlooked in favor of that of photojournalists dispatched by news organizations, but it is no less captivating and insightful. Indeed, much of it presents dimensions of warfare that news photographers must bypass; thus it fills in the spaces between the flashes of immeasurable agony upon which war zone photojournalism often focuses. From depictions of the mundane labors of daily life to intimate portraits of young soldiers, the images military photographers have created over the years humanize a reality that those of us who have never been in battle cannot truly comprehend.

The images in this book are also far more articulate than the text in describing the African American military saga. They vividly reveal America's effort to blot the contributions of its black citizens from history. Despite the remarkable integration of the Continental Army, the absence of African Americans in art depicting the Revolutionary era is nearly absolute. Only those individuals who served alongside celebrated leaders such as Washington and the French general Lafayette are visible, and then only as meek servants. The reality of their contribution is far different.

Not until the Civil War do we begin to see regular efforts to visually document the existence of African Americans in military settings, and then, largely, only as part of Northern society's fascination with slaves fleeing the South through service in the Union Army. And while successful experiments with battlefield integration occurred in most conflicts, only with the Korean War do photographers begin, sporadically, to capture white and black service members working, fighting, and coexisting side by side. Throughout the history, we note the dearth of images depicting the contributions made by black women—or women of any race, for that matter.

But finally, the copious heroic portraits of Colin Powell and other minority service members found in the photo library of today's military reflect a vastly different institution than the one that has gone before. Even with the problems it continues to face, it is arguably far ahead of the nation it serves in embracing racial diversity and, indeed, harnessing that diversity as a valuable resource. These strides represent the ultimate payoff for the campaigns led by advocates like Douglass, DuBois, and Randolph. For not only has the U.S. Armed Forces made this progress as an institution, but—by producing officers such as Powell and the thousands of other African Americans who have used military service as a launching pad to successful civilian careers and lives of civic engagement—it has also, in fact, pushed forward the painstaking process of redrafting this nation's shameful racial legacy into a future filled with promise.

CHAPTER

1

CHOOSING
SIDES

*The Revolutionary
War Era*

Boston was still cold and snowy on the night of March 5, 1770, its residents cringing from what promised to be a prolonged winter. It was a tumultuous time, as tensions between the inhabitants of the Massachusetts colony and the British soldiers stationed there were steadily heightening. Rabble-rousing businessmen such as Samuel Adams had helped stir up opposition to ever increasing British taxes. And the notorious arrogance of the so-called redcoats charged with watching over the city enflamed the resentment of Adams and his cohorts. So when a dispute erupted that evening between the night watchman at the British headquarters and a colonist passerby, the icy peace of King Street exploded into the first firefight of the American Revolution.

The first official account of what Adams later dubbed the Boston Massacre comes from an investigation ordered by Boston's colonial officials. From that account forward, details of what happened in front of Custom House that night—and, more directly, how it happened—were sketchy and conflicting. What is clear is that when the confrontation ended, five men, all colonists, lay dead: Samuel Gray, Samuel Maverick, James Caldwell, Patrick Carr, and Crispus Attucks.

Attucks, a sailor who had been going by the name of Michael Johnson, was a fugitive from slavery.

There were actually three near-riots on the night of March 5. Mobs from each confrontation ultimately converged on the British military headquarters at King Street, where they began taunting and throwing snowballs at the guards. Attucks, whose ship was docked in Boston Harbor, was with a group of sailors in a tavern when the town's alarm bell rang. The men ran out to find the developing mob. Attucks made his way to the front of the crowd and, wielding a piece of firewood, led the group in daring the frightened soldiers to fire. As British Captain Thomas Preston ordered his men to stay calm, the mob's agitation grew. Attucks, in an attempt to escalate the conflict, began whacking a soldier's bayonet with his club and mocking him more intently. A tussle developed between the two, and Attucks emerged with the bayonet as the soldier fell to the snow. Invigorated, the mob's taunts rose.

According to the initial investigation, it is likely that a soldier confused the mob's shouts of "Why don't you fire?!" with a command to do so from Captain Preston. Others at the time charged that Preston in fact gave the order. And some historians believe that the embarrassed soldier whom Attucks bested rose, reclaimed his weapon, and fired on his attacker, prompting a barrage from the other troops. Attucks, according to the March 12 issue of Adams's patriot pamphlet, the *Boston Gazette*, had been

Paul Revere's 1770 sketch of the Boston Massacre depicts those present at the event as white.

The just man shall be in eternal remembrance

The brave Soldier of the Revolutionary War 1770.

Cripus Attucks, an escaped slave, is considered the first person killed in the conflict between Britain and her colonies.

RAN-away from his Master *William Brown* of *Framingham*, on the 30th of *Sept.* last, a Molatto Fellow, about 27 Years of Age, named *Crispas*, 6 Feet two Inches high, short curl'd Hair, his Knees nearer together than common ; had on a light colour'd Bearskin Coat, plain brown Fustian Jacket, or brown all-Wool one, new Buckskin Breeches, blue Yarn Stockings, and a check'd woollen Shirt. Whoever shall take up said Run-away, and convey him to his abovesaid Master, shall have *ten Pounds*, old Tenor Reward, and all necessary Charges paid. And all Masters of Vessels and others, are hereby caution'd against concealing or carrying off said Servant on Penalty of the Law. *Boston*, *October* 2, 1750.

Attucks's slaveholder published this 1750 ad offering a bounty for his capture and return.

"killed instantly; two balls entering his breast, one of them in special goring the right lobe of the lungs, and a great part of the liver most horribly." Paul Revere's sketch illustrating the confrontation, published in the same pamphlet, depicts all of those killed and wounded as white.

Attucks, however, was a mixed-race, or "mulatto," man. His father was African and his mother was Native American. In colonial America, that made him a slave, and a Framingham, Massachusetts, slaveholder, Deacon William Brown, claimed ownership. Attucks had escaped from Brown's clutches some twenty years before his death on King Street and taken up life as a sailor—where blacks were more than welcome—to make up for the white labor shortage that resulted from a widespread distaste for the perils of sea life. We owe perhaps the most colorful descriptions of Attucks to dubious sources. One of these is a bounty ad Brown placed in 1750 offering a ten-pound reward for the return of "a Mulatto Fellow, about 27 years of age, named Crispas, 6 Feet two Inches high, short, curl'd Hair, his Knees nearer together than common: had on a light colour'd Bearskin coat."

The other description came from president-to-be John Adams, who served as defense counsel for the British soldiers involved in the March 5 riot. An ardent advocate of the rule of law, Adams put aside his patriotism to defend the soldiers, securing a legal victory still credited as one of history's most skillful. His argument walked the fine line between damning the British military presence and defending the redcoats' individual actions. This defense helped to

Attucks is actually depicted as African American in this nineteenth-century drawing, published in William Nell's groundbreaking history of blacks in the Revolution.

paint a horrifying picture of the mob the soldiers faced, a depiction intensified by what may have amounted to America's first legal race baiting.

"To have this reinforcement," Adams thundered in his closing argument, describing the mob, "coming down under the command of a stout Mulatto fellow, whose very looks was enough to terrify any person, what had not the soldiers to fear? He had hardiness to fall in upon them, and with one hand took hold of a bayonet, and with the other knocked the man down: This was the behaviour of Attucks; to

whose mad behaviour, in all probability, the dreadful carnage of that night is chiefly ascribed."

John Adams's cousin Samuel and his fellow patriot agitators couldn't have agreed more—but, rather than damning him as a troublemaker, they lionized Attucks as the Revolution's first martyr. Later, as the ensuing war raged, Bostonians gathered annually to memorialize Attucks and the others killed during the Boston Massacre. Then and now, his memory has been showered with the sort of praise that future black martyrs for America have never received.

Few black Revolutionary heroes received recognition such as the memorial built in the Boston Commons in 1888 to honor Attucks and his fellow "martyrs."

A War for Independence

By the time a British soldier fired "the shot heard round the world" at Lexington in 1775, an American war for liberty and equality had been raging for nearly a century. From the slave trade's first violent clashes in West Africa to the slave insurrections that plagued Britain's colonies, scores of black men and women had already chosen to take up arms in an effort to win freedom. It comes as no surprise, then, that as the dispute between Britain and her American subjects erupted into war, both free and enslaved Africans in the colonies decided to join in. Some, betting that the rhetoric of the times would carry meaning for them as well, stood with the patriots. Others, tempted by offers of emancipation in exchange for service, or unconvinced that war's intoxication would actually move their owners to release them, cast their lot with the British occupiers. Still others served for more mundane reasons—such as the slaves who were forced to enlist in their owners' stead, or the free blacks who were drawn by the same $6.67 per month salary that enticed their white counterparts. (For the most part, neither black nor white soldiers ultimately received these promised payments.) Astonishingly, as with much of African American history before the abolition movement of the nineteenth century, the often heroic and dramatic actions of this sizable group of African American people have been largely forgotten.

Roughly five hundred thousand of the 2.5 million people living in the colonies at the war's outset were black. Beyond the broad horrors of the chattel slave system, we know little about who these men and women were and what their lives entailed. We do know, however, that tens of thousands of them par-

Die Einwohner von Boston werfen den englisch-ostindischen Thee ins Meer am 18. December 1773.

Revolutionary Era art depicted African Americans as animalistic or childlike, such as in this drawing of the Boston Tea Party.

While the fact of their army's integration was an unending source of tension for the new nation's planners, they had little choice in the matter. Britain, even without committing significant resources to the campaign, could easily outman them. Furthermore, a significant portion of the colonists themselves were either indifferent to the dispute or fully in support of the Royal Government. So the architects of America's revolution could ill afford to limit their recruitment. At the same time, however, if the new nation was to succeed, the southern colonies were going to have to be appeased. And more than anything, the plantation class that led in that region wanted to preserve the economy to which it owed its existence—an economy buttressed by brutally enforced slave labor. Arming those very slaves—or, worse, enticing them to service with hopes of liberty—was anathema. And so, the Continental Congress and state legislatures uncomfortably wrestled with this paradox throughout the war. They ultimately sidestepped the issue by drafting one decree after another intended to control black recruitment while simultaneously ignoring the unchecked enlistment of African American fighters in both the national and state armies.

But the Continental Army's integration did not make it a bastion of racial equality. Black soldiers were still considered inferior to their white colleagues. They were rarely promoted yet often given the most dangerous assignments. When sick, they received the worst treatment. When out of battle, they drew the most menial and degrading work. And when the battle reports were written, they rarely received credit. Despite this treatment, countless black American soldiers, motivated by factors about which we can now only speculate, fought tirelessly for America's independence, performing strikingly heroic deeds from the war's first battle to its last.

ticipated in the Revolutionary War—as laborers, seamen, servants, infantrymen, gravediggers, spies, and in countless other roles. While a greater number fought for the British, a significant portion of the American forces were black. By 1779, it is believed, one in eight soldiers in the Continental Army were African American. It would, in fact, stand as the most integrated U.S. fighting force until the Vietnam War.

6

Lexington, Concord, and Bunker Hill

The Revolutionary War began in earnest on April 19, 1775. The British, having learned that the banned Massachusetts Congress was raising an army to lead a colonial rebellion, decided to storm the towns of Concord and Lexington in order to commandeer the colonists' gunpowder. (Gunpowder was a rarity in the American colonies, as the British had limited its import in order to control the potential for rebellion.) A step ahead of the British, the nascent rebel force had stationed Paul Revere to monitor the redcoats' advance. When British forces began moving late on the night of the eighteenth, Revere famously rode ahead on horseback, giving the elite minutemen stationed at Concord and Lexington advance warning. Throughout the following day, the British and rebel militiamen met on battlefields around Massachusetts in brief skirmishes. The Battle of Lexington lasted about fifteen minutes, the Battle of Concord five. The British routed the Lexington militia, but the rebels successfully blocked Concord Bridge. As the British marched back toward Boston, bands of rebels struck at them in guerilla ambushes, taking a small toll and then retreating for cover.

African Americans, enslaved and free, participated in all of these battles. Famous figures such as preacher and poet Lemuel Haynes joined scores of black history's faceless names—people such as Cato Bordman, Pomp Blackman, Cuff Whitemore, and Cato Wood—in fighting and dying alongside white colonists to launch America's war for independence.

Most of these men's stories have been lost, their names and lives omitted from the Revolution's first accounts forward. Modern historians, however, have

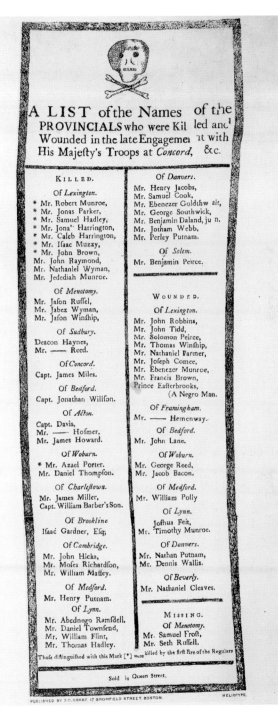

Prince Estabrook was America's first black casualty of war. His is the only name not given the title "Mr." in the list of dead and wounded at Lexington and Concord.

been able to piece together some names from lists of dead and injured compiled by field commanders. While whites were listed as "Mr." and then a surname, blacks were usually identified by first name and listed as "a Negro." Nevertheless, in a few cases, building on the work of pioneering nineteenth-century African American historian William Nell, scholars have salvaged enough snippets of these men's lives to at least offer a few brief profiles.

PRINCE ESTABROOK

The supposedly elite minutemen gathered at Lexington in April 1775 consisted of a mere seventy-seven poorly trained men and boys. Among them was a slave from the area named Prince Estabrook.

Eight rebels were killed and nine wounded at Lexington. While Estabrook escaped unharmed, he appears on a list of those wounded in the subsequent Battle of Concord. He is thus believed to be the first African American casualty of war. In a broadside listing the "Provincials" wounded and killed in the battle, Estabrook is listed as "Prince Easterbrooks, a Negro man." He is the only name on the list not identified as "Mr."

In an October 1883 issue of *Harper's* magazine, artist Howard Pyle published a drawing of the famous battle on Lexington Green. Unlike most pre-twentieth-century renderings of Revolutionary War battles, which almost as a rule ignored the black fighters' existence, Pyle's drawing includes an image of Estabrook. Pyle depicts the soldier as a stern-faced man, standing in the front lines of a group of minutemen, a number of which have fallen. Sporting a long coat, he appears to be either among a group of soldiers hit by British volleys or pausing to observe those fallen comrades.

Howard Pyle's drawing of the battle on Lexington Green depicts Estabrook as an essential part of the battle.

PETER SALEM

With the British encamped in Boston following Lexington and Concord, the rebels surrounded the port city in an effort to drive them out of Massachusetts. One of the war's most well known engagements, the Battle of Bunker Hill, grew out of this effort. Over a dozen African Americans served in that dramatic affair, under the leadership of Colonel William Prescott, who famously ordered his troops to hold fire "till you see the whites of their eyes." A twenty-five-year-old Framingham, Massachusetts, slave named Peter Salem was among the few African Americans whose valor at Bunker Hill has been recorded in the annals of history.

This is a dummy caption. Final captions are TK.

Peter Salem famously slaying the arrogant British major John Pitcairn.

Salem, whose last name comes from his birthplace, was purchased by Major Lawson Buckminster just as the war began. He and Buckminster were momentarily made equal by battle when they fought together at Concord. Following Concord, Salem enlisted in the integrated First Massachusetts Regiment and joined the 1,500 or so militiamen dug in at Bunker Hill. He is credited with slaying the arrogant British leader of the forces at Lexington and Concord, Major John Pitcairn.

The bloody battle began with British warships firing volleys onto the hill, attempting to dislodge the rebels, who outmanned them, before sending in

John Trumbull's 1801 painting of the Battle of Bunker Hill includes both Peter Salem and Salem Poor. It is one of few contemporary portraits of the war to include black soldiers.

marines. Hunkered down, Salem and his cohorts patiently followed Prescott's order and awaited Pitcairn's charge up the hill. When the redcoats got within around fifty yards, they opened fire, decimating the British front lines. It took three charges up the hill before the rebels, running out of ammunition, began to retreat. As the rebels retreated, Pitcairn, according to Samuel Swett's 1818 account of the battle, thrust his sword in the air and proclaimed, "The day is ours." At that moment, Salem took aim and "shot him through." Militia commanders would later honor Salem by presenting him to General George Washington.

In 1786, John Trumbull, who was among those who watched the battle from Boston's rooftops and surrounding hillsides, painted what is perhaps the Revolutionary War's most memorable image. His *Battle of Bunker Hill* still hangs in the U.S. Capitol building's rotunda in Washington, D.C. It is hailed as one of America's most gripping, and realistic, artistic renderings of war. In it, Trumbull depicts two African Americans. One, a musket bearer, is poised behind a white officer in the foreground of the painting. Another is less prominently placed under the flag at the top of the painting. There has been some dispute over which of the two men is intended to be Salem. Later engravings of the work omitted Trumbull's black heroes. Nevertheless, the painting is credited with bringing black military contributions to the minds of an otherwise oblivious Revolutionary-era America.

SALEM POOR

Salem Poor is believed to be the other black soldier depicted in Trumbull's *Battle of Bunker Hill.* Like

Peter Salem, Poor's militia commanders celebrated his heroism during the battle and lauded him before the rebel nation's leaders.

Poor, a twenty-eight-year-old free man from Andover, enlisted himself in the Massachusetts militia, under the command of Captain Benjamin Ames, not long before Bunker Hill. While the details of his actions are not known, he is credited with having killed British Lieutenant Colonel James Abercrombie. On December 5, 1775, Colonel Prescott led fourteen officers in asking the General Court of Massachusetts to honor Poor as "a Brave & gallant Soldier." The petition offers rare written proof of African Americans' bravery during the War of Independence.

"We declare," the petition read, "that a Negro Man Called Salem Poor . . . behaved like an Experienced Soldier, to Set forth Particulars of his conduct Would be Tedious. Wee would Only begg leave to Say in the Person of this said Negro Centers a Brave & gallant Soldier. The Reward due to so great and Distinguished a Caracter, Wee Submit to the Congress."

There is, however, no record of Poor ever receiving such a reward. Poor would nevertheless continue fighting with the rebels throughout the war. He was among the storied survivors of the winter of 1777–78 at Valley Forge, where at least 2,500 soldiers and 500 horses died in six months from exposure to the weather, starvation, and disease.

BARZILLAI LEW

Peter Salem and Salem Poor were joined at Bunker Hill by a number of other black soldiers whose particular contributions were never recorded. They included men such as Seymour Burr of Connecticut, Alexander Ames and Titus Coburn of Andover, Massachusetts, Cato Howe of Plymouth, Massachusetts, Jude Howe of Exeter, Massachusetts, and several more. Throughout the battle, their spirits were driven by the playing of a black fifer and drummer named Barzillai Lew.

Lew, a thirty-two-year-old free black man born of free parents, was a veteran of the French and Indian Wars, as was his father. According to historian Gail Buckley, the Lew family—originally from an all-black settlement in Dracut, Massachusetts, just outside of Boston—has fought in every major American war since the Revolution.

The Lews were a musical family, and when Barzillai joined the Twenty-seventh Massachusetts Regiment in May of 1775, he enlisted as a fifer and drummer. He first fought at Ticonderoga, considered the rebels' first victory, under the command of Ethan Allen and Benedict Arnold. A handful of other black soldiers joined him in that engagement, including the preacher Lemuel Haynes and Abijah Prince Jr.—son of black America's first poet, Lucy Terry Prince. At Bunker Hill, Lew spent the battle firing out the now famous tune, "There's Nothing Makes the British Run Like Yankee Doodle Dandee."

Future Leaders and Mythological Heroes

Joining the hordes of nameless and faceless black Americans who fought in all the Revolutionary War's participating armies were a number of African Americans who would achieve a measure of fame in political and religious circles during the postwar years. They fought for the same set of complex reasons as did all the other black troops, motivated by considerations ranging from the belief in a coming liberty to the desire for individual freedom or financial gain. Their notoriety has helped bring attention to the black contribution to the Revolutionary War.

JAMES FORTEN—ABOLITIONIST AND SAILOR

From the beginning of sea travel, blacks filled the crews of sailing vessels disembarking to and from colonial ports. Life at sea was a hard one, and few whites sought work there. As a result, ship captains were forced to welcome blacks in order to meet labor shortages. The same was true when the Continental Congress raised a navy in 1775. At no time did the Congress, or any of the state legislatures that raised their own navies, bother to stipulate rules for recruiting or enlisting African Americans. Similarly, as Congress and the states hired privateers to augment their official navies, the legislators who were so concerned with black army enlistment never bothered to draft rules restricting privateers' recruitment of either free or bonded blacks. These private vessels, therefore, were a particularly attractive haven for escaped slaves. Ship captains—hungry for the rewards being offered for captured British ships and sailors—unquestioningly welcomed them aboard. The same can be said of the era's marines, which Congress created as a sort of infantry force to ride aboard the navy's vessels, man their guns, and board enemy ships. Marine officers canvassed the colonies, recruiting for the undesirable job, paying no mind to a recruit's race or status as freeman or slave. The first documented black marine, a man named Keto, was in fact an escaped slave from

Wilmington, Delaware. He joined the crew of Captain Miles Pennington's *Reprisal* and was one of thirteen African Americans to serve as a marine during the Revolutionary War. They would be the last blacks to do so until World War II.

The lack of rules regarding black enlistment, however, means navy and privateer records do not list crew members' races. Therefore, while historians agree on a widespread African American presence at sea, there is little in the way of hard numbers on black sailors. Evidence of their existence, while voluminous, is anecdotal. We know, for instance, that black sailors were no more likely to be promoted to command positions than were their army colleagues. But in state navies and aboard privateers, they were often recruited as pilots because of their intricate navigational knowledge of difficult local waterways.

Future abolition movement leader and Philadelphia free black community politico James Forten offers one example of black service at sea. Born free in Philadelphia in 1766, the Quaker-educated Forten went to sea at age fifteen, toward the end of the war. He enlisted as a "powder boy" onboard Stephen Decatur's privateer *Royal Louis*. He was one of twenty African Americans in the crew of around two hundred. Forten's job, running gunpowder to the ship's arms, was a common one for black sailors. As in the army, they by and large drew either the most menial or the most dangerous assignments.

The *Royal Louis* engaged in two particularly bloody battles with British ships. In the second, a mismatched engagement with the British frigate *Amphyon*, Captain Decatur surrendered and Forten was taken prisoner along with the rest of the crew. For the most part, while white prisoners were exchanged with the Americans, the British sold black prisoners into slavery in the West Indies. This would

have been Forten's fate but for an odd personal encounter with the son of the *Amphyon's* captain. The two teenagers played marbles together, and the boy was impressed with young Forten's skill. He appealed to his father to allow Forten to return to England with him. Forten later wrote that he vocally protested this opportunity, declaring, "I am here a prisoner for the liberties of my country; I never, never, shall prove a traitor to her interests." Ultimately, he landed in the brig of the prison ship *Jersey*, where he stayed seven months with approximately three thousand other captives.

Forten was eventually freed as part of a large prisoner exchange between the British and the Americans. Released on Long Island, he walked home to Philadelphia and launched a long and storied career as an abolitionist activist and civic leader in Philadelphia's free black community, from which the first national black political and religious organizations grew in the postwar years.

LEMUEL HAYNES—PREACHER, POET, AND SOLDIER

While he holds an important place in black history, Lemuel Haynes actually earned his contemporary fame in the white world. A mixed-race man—his mother was a Scottish servant and his father an African slave—Haynes was the first black minister ordained into a mainstream congregation, and he won acclaim preaching to white audiences for over three decades. This at a time when a "mulatto" held the same place in America's racial caste system as that of any other person of African descent.

Born in West Hartford, Connecticut, in 1753, Haynes never met his black father and was aban-

Firebrand minister Lemuel Haynes. Historians only recently discovered his revolutionary writings, born from his experience on the frontline.

doned by his white mother—both of whom apparently had no desire to raise the offspring of what was then an illicit if common sexual relationship. A white foster family in Granville, Massachusetts, actually raised Haynes, keeping him as an indentured servant working on their farm. During his stay with the family, Haynes educated himself by fireside and developed a passion for the Gospel. He began occasionally preaching before the family's church while still a teenager.

When his indenture expired in 1774, the twenty-one-year-old Haynes went off to join the minutemen. He trained for just a brief period before joining the patriots at the Battles of Lexington and Concord. He went on to fight at Ticonderoga with Ethan

Allen's Green Mountain Boys. Shortly after Lexington, Haynes—who would be a prolific essayist and orator throughout his life—wrote a poem about the engagement, entitled "The Battle of Lexington, A poem about the inhuman tragedy perpetrated on the 19th of April 1775." The unpublished piece, thirty-seven stanzas in length, champions the patriot cause as a noble struggle of slave against master, declaring, "Thrice happy they who thus resign / Into the peaceful Grave / Much better there, in Death Confin'd / Than a surviving Slave." While Haynes ignores in this poem the obvious similarity between the situation most Africans in America faced and that of the rebels he eulogized, he later penned a now acclaimed essay calling for the expansion of revolutionary ideals to include freedom for blacks. He wrote the essay, "Liberty Further Extended," sometime in 1776; historians did not discover the unpublished tract, however, until the 1980s.

Haynes's 1776 denouncement of slavery was all but his last public statement on the topic—or race at all, for that matter. After the war, in 1785, he was ordained a minister in the Congregationalist Church of America. He held the pulpit in a Connecticut church for a few years, before migrating to the Rutland, Vermont, church that would be his home for the next thirty years. Much of his national prominence began with his notorious rebuttal of a visiting Universalist preacher's sermon, in which he characterized the doctrine of "universal salvation" as the work of the devil. The address, "Universal Salvation, a Very Ancient Doctrine (of the Devil)," was typical of Haynes's unforgiving and often bitingly sarcastic oratory. It was reprinted in over seventy editions from the time of its deliverance in 1805 until 1865.

Haynes was embraced by white society at all levels for most of his life and never lived in a segregated black world such as that almost all African Americans navigated. However, when he was ultimately forced out of his Rutland pulpit, he believed that the congregants dismissed him because of his race. He was said to have mockingly memorialized his tenure, quipping, "He lived with the people of Rutland thirty years, and they were so sagacious that at the end of that time they found out that he was *a nigger*, and so turned him away." Nevertheless, before his departure from Rutland, Haynes gave over five thousand sermons to his white congregation, was a member of several white New England society groups, and became the first African American to receive a Master of Arts degree when Middlebury College granted him an honorary MA in 1804.

BLACK SAMSON

Ironically, soldier-statesmen such as Haynes and Forten, in offering recognizable examples of black Revolutionary War service, were aided by a handful of legendary figures who may or may not have actually existed. Regardless of their veracity, these tales of black heroism and superhuman strength were widely embraced by Revolutionary-era Americans, soldier and civilian alike. And like the community leaders who fought, their fame has endured.

One of these folk heroes is "Black Samson" of the Battle of Brandywine in Delaware. While his name appears nowhere in military records, Black Samson plays a bit role in a regional tale of patriot betrayal and vengeance. According to the story, a white man named Isaac Maryland was betrayed by a British spy whom he and his daughter had taken into their confidence, leading to Maryland's death by burning while hiding from British troops. Maryland

had taught Samson, and his daughter had given him food when he was down on his luck. So the "giant Negro" took the murder personally.

As legend has it, during the Battle of Brandywine the following day, Samson, "armed with a scythe," heroically "sweeps his way through the red ranks like a sable figure of Time." Later, "in the height of the conflict," Samson reenters the American ranks with the treacherous spy as his prisoner. Following the battle, the patriots tied the spy's arms and legs to a pair of hickory trees they had bound at the top. After lashing him, they cut loose the trees and allowed his body to be torn apart.

Late-nineteenth-century black poet Paul Laurence Dunbar further memorialized the mythic figure with his poem "Black Samson of Brandywine." Dunbar's stanzas lyrically invoke Samson's heroic image, as in this one:

> There in the heat of the battle
> There in the stir of the fight
> Loomed he, an ebony giant,
> Black as the pinions of night
> Swinging his scythe like a mower
> Over a field of grain
> Needless the care of the gleaners,
> Where he had passed amain.

JACK SISSON

Another black figure to make it into Revolutionary folklore was Jack Sisson (also known as "Tack Sisson" and "Prince"). While Sisson's deeds may or may not have been exaggerated, unlike Black Samson, he did in fact exist.

In July 1777, Sisson joined a squad of around

forty patriots serving in Rhode Island under a lieutenant colonel named Barton in a raid to kidnap British Major General Richard Prescott. The commandos boarded boats, one of which Sisson steered, and snuck under the cover of night past British warships and into redcoat headquarters at Newport. They disembarked near Prescott's quarters, and as the rest of the men surrounded the house, Barton, Sisson, and a third man set out to apprehend the major general. After the men dispatched with the sentry, Sisson—who legend describes as a "stout active Negro"—broke the door down by striking it with his head. The men entered, took Prescott in his britches, and escaped with their prize. Sisson went on to serve in the First Rhode Island Regiment—the Continental Army's only all-black regiment.

Sisson and Barton's daring mission would become a popular Revolutionary-era ballad. According to historian Sidney Kaplan, among the jingle's verses were the lines:

> A tawny son of Afric's race
> Them through the ravine led,
> And entering then the Overing house,
> They found him in his bed.
>
> But to get in they had no means
> Except poor Cuffee's head,
> Who beat the door down, then rushed in
> And seized him in his bed.
>
> Stop, let me put my breaches on,
> The general did then pray.
> Your breeches, massa, I will take,
> For dress we cannot stay.

The Black Loyalists

Just two months after Bunker Hill, the Continental Congress decided to raise an army rather than fight the war with state militias. It appointed Virginia militia leader and congressional delegate George Washington as the commanding officer. From the start, Washington and his fellow rebel leaders agonized over whether or not blacks should be officially allowed to serve. It was during this process that Washington, himself a slaveholder, began a well-documented personal conversion to the belief that slavery should be abolished and that blacks were equal to whites. He would be near his deathbed before fully developing those beliefs; and he would not act on them until death itself, when he freed his slaves through his will.

When he took command of the Continental Army in 1775, however, Washington quickly put a stop to the recruitment of blacks, along with British deserters and vagabonds. In September of that same year, the Continental Congress, led by southern delegates, outright banned "negroes, Boys unable to bear arms [and] Old men" from serving in the Continental Army. These orders, of course, did not stop field commanders desperate for soldiers from accepting black volunteers, nor would it be the end of the rebel leaders' debate over whether blacks were officially welcome to fight.

The principal concern of southern colonists was that they not arm slaves. By this point, blacks outnumbered whites in both South Carolina and Georgia. Better to remain under the British boot, southerners reasoned, than to foment rebellion among such a mighty black population. And their concerns were probably well put. As the coming century would reveal, this population of Africans in America was by no means docile. Violent revolt was, in fact, in the forefront of several slave leaders' minds.

THE ETHIOPIAN REGIMENT

Not long after the Continental Congress's decision to bar black enlistees, the Royal Governor of the Virginia colony took a very different tack. On November 7, John Murray, Earl of Dunmore, issued a decree that declared martial law in the colony and granted freedom to all male slaves who escaped and joined the British forces.

Dunmore intended to do more than recruit men for his army; he also hoped to destabilize the colony and preoccupy its rebels with guarding their slaves. It was a technique the British and other Europeans had used in skirmishes with one another since their arrival in the Americas. Indeed, the tactic pushed Britain and Spain into a low-intensity war during the early 1700s. Following the establishment of the Carolina colony at the opening of the eighteenth century, Spanish officials in the colony of St. Augustine (located in today's northern Florida) offered freedom to all escaped British slaves. The steady stream of fleeing slaves so enraged Carolina's British colonists that they eventually attacked St. Augustine, setting off a series of skirmishes that lasted decades. (The colonial legislature also responded with the creation of some of history's most barbaric laws, at one point offering bounty hunters twenty pounds for an escaped slave's scalp with two ears attached.) As a result, in 1738 St. Augustine established the first black military installation in the Americas, the community of Gracia Real de Santa Teresa de Mose, a northern outpost for St. Augustine.

Known as Fort Mose, or the "Negro Fort" to the British, it housed around forty black families at its outset. Fort Mose lasted four decades, under the command of Captain Francisco Mcncndcz, who had led St. Augustine's slave militia.

Decades later, slaves in Britain's southern colonies faced a more delicate decision than that of their predecessors. Should they gamble on freedom in a liberated America, or trust the British, who had brought them into slavery in the first place? The northern rebel leaders' talk of liberty and equality sounded as though it would apply to all, but the Continental Congress's actions, certainly that of its southern delegates, made it clear that freedom for the Africans among them was not one of the Revolution's goals. So Lord Dunmore's offer of liberty in exchange for service was met with a strong response. At least three hundred slaves fled to Dunmore's naval fleet in Norfolk Harbor. They became known as the "Ethiopian Regiment" and wore uniforms emblazoned with an insignia that read "Liberty to Slaves."

Dunmore's proclamation turned him from a popular local official to public enemy number one among southern colonists. Not only had he stood with the British, he had taken the far more damning step of arming slaves and fomenting insurrections. The energized local militia by and large routed Dunmore's forces, eventually robbing him of any land base whatsoever and causing him to fight the war from his fleet of ships floating off Norfolk's shores. By the following spring, under attack by both colonists and a smallpox outbreak, the short-lived Ethiopian Regiment had been trimmed to around 150 men. That summer, Dunmore and his fleet set sail to the north, reluctantly abandoning Virginia to the rebels.

BOSTON KING

Dunmore may have been defeated in Virginia, but he nevertheless flung open the gates to freedom in the eyes of many southern slaves. These men and women began scrambling to British lines all over the South following his proclamation. Three years after Dunmore's evacuation, in 1779, Britain's commanding officer, Sir Henry Clinton, again made the invitation official. Clinton's Philipsburg Proclamation promised freedom to all colonial slaves who escaped and joined British forces, going yet another step further than Dunmore's by also expressly forbidding the sale or claim of any slave who had crossed British lines. It is unclear exactly how many slaves fought with the British as a result, but as many as fourteen thousand blacks left with the redcoat army at the war's end. The Hessian mercenaries who were supporting Britain's soldiers even formed a black drum corps. Ultimately, historians estimate that tens of thousands of slaves escaped the South during the course of the war, either joining the British to fight or simply fleeing with them at the war's end.

Among those thousands was an escaped slave from Charleston, South Carolina, named Boston King. He fled to the British while still a teenager, after they took Charleston in 1780. While King was visiting his parents, who lived as slaves on a property just a short distance from his owner's home, the white servant who was escorting him disappeared with the slaveholder's horses. Certain that he would be blamed, King simply ran away rather than return late or without the horses. Shortly after he joined the British, however, a smallpox epidemic hit among the black soldiers. They were quarantined a mile away from the regular camp to prevent its spread to the whites, where there were neither enough nurses to treat the black soldiers nor adequate security to pro-

J.H. Carl's 1784 rendering of Hessian mercenaries who aided the British includes a member of their black drum corps.

tect them from rebel raids. Still, King survived.

Later, during the chaos of a regiment movement, King was accidentally separated from his normal unit. He landed in the charge of a militia made up of southern loyalists, whose feelings about slavery were not far removed from their rebel brethren. The commander, a man named Captain Lewes, planned to desert the British and made it clear King would return to his place in the slave caste system. King managed to escape Captain Lewes, however, and reveal his plot to the British commanders, who subsequently foiled the plan. In a similar act of bravery, when his regiment was pinned down and outnumbered 1,600 to 250 by the Americans, King snuck through rebel lines to take word to reinforcements. He had been promised great rewards for taking the mission, but as with Salem Poor at Bunker Hill, he never received those honors.

When the British later surrendered Charleston, King was among four thousand black refugees who joined them in retreating to New York. There he took odd jobs supporting the military, married his wife, Violet, and awaited the war's end. He was briefly captured by American rebels again, but he once more managed to escape and return inside British lines. When the war ended in 1782, Britain's General Guy Carleton negotiated a deal with Washington that allowed King and the other tens of thousands of slaves who joined the British before the treaty's November 30 signing to remain in the care of the Royal Crown. (Slaves who had fled to the British after that date were returned to their American slaveholders.)

Carleton created a "Book of Negroes" that contained the names and identifying information for all of the blacks who set sail with his forces from New York. In it, King, then twenty-three, is identified as a "stout fellow" and his wife Violet, thirty-five, is identified as a "stout wench." Boston and Violet were among approximately three thousand black American refugees the British settled in Nova Scotia, Canada, following the war. Others went to various places in the empire. The Kings were to be given land and supplies, but the area in which they settled was devastatingly cold and barely arable. Eventually, in 1792, the couple joined thousands of black families in relocating to Sierra Leone. They had both become evangelical Christians, and King was a Methodist preacher. As with many of the black Americans who later founded the neighboring West African country of Liberia, they hoped to help convert Africans to Christianity.

If the British failed to give King and his colleagues at Nova Scotia exactly what they promised, other slaves who had fled to the British lines received far worse deals. In some cases, they were forced to return to their former masters, in others they were simply abandoned and left to starve. Historian Sidney Kaplan cites the journal of one Hessian officer, who notes, "We drove back to the enemy all of our black friends, whom we had taken along to despoil the countryside. We had used them to good advantage and set them free, and now, with fear and trembling, they had to face the reward of their cruel masters."

Alongside Washington and His Generals

Lord Dunmore's November 1775 proclamation drastically altered Washington's thinking on whether blacks should be allowed to serve in the Continental

Army. Manpower was already a critical concern of Washington's and would remain so throughout the war. The Continental Army never grew to larger than thirty thousand soldiers, and at times shrunk to as few as five thousand. While the British dedicated only just over forty thousand troops to quell the rebellion, Washington's strategy of prolonging the fight until the redcoats cut their losses and left America required one thing more than any other: reinforcements. He was in no position to ban a fifth of the colonial population from service, particularly if the British were going to actively recruit from those castaways.

So just one month after Dunmore's proclamation, Washington petitioned the Continental Congress to reverse its earlier decision forbidding blacks from fighting. In January 1776, the delegates capitulated and declared that free blacks who were already in the service when the restriction was passed could return to their posts. Each state legislature wrestled with the same issue as they struggled to meet congressionally mandated enlistment quotas for the new army. They all passed variations on the Continental Congress law, officially restricting black participation in one manner or another. But laws aside, desperate commanders welcomed new black volunteers throughout the war, just as they continued allowing slaves to serve in place of their masters. Historians believe, ultimately, that more than five thousand African Americans participated in the eight-year struggle as a result.

WILLIAM LEE AND WASHINGTON

Some of these black soldiers fought literally alongside Washington throughout the war. One such man was his slave and personal assistant William Lee. Lee,

whom Washington had purchased in 1768, was with Washington from the first day of the war to the last and returned to Mount Vernon to continue as his slave afterward. Upon his death in 1799, Washington finally freed his 277 slaves, including Lee. His will notes Lee's "faithful service during the Revolutionary War." That service may have left Lee wounded, as the will also notes "accidents which have befallen him, and which have rendered him incapable of walking or of any active employment."

Two portraits of Washington include depictions of Lee. Both stand as unfortunate examples of the way in which blacks were largely portrayed in seven-

John Trumbull's 1780 portrait of George Washington depicts William Lee as a meek, childlike servant.

Edward Savage's 1796 portrait of the Washington family depicts Lee as a noble but servile aide, removed to the background.

teenth- and eighteenth-century art. African Americans typically were depicted as comic buffoons or were relegated to the painting's fringe, barely visible as meek and humble servants withdrawn into the background. In Trumbull's 1780 portrait of Washington, he envisions Lee as the latter stereotype—hiding behind the gallant general's horse wearing a turban and a childlike expression. Edward Savage's 1796 portrait of the Washington family similarly situates Lee in the background, his features beyond a dark complexion, barely visible.

PRINCE WHIPPLE ON THE DELAWARE

Another African American that served alongside the Continental Army commanders was a slave named Prince Whipple. The young man had been sold into slavery at age ten by a ship captain in whom his wealthy African parents had placed their trust. They hired the man to ferry their boy to America so that he would be able to receive a Western education. Instead, the captain sold Prince to William Whipple, who subsequently became a signer of the Declaration of Independence and a general in Washington's army. General Whipple brought Prince to battle with him as his bodyguard, and they spent the war alongside each other, traveling with Washington's inner circle. Following the war, Whipple would join a group of slaves in petitioning the New Hampshire state legislature for freedom. It was one of several such petitions slaves and free blacks put before state legislatures in the post-Revolutionary era.

Both Whipple and Lee were among a number of African American soldiers present for one of Washington's most stirring feats as a general. The months following the July 1776 Declaration of Independence were dreadful ones for the

Continental Army. The British went on the offensive that summer and fall. And by the time the cold, dreary winter settled in, Washington's army had been driven from New Jersey into Pennsylvania and Congress had been thrown out of Philadelphia. These were, as Thomas Paine wrote, "the times that try men's souls." Washington knew he needed a victory.

So he assembled 2,400 soldiers and launched an unorthodox surprise offensive on Trenton, New Jersey. The soldiers piled into rowboats on Christmas Eve 1776 and crossed the Delaware River into New Jersey, fighting through mounds of ice and blinding snow. They then marched to Trenton and, on the evening of December 26, attacked the Hessian mercenaries that had reinforced the redcoats. It is con-

Prince Whipple was among the oarsmen in Washington's boat as he crossed the Delaware on Christmas Eve, 1776. He is shown here at the front of the boat, to Washington's right.

Thomas Sully's 1819 portrait of Washington and his troops on the banks of the Delaware also includes Whipple as an active participant, riding horseback alongside of Washington.

sidered Washington's most brilliant moment, as both a military strategist and a national leader. And Whipple was one of the oarsmen in the boat Washington rode across the Delaware to that battle.

The event, including Whipple's role, has been memorialized in two famous early-nineteenth-century paintings. The most renowned of the two works is Gottlieb Leutze's 1851 painting, which depicts Washington standing in the middle of a rowboat, American flag waving at his side, while a group of oarsmen battle the stormy, near-frozen waters of the Delaware. In the front of the boat, at Washington's right, is Prince Whipple. In stark contrast to Trumbull's and Savage's depictions of Lee, this image portrays Whipple as a vital and active participant in the scene. The second painting is an 1819 work by Thomas Sully, which depicts Washington and his troops on the banks of the Delaware as they prepare to march on Trenton. In the far right margin, riding horseback alongside Washington, is a black man believed to be Whipple.

JAMES LAFAYETTE AT YORKTOWN

James Lafayette was yet another African American present with Washington and his commanders at a key victory. A Virginia slave, James Lafayette worked as a spy for the French officer Marquis de Lafayette during the 1781 siege at Yorktown, Virginia, which

This 1783 portrait of French General Lafayette at Yorktown shows his slave spy, James Lafayette, as a servant rather than combatant.

led to British General Charles Cornwallis's surrender and essentially brought the war to a close.

France recognized the rebel United States in 1778; it was the first country to do so. With recognition came a host of French soldiers and military expertise—a boon that would decisively tip the Revolutionary War's balance. In September 1781, Washington's army was augmented by a large French force, led in part by General Lafayette, while facing down the British in Virginia. With the French troops, they outnumbered the Brits two to one. Over the course of the monthlong siege, James Lafayette ferried back and forth between Cornwallis's headquarters and the French and Americans in Richmond. He was a double agent, having convinced Cornwallis he was spying for the British, all the while actually working for General Lafayette. "His intelligence from the enemy camp," General Lafayette later wrote, "were industriously collected and more faithfully delivered. He perfectly acquitted himself with some important commissions I gave him and appears to me entitled to every reward his situation can admit of."

Nothing of James Lafayette's espionage skills is apparent in Jean-Baptiste Le Paon's 1783 work *Lafayette at Yorktown*, however. Though the portrait allows James more humanity than usual, giving him distinguishable features and a striking uniform, it again places the black war hero in the margins, tending to the general's horse and looking up in amazement at a man who had actually so praised his own ingenuity. In contrast, a later portrait of James Lafayette himself—John Martin's 1824 work— shows a graying, distinguished gentleman with the confident if stern expression that might have typified someone with his daring life experience.

John B. Martin's 1824 portrait of James Armistead Lafayette offers a more genuine rendering of the American double agent.

Black Regiments

Although the Revolutionary War's Continental Army and various state militias combined to create the most integrated American military until Vietnam, there were still two all-black fighting units among the rebel forces—one in Rhode Island and one in Massachusetts. Following the British occupation of Savannah in late 1778, the Continental Congress recommended that Georgia and South Carolina raise black units to boost scant southern forces as well, but the state legislatures refused. The French also brought a six-hundred-man "Black Brigade of Saint Dominique" to help the Americans defeat the British. Among these men were a number of those who would later lead a successful slave revolt on that island.

FIRST RHODE ISLAND REGIMENT

The original "all-black" unit, formed in early 1778, was the First Rhode Island Regiment, which fought from that time all the way through the war's end at Yorktown. Rhode Island's state legislature cast its decision to create the regiment in grand terms, noting in February 1778 that history held "frequent precedents of the wisest, the freest, and the bravest nations having liberated their slaves, and enlisted them as soldiers." Legislators declared that all slaves who enlisted would be immediately emancipated, with the state compensating the owners. And, since they were free, black recruits would also receive equal pay to white soldiers.

So it may seem that the state's bold move in opening the ranks to slaves was motivated by a desire to strike a blow against racism. That may in fact be true, but an at least equally significant factor was the state's failure to meet its quota for enlistees. The previous winter had been a brutal one for the Continental Army. Camped at Valley Forge, Washington's soldiers ceased fighting a war and simply struggled to stay alive. Many failed. Due to a lack of supplies to protect them from the elements, massive food shortages, and rampant disease, at least 2,500 soldiers died at Valley Forge. As the dreadful season broke, Washington desperately needed new recruits. At the same time, Rhode Island, with the largest black population in New England, was in equally dire straits. The British, and their Hessian mercenaries, had the state under siege, controlling two-thirds of its land. In part as a result, the state had been unable to fill the ranks of its two battalions. So General James Varnum suggested that Washington allow Rhode Island to combine those battalions and recruit blacks to form a new unit. Washington agreed, and by that spring Colonel Christopher Greene began training his new troops. A number of state legislators objected, but Governor Nicholas Cooke and his allies in the body carried the day.

In August 1778, the regiment, with ninety-five

This 1781 portrait of American troops at Yorktown includes a member of the black First Rhode Island Infantry Regiment.

ex-slaves and thirty freemen, was thrown into action when it formed the first line of defense in the Battle of Rhode Island. Despite its scant preparations, the First Rhode Island Regiment took part in what General Lafayette called "the best fought action of the war." The Hessian mercenaries directed the brunt of their offensive at the First Rhode Island's position but were repulsed on three different charges. Ultimately, the British and Hessians won the four-hour battle, but their casualties were five times as high as the Americans'. "By the best information," American General John Sullivan declared following the battle, in a communiqué intended to dispel malicious rumors that the black troops had not fared well, "the Commander-in-Chief thinks that the Regiment will be intituled to a proper share of the Honours of the day." However, as with most black contributions to America's War of Independence, the First Rhode Island's valor has since been largely ignored.

The First Rhode Island, envisioned as a segregated black regiment, was of course nothing of the sort. The state's white citizens did not embrace the idea as readily as had Governor Cooke and the legislature, and the coming election found over half of those lawmakers thrown out of office. The newly constituted chamber quickly repealed the resolution creating the First Rhode Island. As a result, no new black recruits entered the regiment after June of 1778. Nevertheless, the regiment, reinforced with white recruits, would fight straight through to Yorktown. A French sublieutenant named Jean-Baptiste Antoine de Verger sketched a rendering of American troops at Yorktown. In it, on the far left, is a black soldier who is presumably a member of the First Rhode Island.

Connecticut attempted a similar, if less sweeping, experiment at segregating black troops. In 1780,

officers in the state's Fourth Regiment splintered the unit's fifty-two African Americans off into a separate but internal company. The all-black Second Company, Fourth Connecticut Regiment existed for only two years, at which point the black soldiers were reintegrated into the larger regiment. It is unclear what triggered the Second Company's disbanding.

BUCKS OF AMERICA

Perhaps the most elusive piece of Revolutionary-era black history is the story of a group of Bostonians called the "Bucks of America." We don't know for sure who its members were, what their function was, or how many of them existed. We don't even know when the group was created or how long it lasted. All we know for sure is that the Bucks did exist, and that

A medallion likely worn by members of the all-black
Bucks of America.

The flag of the Bucks of America, a unit whose history has been all but lost.

Massachusetts Governor John Hancock honored them in 1783.

Historians have surmised that the Bucks were an all-black paramilitary group charged with protecting property in Boston, likely established following the British evacuation of the city in 1776. Pioneering nineteenth-century black historian William Nell is credited with unearthing what few details about the group are available. In his 1855 seminal account of African American participation in the Revolutionary War, Nell writes of an exhibit in Boston of "relics and mementos" from the war that included a flag presented by Hancock to "an association of colored men, called the 'Protectors,' who guarded the property of Boston merchants." The flag, which Nell obtained from a "Mrs. Key"—who was present at Hancock's original honoring ceremony—has been housed at the Massachusetts Historical Society since Nell donated it in 1862. It is silk, with an insignia depicting a pine tree and a running buck. The initials "J.H." and "G.M." are written over the symbol, along with the name "Bucks of America." The Massachusetts Historical Society also possesses a silver medallion with the same insignia and the initials M. W. The medallion is likely a badge that members wore on their coats, and M. W. the initials of a given soldier. The initials on the flag are likely those of John Hancock and the one member whose name historians believe they know—the group's leader, George Middleton.

Nell's account mentions that the Bucks' commander was a black man named Colonel Middleton. Nell doesn't offer Middleton's first name, and military records reveal no black officer by that or any other name in the Revolutionary War. However, it is likely that Colonel Middleton was George Middleton, a civic leader in Boston's free black community. He was a member of Prince Hall's African Lodge of Freemasons—the first black Masonic temple and an important center of black political activity in the post-Revolutionary era—and later served as its grand master. His officer rank was likely directly assigned by Hancock, merely to designate him as the leader of the paramilitary group.

THE BLACK BRIGADE OF ST. DOMINIQUE

In the fall of 1779, the French sailed thirty-three ships to Georgia in order to help the Americans retake the port town of Savannah. The French forces included 2,979 "Europeans" and 545 "Colored," known alternately as the Volunteer Chasseurs and the Fontages Legion, after their commander Viscount Francois de Fontages. The group had been recruited from Santa Domingo and contained several future leaders of the island's slave revolution, including independent Haiti's first king, Henri Christophe.

France's black regiment did not participate directly in the ill-fated battle to retake Savannah. But as the British drove the Franco-American force backward, the Fontages Legion, stationed in the rear guard, stepped up to provide cover and prevented a slaughter. Both the then twelve-year-old Christophe and future general Martial Besse of France were injured in the fray. Years later, local officials in Charleston, South Carolina, would greet Besse, during his visit as a representative of the French military, with a demand that he pay the same bond all free blacks entering the state were then required to post.

WARS OF A
YOUNG NATION

*Slave Uprisings and
the War of 1812*

At forty-eight years old, Dangerfield Newby probably considered himself too old for warfare. He'd been through a lot as it was. Born a slave, the son of his white owner, he was freed upon his father's death. He lived on a farm near Harpers Ferry, Virginia, and worked assiduously toward one goal: raising the $1,500 he needed to buy his wife and children, including a newborn, out of slavery. So when the militant white abolitionist John Brown and his band of raiders planned their attack on the federal armory near Newby's farm, Newby decided he'd help out by spying but wouldn't join the actual fighting. Maybe Newby believed Brown's men would fail, or perhaps he thought he was too close to getting his family back to risk death. Whatever his calculations, they were drastically altered by a desperate letter from his wife.

Harriet Newby told her husband that she expected to be sold to a southern slave dealer any day; the family, as had been countless other black families, would be forever broken apart. "Dear husband," she wrote, "It is said Master is in want of money. If so, I know not what time he may sell me, and then all my bright hopes of the future are blasted, for there has been one bright hope to cheer me in all my troubles, that is to be with you." Seeing no other option, Newby cast his lot with armed struggle. He would be the first of Brown's men slain by federal troops brought in to quell the uprising.

The United States of America was home to approximately 1.4 million people of African descent by the beginning of the War of 1812. While the vast majority were slaves, over two hundred thousand lived free, primarily in black enclaves of northern cities. But whether emancipated or bonded, these black Americans were acutely aware that the liberty and equality for which the young nation had fought at the eighteenth century's close did not yet extend to themselves. The republic's architects made this clear from the start, when they struck Thomas Jefferson's condemnation of the British slave trade from his first draft of the Declaration of Independence. Later, when the authors of the U.S. Constitution met in 1787, they formally codified the exclusivity of their newfound liberty. At the time, a handful of northern states had already begun to restrict the further import of slaves and to mandate gradual manumission of those held in bondage. But the Constitutional Convention refused to take such steps, instead declaring that the slave trade would be left unchecked until at least 1808. Delegates further agreed that the law would formally consider blacks held in bondage to be the owner's property, just as any other possession. Meanwhile, the world free

Forty-eight-year-old Dangerfield Newby was the first of John Brown's men killed in the Harpers Ferry raid.

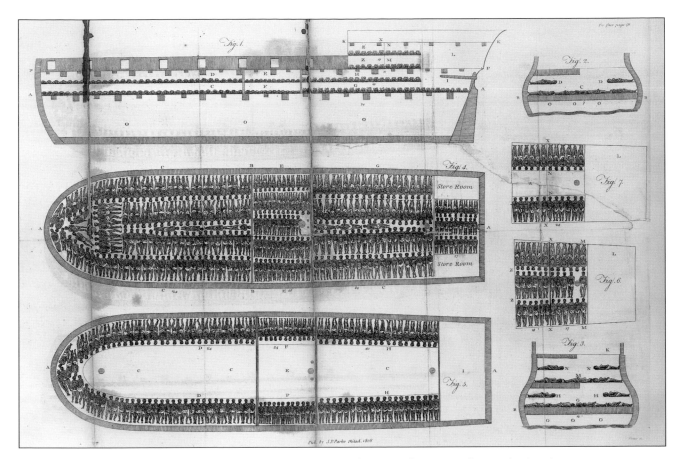

Africans were packed tightly into slave ships for the Middle Passage—the voyage from West Africa to the Americas.

blacks could navigate was circumscribed by state-level legal and cultural boundaries that limited where and how they could live, work, socialize, and study. African America's freedom struggle, which had for a time coincided with that of America at large, was now once again separate.

As with the Revolution itself, black Americans reacted to this postwar racial landscape in vastly different ways. Some continued to embrace the professed values of the American republic and availed themselves of its prescribed routes for grievance. Revolutionary War veteran Prince Whipple was among the countless African Americans who, bound together in small lobbying groups, appealed to state legislatures for the emancipation of themselves or their loved ones. Others, such as war vet James Forten, joined the nascent Abolition Movement, organizing within the increasingly vibrant free black communities of urban centers such as Philadelphia, Boston, and New York City. Still more, particularly in the South, turned to the newly organized and independent black church for guidance. But many black Americans—some of whom were civic, political, and religious leaders themselves—made the same choice as Dangerfield Newby. For them, the struggle for freedom would necessarily involve armed conflict.

New slaves did not accept their bondage passively, as depicted in this abolition movement card. Many revolted in large and small attacks.

Battles of the Black Revolutionary Era

The American Revolution was hardly black slaves' first encounter with armed insurrection. From the very beginning of the Atlantic slave trade, Africans had attempted to steal their freedom by force. The correspondence and diaries of British slave traders are replete with tales of bloody clashes with hostile West African armies. As the trade unfolded, insurrections aboard slave ships, during the infamous "middle passage" between Africa's west coast and the Americas, grew in regularity as well. One imagines that the leaders of these uprisings must have been military commanders or soldiers in their original communities.

The slaves were no more docile once they reached the Americas. In fact, the earliest known slave revolt in the area that would become the United States coincides with what historians also believe to be the arrival of African slaves in that area. In 1526, five hundred Spanish explorers, Native American guides, and African slaves set sail from the Spanish

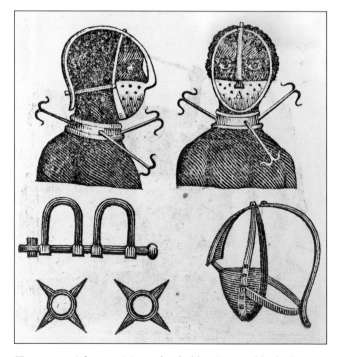

To prevent violent uprisings, slaveholders invented barbaric restraints for Africans, such as the infamous iron mask.

REPRESENTATION of an INSURRECTION
on board
A SLAVE-SHIP.

Shewing how the crew fire upon the unhappy Slaves from behind the
BARRICADO, *erected on board all Slave ships, as a security whenever*
such commotions may happen.

Despite all of the slave traders' extreme measures, Africans still regularly launched uprisings during the Middle Passage.

West Indies in search of a route to the East. They made it as far as the southeastern tip of North America—the area that is now Georgia. There they built a temporary settlement just below modern-day Savannah called San Miguel de Gualdape. The Native Americans who had been pressed into service as guides and translators promptly deserted the settlement, while food shortages and disease began to take their toll. Soon, the settlement's leader died and a succession struggle erupted. Amid this chaos, the African slaves planned and launched a rebellion. The colonists quelled the uprising, but several slaves escaped into the interior, becoming what must be considered the first African Americans.

Such rebellions continued apace from the onset of the British colonies in the early seventeenth century straight through the dawn of the Civil War. It can be said, then, that black America's heritage is as much defined by defiant revolt as it is by oppressive slavery. One of the most notorious slave revolts in colonial America occurred in New York in 1712. A group of what is believed to have been twenty-three slaves gained access to weapons—firearms, knives, swords, and hatchets—and staged an uprising near Westchester. At around one o'clock in the morning on April 6, they set fire to a barn, drawing the townspeople out of their homes. When the whites arrived at the barn, the group came out of hiding and attacked. In his report to Britain, New York Governor Rob Hunter testified that "not above nine Christians were killed, and about five or six wounded." Twenty-one of the participants were caught and publicly executed; two others took their own lives before being apprehended. The relatively minor plot set off a fury of paranoia throughout Britain's American colonies. In some cases, such as Massachusetts and Pennsylvania, it ultimately led

lawmakers to limit the further import of slaves. In others, such as New York and around the South, it led to more draconian laws to prevent future uprisings.

No effort to eradicate slave revolts was successful, of course. Many plots were foiled before they were launched, but slaves went on planning them nonetheless. Another revolt that deeply shook the colonies took place just outside of Charleston, South Carolina, in 1739. Known as the Stono Rebellion because it began near the Stono River, the uprising was part of the ongoing dispute between Britain's southernmost colonies and Spanish Florida—where officials had offered freedom to British slaves, in a successful effort to encourage runaways and foment chaos within the colonies. The approximately twenty slaves who took up arms on September 9 were believed to have been making their way to Fort Mose, the black military settlement that served as the Spaniards' northernmost defense. The group launched its mission dramatically, storming a storehouse, commandeering the weapons held there, killing the proprietors, and leaving their severed heads on the front steps. The slaves then marched south, growing in number and killing whites they encountered along the way. By that afternoon, they had grown to a force of around one hundred.

Despite their increasing size, the slaves' march made it only about ten miles before being subdued by the colonial militia. For reasons that have been debated by historians since, the group stopped in a field, allowing the militia to catch up and overpower them. Contemporary accounts asserted that the rebels had pillaged liquor from plantations along their march and become drunk. More recently, historians have argued that the group's pause to raise a flag in an open field was consistent with Central

African war customs. Still others have speculated that the group delayed their march in order to allow more escaping slaves to join them. Regardless, when the colonial militia caught up, it was still unable to take all of the rebels into custody. It would be a full week later before the militia would defeat the largest splinter group of slaves, in a battle about thirty miles farther south. A number of the combatants were believed to have made it to Fort Mose.

But while armed uprisings such as those in New York and South Carolina were a staple of pre-independence America, they were launched with a new gravity in the liberated nation. The successful 1809 revolution in Santa Domingo (now Haiti) had terrified white Americans, who feared it would encourage a similar widespread uprising in the United States. And for blacks, slavery had shown its resilience by surviving both the Revolutionary War and the subsequent nation-building process. As abolitionists debated the most effective route to its destruction, the planners and executors of the new century's insurrections spoke with their actions. For them, the only remaining solution was the one the nation's founders had employed as well: revolution.

GABRIEL'S REVOLT

Two of the nineteenth century's most well known slave insurrections—one in Virginia, the other in South Carolina—were uncovered and stopped before they began. In both cases, however, historians believe the plans had reached hundreds, if not thousands, of combatants before they were foiled. This widespread participation, combined with the detail with which the revolts were planned, have led some analysts to suggest that both stand as the most likely of America's slave uprisings to have succeeded.

The first of these plots was planned and led by a young Virginia slave named Gabriel Prosser. Born in 1776 near Richmond, on the plantation of Thomas Prosser, Gabriel learned to be a blacksmith as well as to read and write while still a child. These exceptional skills meant that as he grew older, Prosser could hire Gabriel out to work in town. This common if officially frowned upon practice allowed slaveholders to make extra money off of their human capital and let those hiring the slaves cut costs on jobs that required skilled labor—for which white tradesmen charged much higher rates. Critics feared the system risked impacting slaves in exactly the way it did Gabriel—radicalizing their worldview by bringing them into contact with free blacks and white laborers.

But Gabriel's belief that his freedom would come only as the result of revolution was nursed not only by this exposure but also by the rhetoric of the Revolutionary War era in which he grew up and the example set by Santa Domingo's slaves. His conviction was solidified, historians believe, by a 1799 run-in with Virginia justice. He, his brother, Solomon, and a third Prosser slave had been caught stealing a pig. Gabriel resisted arrest and bit off the ear of one of the white men who caught them. He escaped prison through a statute that allowed slaves the leniency of only being publicly branded if they could recite a biblical verse. Shortly thereafter, he began plotting his insurrection.

The plan was relatively straightforward. Forces in Richmond would seize the governor's mansion and take Governor James Monroe hostage, to use as leverage. Meanwhile, armies in Norfolk and Petersburg would secure those cities. An envoy would be sent to surrounding Native American nations to ask for their help. Gabriel was convinced that once the assault pushed past the opening stages, he would receive such aid, as well as support from working-class whites in Virginia. Joined by Solomon, another Prosser slave named Ben, and two other slaves named Jack Dither and Ben Woolfolk, Gabriel recruited soldiers from all over southern Virginia. A few whites did in fact join, as did some free blacks and many black Revolutionary War veterans. According to testimony in Gabriel's later trial, he may have built an army of as many as fifteen hundred men.

The attack was planned for the night of August 30, 1800. But a massive thunderstorm hit southern Virginia that night, and the rebels decided to postpone one day. That was enough time for catastrophe to strike. Two slaves who knew of the plot revealed it to their owners, who informed Governor Monroe. The governor had ignored rumors of a slave uprising the day before but reacted to this news. The state militia sprung into action and within a week arrested some thirty conspirators. Gabriel himself avoided trackers all month but was finally apprehended when a slave aboard a ship in which he was hiding spotted him and turned him in, hoping to win a $300 bounty. White officials, of course, matched the man's treachery and paid him only $50 of the promised money.

The state offered full pardons to a handful of Gabriel's conspirators in exchange for testifying against the rest. Ben Prosser and Ben Woolfolk took the deal and were the lead witnesses. Ultimately, a juryless court tried sixty-five slaves and hung twenty-seven of them, including Gabriel. Reportedly, during the trial one man was asked if he had anything to say in his defense, to which he replied, "I have nothing more to offer than what General Washington would have had to offer, had he been taken by the British officers and put to trial by them. I have ventured my life in endeavouring to obtain the liberty of my countrymen, and am a willing sacrifice in their cause; and I beg, as a favor, that I may be immediately led to my execution. I know that you have predetermined to shed my blood, why then all this mockery of a trial?"

DENMARK VESEY'S REVOLT

In 1821, Charleston, South Carolina, was again rocked by a major slave rebellion. In this case, the plan—uncovered by white officials just as it was being launched—was likely the most ambitious ever conceived, involving more people than any slave insurrection in American history. It was led by a free black man from the Virgin Islands named Denmark Vesey.

Vesey was taken captive from his home in St. Thomas at the age of fourteen, in around 1781. His captor, a slave ship captain named Joseph Vesey, sold the boy into bondage in Santa Domingo. Young Vesey lived there for only a brief period but undoubtedly long enough to be exposed to a building discontent among that soon-to-revolt black population. His stay in Santa Domingo was cut short because the man who purchased him became annoyed by the boy's epilepsy. The slaveholder demanded that Captain Vesey buy back the damaged goods he had sold. So Denmark Vesey sailed with his captor's slave ship for the next couple of years, traveling the region and learning new languages and cultures. In 1783, Captain Vesey settled in Charleston, keeping Denmark as his slave.

In Charleston, the sixteen-year-old Vesey learned carpentry and developed a reputation as a highly skilled craftsman. In 1800, he used $600 of

$1,500 he won in a lottery to purchase his freedom, a price the town's mayor later declared to be far below his actual value. He worked as a carpenter in town and earned another reputation along the way—what witnesses in his trial would describe as that of an "uppity nigger." This notoriety stemmed from Vesey's willingness to regularly engage white townspeople in public arguments. He had become an increasingly vocal proponent of black liberation, both from slavery and from the bottom of America's caste system, and spoke openly about it. By 1818, Vesey had begun quietly discussing the potential for a slave rebellion in Charleston, and by 1821, he and a group of five other men had begun plotting the details of their insurrection.

All of the six conspirators, even those still in bondage, held some degree of education and status. They were all active members of the African Methodist Episcopal church. Two of the men, Ned and Rolla Bennett, were slaves on the plantation of South Carolina Governor Thomas Bennett—who was known for his belief in a "soft" slavery in which bonded men and women could achieve some degree of education and be allowed to pursue Christianity. Peter Poyas and Monday Gell were, as Vesey, respected craftsmen. And Jack Pritchard, also known as Gullah Jack, was both revered and feared among blacks for his believed supernatural powers. Indeed, as the men recruited participants, Gullah Jack proclaimed he had secret powers that would make him invincible and that he would be able to pass those powers on to soldiers once the rebellion began.

The men recruited from all over the state. At meetings, Vesey read from the Declaration of Independence, quoted antislavery members of Congress, and offered interpretations of the Christian Bible that he argued supported armed insurrection. He assured recruits that once the war began in Charleston, the now-liberated Haitians (and perhaps even African armies) would come to join the battle. All of these messages were apparently wildly convincing. Judging from testimony during the conspirators' trials, the men may have recruited as many as nine thousand participants. Vesey made certain that we would never know for sure, however. He is believed to have kept logs of, among other things, the names of those who signed up to join his army, but he burned all of those documents when whites uncovered the plot.

As the recruitment went forward, blacksmiths crafted weapons, while others procured what guns they could and Vesey and his inner group plotted the details. The attack was to begin on Sunday, July 14, 1822. A Sunday meant many whites would be traveling out of town and that hordes of blacks coming into town would not draw suspicion, since they normally converged on Charleston to attend church. They would target government leaders and armories. Poyas and Ned Bennett were to lead groups to take two arsenals. Rolla Bennett was to lead another group in assassinating the governor and mayor, then block the bridge leading into town.

But, as with Gabriel's plot, Vesey and his colleagues were betrayed. One of the slaves who had heard about the conspiracy informed his overseer. The man, Peter Prioleau, worked in the plantation owner's house—a position usually reserved for more loyal servants. Other blacks often looked upon such "house slaves" with suspicion, and Vesey had avoided recruiting them.

Poyas and others were arrested, but they convinced authorities that the plot was a myth. Shaken but undeterred, Vesey moved the date of the attack up to June 16. But when they mobilized in the

predawn hours of that morning, the rebels found heavily armed white guards all over the city. They withdrew, but the local militia eventually rounded them up. Amid the ensuing hysteria in white Charleston, a special tribunal weighed charges against 131 black South Carolinians in the course of five weeks. The state's case was based primarily on the testimony of one of the conspirators, Monday Gell. Officials released thirty-eight people for lack of evidence but tried ninety-three others—acquitting twenty-six and convicting sixty-seven. Eleven of those acquitted were nevertheless banished from the state, along with forty-three others. Officials publicly hung thirty-five people, including Vesey and all of the key conspirators. (Likely among the exiles was radical black journalist David Walker, whose 1829

treatise *An Appeal to the Colored Citizens of the World* would terrify white southerners and embolden antislavery advocates. The book-length essay offered an early articulation of many of the ideas espoused by the late twentieth century's black power movement.)

NAT TURNER'S REVOLT

Ironically, the early nineteenth century's most well known slave revolt, and the one to make it the furthest beyond the planning stage, was also the one that involved the least preparation. The careful plotting that marked Gabriel Prosser's and Denmark Vesey's insurrections was completely absent from the bloody rampage led by Nat Turner in 1830. In many

Nat Turner's 1830 uprising, represented in this 1831 illustration, was among the era's most bloody. He and his men killed fifty-seven white men and women, many in their sleep.

ways, it was more of a mass murder than an actual rebellion. But the attack is also unique because Turner, a Virginia slave with messianic visions, left an oral history of how and why he launched it. While awaiting execution, Turner offered white journalist Thomas Gray an interview, recounting the details of his life and the grizzly two-day uprising he led. Gray published that famous interview as *The Confessions of Nat Turner*.

Turner was born in 1800 on a Southampton County, Virginia, plantation. From an early age, he and his parents believed him to be an exceptional child. One day, while playing with other slave children, Turner recounted the details of an event that had occurred before his birth, leading his mother—as well as his devoutly religious owner—to conclude he was a prophet. They began to treat him specially and segregate him from the other children when he was not working. He was a remarkable student who learned easily and busied himself with scientific experiments, attempting to make things such as paper and gunpowder.

As Turner grew older, he continued to segregate himself from his colleagues. One day, according to Turner, while working alone in the field, a spirit approached him and declared, "Seek ye the kingdom of Heaven and all things shall be added unto you." The vision solidified his belief that he was a prophet "ordained for some great purpose in the hands of the Almighty." Meditating on the issue, he decided that he was meant to lead his fellow slaves out of bondage. "I began to direct my attention to this great object," Turner told Gray, "to fulfill the purpose for which, by this time, I felt assured I was intended."

But when Turner began spreading the word of his destiny, the plantation overseers placed him under special watch. He escaped into the woods and

stayed there for thirty days. In this seclusion, Turner's messianic visions intensified and ultimately prompted him to voluntarily return to the plantation, where he could fulfill his mission. Over the next several years, a series of spiritual encounters would lead him to believe the apocalypse was approaching. "I saw white spirits and black spirits engaged in battle," he said in describing the most dramatic of these, "and the sun was darkened—the thunder rolled in the heavens, and blood flowed in streams." Another came while he was working in the fields one day. He saw drops of blood on the corn "as though it were dew from heaven." Wandering into the woods, he found hieroglyphic drawings on the leaves, depicting scenes he had seen previously. This experience solidified his belief that a judgment day was approaching, "when the first should be the last and the last should be first."

Finally, a solar eclipse in February of 1830 led Turner to act. He bandied around loose plans for an uprising on July 4 of that year with a small group of slaves. But the men couldn't agree on a plan, and when Turner became ill, they decided to postpone it. Then, on the thirteenth of that August, the sky turned an odd color and Turner decided his mission could be delayed no longer. A week later, on the night of the twentieth, he and seven others snuck into their plantation owner's house and murdered the sleeping family. The group then went from house to house, killing entire white families and picking up additional men as they traveled. Over the next two days, the band grew to about forty people and killed fifty-seven whites. On the twenty-third, however, a militia caught up with them and took most into custody. Turner and some others escaped during the fray, and the white militia killed over one hundred blacks while hunting them down over the next month and

An 1876 illustration of Turner being apprehended by a white official.

a half. When Turner was finally apprehended, white officials hung him and then skinned him. They hung fifty-five blacks in all for the uprising.

The War of 1812

The tensions between America and Britain that erupted into war in 1812 were really a continuation of the two nations' eighteenth-century conflict. The core issue was the same one that had divided the redcoats and the colonists in New England: Britain's right to impose its economic will on the occupants of North America. By the 1800s, that dispute focused on maritime laws. Americans were becoming increasingly irritated about the British Navy's bullying of their ships. The British, locked in an ongoing battle with France to control the flow of goods in and out of Europe, were attempting to enforce rules that pushed

American trade with Europe through Britain. In the process, they were also regularly boarding American vessels to reclaim deserters from the British Navy; Americans complained that the Brits used this cover to capture U.S. sailors and impress them into service.

As was the case with Crispus Attucks and the Revolutionary War, African Americans were central figures in the event that pushed this dispute down the road to war. In June 1807, the U.S. frigate *Chesapeake* pulled out of the Norfolk, Virginia, navy yard and met with the British ship *Leopard*. The *Chesapeake's* captain refused to allow his ship to be searched, so the *Leopard* opened fire. After subduing the *Chesapeake*, the Brits boarded, declared themselves in search of deserters, and apprehended four sailors. One of those men was in fact a British deserter, but the other three men—David Martin, John Strachan, and William Ware—were black Americans. They would remain in British custody until 1811. The incident prompted the first in a series of bellicose diplomatic steps by America that culminated in a declaration of war five years later in June of 1812.

A WHITEWASHED ARMY

The years leading up to the War of 1812 had witnessed the dismantling of America's integrated armed forces. In 1792, Congress passed a bill creating a "uniform militia" to serve the national defense. The law mandated enrollment of "each and every free able-bodied white male citizen" between the ages of eighteen and forty-five. While it did not specifically ban blacks, most militia leaders read as much into it. Ironically, only southern militias continued to allow blacks to enlist—as laborers assigned to jobs too menial for white men, or as musicians.

So when the War of 1812 broke out, the military's land forces, which suffered a string of lopsided losses in the war's first year, were almost exclusively white. But when the British marines, some of whom were black, seized and burned Washington, D.C., and Philadelphia in 1814, two states rediscovered the urgency that motivated earlier military leaders to open their ranks to African Americans. New York created two black regiments, with a total of around two thousand soldiers. Both free and bonded men were welcomed to enlist, and slaves were promised their freedom if they served three years. Similarly, Pennsylvania created a black regiment of around 250 soldiers. However, the Treaty of Ghent, signed that December, cut short plans for these regiments, and none of them actually saw combat.

Still, there were two places in the American military that African Americans did serve during the War of 1812. While blacks were shut out of the uniformed army, the War Department employed a free black man named Caesar Lloyd Cummings. History has left us almost no information about this man, but he was one of the department's six civilian employees. The second place blacks served was in the U.S. Navy. There, the long tradition of welcoming both free and bonded blacks continued throughout the war, and African American sailors likely participated in every major battle.

IN THE NAVY

In 1798, Congress followed up its Militia Act of six years previous with a bill formally establishing the U.S. Marine Corps, which would become a division of the navy. The law barred blacks from serving in the new unit—a rule that would remain in place, fully enforced, until the 1940s. At the same time, Secretary of the Navy Benjamin Stoddert issued an order barring blacks from serving in his entire branch. But unlike the congressional ban on black marines, Stoddert's order turned out to be nothing more than wasted paper. As had been the case for decades, labor shortages would prompt ship captains both inside and out of the navy to go right on welcoming, and sometimes even recruiting, both free and bonded blacks. And this practice would proceed, unofficially sanctioned, right into the War of 1812, when intense fighting would necessitate a more official welcome for black sailors. During the first year of the war, most battles took place between ground troops along the Canadian border. But as the contest entered its second year, the real fighting shifted to the waters of the Atlantic Ocean and Great Lakes. Finding itself at the war's front line and facing ever present recruitment problems, the navy removed even the pretense of banning black service members. The March 1813 order officially opening the navy's ranks triggered a wave of black enlistment, and African Americans soon accounted for an estimated sixth of the branch.

Facing constant labor shortages, Navy vessel captains could ill afford to turn away black sailors.

These black sailors were regularly cited for heroism. In one of the most often referenced examples, the captain of a private ship in the navy's service reported the unimaginable courage of two African American sailors with gruesome battle wounds. Writing to his agent, Captain Nathaniel Shaler of the *Governor Thompkins* described the Atlantic Ocean battle, stating, "The name of one of my poor fellows who was killed ought to be registered in the book of fame, and remembered with reverence as long as bravery is considered a virtue; he was a black man by the name of John Johnson; a 24 lb. shot struck him in the hip and took away all the lower part of his body; in this state the poor brave fellow lay on the deck, and several times exclaimed to his ship mates, 'Fire away my boys, no haul a color down.' The other was a black man, by the name of John Davis, and was struck in much the same way; he fell near me, and several times requested to be thrown overboard, saying he was only in the way of others. While America has such tars, she has little to fear from the Tyrants of the ocean."

But the African American sailors' best-known contribution was their participation in one of the war's most significant battles. In September 1813, Captain Oliver Hazard Perry led an armada of ships on Lake Erie in what was envisioned as the opening shot of an American charge into Canada. A quarter of Perry's approximately four hundred sailors were black. Originally, Captain Perry complained to his supervisor about having to lead such a force, which he derided as "a motley set, blacks, soldiers, and boys." His superior, Commander Isaac Chauncey, testily replied, "I regret you were not pleased with the men sent you . . . for to my knowledge a part of them are not surpassed by any seamen we have in the fleet and I have yet to learn that the color of skin or the cut and trimmings of the coat can affect a man's qualifications and usefulness. I have nearly fifty blacks on this boat and many of them are among the best of my men."

Perry's fleet defeated the British in the Battle of Lake Erie, giving the United States control of the area that is today's Michigan and briefly emboldening the pro-war "hawks," who dreamed of conquering Canada. Following the brutal battle, Perry reversed his earlier position and declared his black sailors "absolutely insensible to danger." In the report, he cited a number of black sailors specifically, including Cyrus Tiffany. An 1873 painting by William Henry Powell, which today hangs in the U.S. Capitol building, depicts Perry and a group of sailors abandoning the flagship *Laurence* during the battle. The work memorializes Tiffany as one of the rowers on Perry's boat.

The Americans' invigorated spirit of conquest was soon squelched when the British, having ended their ongoing conflict with France, began devoting more resources to the war. In August 1814 they burned Washington, D.C., drove out the government, and appeared poised for victory. But on September 11, Captain Thomas McDonough turned the war's tide again when his fleet defeated the British on Lake Champlain. The loss rattled the Brits, and they withdrew advancing forces all along the northern perimeter of the United States. Black sailors, of course, participated in that battle as well. However, they have been memorialized in a much different manner than their colleagues at Lake Erie. McDonough's victory prompted an Albany, New York, theater proprietor named Michael Hawkins to compose a song about the battle, which became one of the era's most popular war jingles. It was performed in blackface, using the mock dialect of a southern black sailor. An 1837 publication of the

Cyrus Tiffany is included in William Henry Powell's famous depiction of the Battle of Lake Eire. One quarter of the sailors in Captain Oliver Hazard Perry's armada were black.

song was adorned with the typical depiction of African Americans in nineteenth-century pop art: The crooning sailor is dressed in rags, bearing a bewildered expression, his hands and feet resembling the paws of an animal.

Following the war's end, blacks would go on serving in the navy, unrestrained. Finally, in 1839, with the nation at peace, Congress again acted to restrict black participation onboard America's fleet. Legislators, led by rabidly pro-slavery South Carolina Senator John C. Calhoun, passed a law that year capping black enlistment at five percent of the total navy manpower.

NEW ORLEANS BATTALION OF FREE MEN OF COLOR

While the black regiments of New York and Pennsylvania never saw battle, a historic group of free black soldiers in New Orleans—veterans of both the Revolutionary War and Santa Domingo's French army—were crucial parts of one of the war's most famous ground battles. Ironically, the bloody Battle of New Orleans, which took place two weeks after the Treaty of Ghent, officially brought an end to the fighting.

As part of its southern offensive, the British

forces set their sights on taking New Orleans, plotting an attack either from the Gulf Coast shores or overland from Alabama—where they were locked in battle with General Andrew Jackson's troops. Throughout its years of French and Spanish control, Louisiana had always enjoyed the service of a black militia, which the French and Spaniards had employed to hunt escaped slaves. When the United States took control of the territory, Governor William Claiborne began campaigning to reestablish the then-disbanded group. By the close of the century's first decade, New Orleans's population was half black. The majority of these men and women (about two thousand out of a population of thirty-five hun-

dred people of African descent) were refugees from Santa Domingo—people who had either supported or fought on behalf of the French during the island's successful 1809 slave uprising. When the war began, Claiborne not only felt this huge black population could help fend off a British onslaught, but he also feared that relegating such a large segment of the city to the sidelines would only encourage another British recruitment effort à la Lord Dunmore. President James Madison agreed, and Claiborne established the Battalion of Free Men of Color.

The battalion was to be led by white officers, with enlistment open to blacks who either had paid taxes for the previous two years or owned $300

More than ten percent of General Andrew Jackson's troops in the Battle of New Orleans were black. Still, drawings of the fight include only typically derisive depictions of blacks.

worth of property. There were, however, three black officers among the group: Second Lieutenants Isidore Honoré, Vincent Populus, and Joseph Savory. Populus would go on to become the first field-grade officer in the U.S. military. He and Honoré had both served in the original New Orleans black militia. Savory, who would be hailed as a hero in the Battle of New Orleans, was a veteran officer of the French army in Santa Domingo, however, who had fought against the rebelling slaves. Since fleeing the island, he had taken up with a reputed band of pirates and developed a name as a particularly fierce marauder.

In the fall of 1814, with the British attack apparently imminent, Madison tasked General Jackson to lead Louisiana's defense. Claiborne urged Jackson to utilize his black militia. Jackson, who had discovered heroic black soldiers among his forces in Mobile, was more than willing to do so. He created two all-black corps and offered free blacks who volunteered the same bounty paid to white enlistees: $124 and 160 acres of land at the war's close. "Through a mistaken policy," he told the black troops, "you have heretofore been deprived of participation in the glorious struggle for national rights in which our country is engaged. This no longer shall exist. As sons of freedom, you are now called upon to defend our most inestimable blessing." On December 18, just a week before the battle would begin, Jackson had another special address read to the black troops, using still more grand language. "To the Men of Color, Soldiers!" it began,

> **From the shores of Mobile I collected you to arms; I invited you to share in the perils and to divide the glory of your white countrymen. I expected much from you for I was not misinformed of those qualities which must render you so formidable to an invading foe. I knew that you would endure hunger and thirst and all the hardships of war. I knew that you loved the land of your nativity, and that, like ourselves, you had to defend all that is most dear to man; but you surpass my hopes. I have found in you, united to those qualities, that noble enthusiasm which impels to great deeds. Soldiers! The President of the United States shall be informed of your conduct on the present occasion, and the voice of the representatives of the American Nation shall applaud your valor, as your General now praises your ardor. The enemy is near; his sails cover the lakes; but the brave are united; and if he finds us contending among ourselves, it will be for the prize of valor, and fame its noblest reward.**

The Battle of New Orleans was actually two conflicts. The first occurred on December 23, 1814, when Jackson discovered the British camped just outside of the city. Caught off guard by the enemy's proximity, he launched a harrowing night assault, setting off a close combat battle that ended in relative deadlock. A few weeks later, on January 8, 1815, the main battle erupted when the British finally stormed the city. Jackson's December 18 address had drawn massive new black recruits, and as a result the army that met that British attack was around ten percent black. Jackson amassed all of his troops outside of town and recruited every able-bodied citizen to build a wall of mud and trees behind which his troops could stand while firing upon the advancing Brits. Two corps of around six hundred black troops

Contrary to popular depictions of the event, around 600 black soldiers formed the center of Jackson's Line—the largest collection of black troops ever to fight for the U.S.

formed the middle of this defense—which came to be known as "Jackson's Line"—forming the largest collection of black soldiers ever to fight for the United States. A third of those wounded in the battle would be from these corps. Popular memory of the battle would not include their sacrifice. Most subsequent prints depicting the heroic moment included blacks only as musket bearers and ammunition carriers, often in childlike or animalistic poses.

Jackson's troops turned the British attack back, striking one of the war's most acclaimed (if strategically meaningless) victories. The British, who never came close to crossing Jackson's Line, lost two thousand men, including their commanding general; Jackson's army suffered only thirteen deaths. Jackson heaped praise upon the black soldiers, offering particularly

glowing reports of Second Lieutenant Savory's heroism in both battles. He also later told President Madison that he was convinced "a free man of color, who was a famous rifle shot and came from the Attakaps region of Louisiana," had killed the Brits' general. Nevertheless, as had by now become a pattern in America's dealings with its African American soldiers, that praise would soon fade. Congress did not applaud the black fighters' valor, as Jackson had predicted, and the "noblest reward" the men received was more lofty rhetoric from their general. They never got a penny or an acre of their promised bounty. And, adding insult to injury, they were forbidden from joining the victory parade. Savory defiantly marched his two hundred men through the center of New Orleans anyway. Shortly thereafter, he left

America and returned to his lucrative pirating career.

The New Orleans Free Men of Color would be the last organized group of black soldiers in the U.S. Army until the Civil War. The army officially disbanded them in 1834.

A Final Uprising: John Brown's Raiders

As the nineteenth century progressed, the slave insurrections that typified its opening decades gave way to

John H. Copeland of John Brown's Army.

By the eve of the Civil War, freesoilers, such as John Brown, had cast aside the abolition movement's pacifism and embraced violent revolution.

a robust abolitionist movement led by pacifist figures such as William Lloyd Garrison. Uprisings, of course, still took place, but no slave rebellion shook the national psyche in the way Prosser's, Vesey's, or Turner's had. None, that is, until the eve of the Civil War. It was then, with a bloody battle over the status of Kansas as a free or slave state already raging, that John Brown launched his famous 1859 raid on the federal armory in Harpers Ferry, Virginia.

John Brown was a man befitting the legend that followed his death. Tall and thin, his sharp facial features gave him a severe profile, which was softened only by the long white beard he began wearing as a disguise later in life. He was a father of twenty children, a number of whom he recruited into his antislavery crusades. A fiery abolitionist-turned-revolutionary, Brown both inspired and frightened those who followed him. By the time he launched his Harpers

Ferry raid, the fifty-nine-year-old white militant had spent most of his life fighting slavery and had long concluded that the institution's demise would come by armed conflict alone. As early as 1847, he confided to fellow abolitionist Frederick Douglass that he planned to launch a national slave revolt, which would begin in Virginia. When he later attempted to recruit Douglass—who firmly believed the only way to derail slavery was to leverage the American system's own laws and values against it—the skeptical orator warned Brown that he was "going into a perfect steel trap."

But Brown could not be deterred by Douglass or others in the antislavery movement who believed violent revolution implausible. He recruited twenty-two men to form his "Provisional Army of the United States"—which included three of his sons—

and attacked Harpers Ferry on the morning of October 17, 1859. Five of the men were African American, including Dangerfield Newby. Shields Green was a twenty-three year old runaway slave from Charleston, South Carolina, who had been living with Douglass in Rochester, New York. He came south with one of Brown's sons to join the group. John Copeland and Lewis Sheridan Leary were classmates at Ohio's Oberlin College. The previous year they had joined a group, dubbed the "Oberlin Rescuers," that freed a captured slave from U.S. Marshals in protest of the Fugitive Slave Law, which allowed slaveholders to hunt down and recapture slaves who had escaped into free states. Free black printer Osborne Anderson, thirty-three, had also been an Oberlin student and had been with Brown in Canada since the previous year. Anderson, who would be one of five raiders to survive the ordeal, later

Lewis S. Leary, Copeland's classmate.

Black printer, Osborne Anderson.

Robert E. Lee led the federal troops and Virginia militiamen who captured Brown's raiders, killing ten of them in the process, as is depicted in this Harper's drawing.

published an account of the attack. He also subsequently fought in the Union Army during the Civil War.

The raid began well, with Brown's men successfully taking the armory, the fire engine house, a rifle factory, and the Baltimore & Ohio Railway Bridge, along with a handful of hostages. But the raiders failed in what may have been their most important charge: stopping the eastbound train before it left town. The escaped train quickly sent a telegraph to Washington, and by early morning on the eighteenth federal troops and Virginia militiamen, led by Colonel Robert E. Lee, had arrived and overpowered Brown's scrappy force. Ten of Brown's raiders were killed in the battle, including both Leary and Newby. Newby was the first killed, a six-inch spike shot

through his neck. On his mutilated body—which either livestock or angry white townspeople ravaged —officials found his wife Harriet's desperate letter. Shortly thereafter, she and her children were sold south.

Copeland and Green were taken captive along with Brown and the three remaining white raiders. All were hanged publicly. In a letter penned on the morning of his execution, Copeland assured his family that he had no regrets. "Let me tell you," he wrote, "that it is not the mere fact of having to meet death, which I should regret (if I should express regret I mean), but that such an unjust institution should exist as the one which demands my life, and not my life only, but the lives of those to whom my life bears but the relative value of zero to the infinite."

JOHN BROWN

Meeting the Slave-mother and her Child on the steps of Charlestown jail on his way to execution.

The Artist has represented Cap.t Brown regarding with a look of compassion a Slave-mother and Child who obstructed the passage on his way to the Scaffold.— Cap.t Brown stooped and kissed the Child— then met his fate.

FROM THE ORIGINAL PAINTING BY LOUIS RANSOM.

Brown, who was publicly hanged, became a martyr as the Civil War ignited. His visage was used in Northern propaganda posters, such as this one, and his name invoked in Union Army marching songs.

"IF WE MAKE HIM A SOLDIER, WE CONCEDE THE WHOLE QUESTION"

The Civil War

Few historical moments encapsulate America's relationship with its black military heroes as well as that of the first nationally recognized engagement between black Union regiments and Confederate troops. In May 1863, General Ulysses S. Grant decided that the rebel fort at Port Hudson, on the lower Mississippi River, was a serious obstacle in his drive toward Vicksburg. As the Confederate Army's last fort in the area, Port Hudson was heavily garrisoned and promised to be a stubborn victim for any attacking force. Grant was undeterred. And he chose two black regiments from Louisiana for the first assault.

None of the men in these regiments had seen significant combat so far. The regiments themselves, however, held a storied place in African American military history. The First and Third Louisiana Native Guard, also known as the Corps d'Afrique, were descendants of the New Orleans Free Men of Color who had defended the city against the British during the War of 1812. Even without fighting experience, they showed the same bravery during the Battle of Port Hudson as had their predecessors in Jackson's Line. Marching over fallen trees and under the fire of rebel guns, they stormed the fort again and again. Repelled by heavy fire each time, the regiments made

Louisiana Native Guard regiments, depicted here at Port Hudson, were the first black troops to gain national recognition during the Civil War.

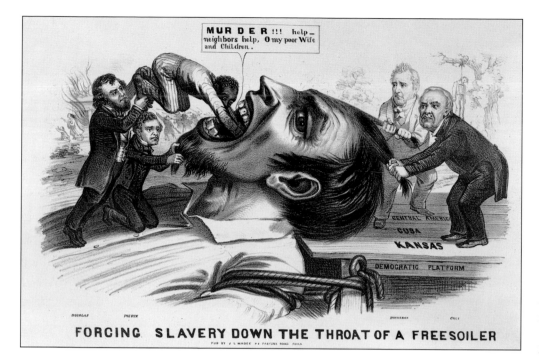

Decades worth of
compromises on slavery
failed to stave off war.
Here, an anti-slavery
propoganda poster.

seven drives and lost one fifth of their members before finally retreating. They had not won the battle, but they had weakened the installation enough to guarantee a second attack's success. And, more important, they had destroyed a thus far reluctant nation's belief that black soldiers could not be trusted to fight on behalf of the Union. "It is no longer possible," the venerable *New York Times* declared, "to doubt the bravery and steadiness of the colored race, when rightly led."

The latter phrase of the *Times* statement was not an insignificant one. Despite the now long history of African American military heroism in both the Revolutionary War and the War of 1812, white America still could not believe that black soldiers were committed and capable fighters in their own right. Their success, the nation concluded, was contingent upon white leadership. It was an assertion that would become the American military's mantra

in the post-Civil War era dealings with black soldiers. But what the *Times* and others chose to ignore was that the Native Guard, owing to its history as a quasi-independent militia, was unique. Black officers were by and large banned in the Union Army; but in the Native Guard, two out of every three officers were black. They had indeed been "rightly led" at Port Hudson.

From the beginning, the issue of slavery set the United States on a collision course with itself. The nation's deep divide over slavery—where it should exist, in what form, and for how long—almost prevented its formation in the first place. Northern Constitutional Convention delegates who wanted to reign in an institution they believed would burden the country's future knew they could do so only if they were willing to move ahead without the southern colonies—which of course they were not capable of doing. Slavery was a deal breaker, so both northern and southern delegates punted it, declaring that nothing would change until at least 1808. President Washington, despite confiding to close colleagues his distaste for slavery, was eager to keep the issue off his agenda as well. Congress would be no more engaging, and in 1836 went so far as to pass a procedural rule banning members from reading antislavery petitions into the record, or acting on them in any way, for that matter. But despite these efforts, American politicians could not ignore slavery. While recurring uprisings kept the issue hot in the minds of the citizenry, the country's constant growth forced its reluc-

President Lincoln sought to define the conflict narrowly, but much Union propaganda tied the war to the Revolutionary era ethos of liberty for all.

tant policy makers to return to the debate over slavery again and again.

The divide, of course, was not primarily a moral one for white politicians. By and large, those who opposed slavery did so because they desired a strong federal government, and because they believed the plantation aristocracy held disproportionate sway over the national economy. They were either northern businessmen longing for a more diverse economy or small farmers struggling under the hegemony of large, slave-labor plantations. As new states joined the Union, these antislavery forces wanted them to enter as "free soil" states, where slavery was banned. Pro-slavery southerners rightly saw this as an attempt to slowly decrease their influence in national government and eradicate their livelihood.

The first threatening strains appeared in 1819. That year, the Louisiana Purchase brought the Missouri Territory, where slavery thrived, into the Union. Bringing the territory in as a slave state would have upset the even balance of free versus slave states. So Kentucky Senator Henry Clay hammered out the Missouri Compromise, under which northern Massachusetts would become the independent state of Maine, a free soil state, and Missouri would enter as a slave state. To avoid future problems, legislators drew a line across the continent at thirty-six degrees thirty minutes north latitude. All future new states above the line were to be free; those below it were to be slave. This tenuous agreement held until 1850, when California's entry as a free state again momentarily threatened the nation's stability. But finally, in 1854, the Nebraska Territory's entry into the Union presented more problems than could be compromised away.

In order to win southern support for the Nebraska Territory's statehood, Illinois Democratic

Senator Stephen Douglas—who was eager to see the area developed in order to ease the planned transcontinental railroad's passage through Chicago—crafted a bill that split the territory into two states: Kansas and Nebraska. Each state could decide its own status, slave or free. Nebraska was certain to declare itself free, but Kansas, sitting adjacent to the slave state Missouri, was questionable. Both pro-slavery and antislavery forces flooded the state in an effort to establish its status, and eventually their disputes opened up into violent conflict.

All of this came to a head with the election of President Abraham Lincoln. Through his 1858 campaign against Douglas for the Illinois Senate seat and his subsequent 1960 presidential campaign, Lincoln had become the face of the "free soil" movement. When he was narrowly elected the sixteenth president, the slave states believed it marked the beginning of their end. South Carolina immediately seceded from the Union, followed shortly by six others. And in February 1861, the willing exiles formed the Confederate States of America. On April 12, South Carolina attacked the Union's Fort Sumter, launching America's bloodiest war to date.

Fighting with One Hand

At the time the war began, four million Americans—one in seven—were of African descent. Three and a half million of those people lived in the South, primarily as slaves. In each of the nation's previous wars, the conflict had held at least some promise of liberation for the masses of African Americans in that region. But this time, black America reasoned, the conflict was wholly about their right to freedom. As a result, all across the North, free blacks eagerly offered their service to the Union Army in the days following the Sumter attack. Lincoln had immediately called on the nation to raise a 7,500-man force. In New York, black leaders responded by offering to assemble and finance three black regiments. In Philadelphia, the Prince Hall African Masonic Lodge—the nation's first black Masons—formed two black regiments and offered their service. In Washington, D.C., a group of one hundred blacks wrote Secretary of War Simon Cameron, asking to join the effort. Similar offers reached governors and local commanders all over the North.

But the 1792 Militia Act—which the army had interpreted as banning black enlistment—remained in place, and thus the North began the war with the same whitewashed army that fought the War of 1812. Lincoln saw no reason to change this. For one, he understandably assumed the North could easily quell the rebellion with a white army. The region was home to over twice as many whites as the South, and to a wide range of industries that were much more useful to wartime production needs than the agrarian South. But more important, Lincoln was loath to inflame the conflict by arming blacks. Such a bold step would have sent what he saw as exactly the wrong message to the seceded states—that Lincoln wasn't ready to compromise in order to bring them back into the Union—and, worse still, may have chased more border states into the Confederacy. As it was, his military response to the attack on Sumter had prompted four additional states to secede.

Abolitionist leaders, however, immediately turned their focus to lobbying Lincoln to enlist African Americans. What better way to break the back of slavery than to allow blacks to fight against it? Years later, as the Confederacy considered arming slaves in a desperate attempt to forestall defeat, rebel

Frederick Douglass relentlessly pressured Lincoln
to allow blacks to fight.

General Clement Stevens would, ironically, articulate the abolitionists' logic best, arguing, "The justification of slavery in the South is the inferiority of the Negro. If we make him a soldier we concede the whole question."

That was how Frederick Douglass felt as well, and as the nation's most well known abolitionist he needled Lincoln on the point at every turn. Not all African Americans agreed, and there was a robust debate within northern free communities over whether blacks should be willing to die to preserve a nation that allowed a racial caste system to persist. But to Douglass, this was the black community's best opportunity to force an end to all of that. He argued that Lincoln needed not only to arm blacks but to explicitly cast the war as one being fought for the slaves' emancipation. Throughout the summer and

fall of 1861, as the Union suffered unexpected defeats, it became increasingly clear that the war was going to be a prolonged one. So Douglass turned up the heat on the president, arguing that the North would lose if it did not utilize all of its resources. "This is no time to fight with one hand, when both are needed," he wrote in a September 1861 essay. "This is no time to fight only with your white hand, and allow your black hand to remain tied."

Early Black Fighters

Despite intense pressure, Lincoln held his ground against enlisting blacks for the better part of the war's first two years. The furthest he went—following the Union's unexpected loss to General Thomas "Stonewall" Jackson at Bull Run, Virginia, in July 1861—was to authorize the enlistment of fifty thousand African Americans for menial labor and noncombat duties such as scouting and blacksmithing. But as with every previous prohibition on black enlistment, the ban was only as strong as the field commanders' willingness to respect it. And several Union officers were unwilling to do so from the very beginning of the war.

Perhaps the most outspoken of these renegade officers was General John Frémont, head of the Western Department. Frémont was a former Republican Party presidential aspirant and an outspoken free-soiler who was allied with the abolition movement. Headquartered in contentious Missouri —one of the border states about which Lincoln worried most—the brash general decided in August 1861 to do just what Lincoln would not. He declared that all slaves who joined the Union Army would be emancipated. His pronouncement enraged both the Confederate forces, who intensified guerrilla

General John C. Frémont, an ardent freesoiler, angered Lincoln by offering emancipation to all slaves who joined his army in Missouri.

attacks in Missouri, and Lincoln, who promptly fired Frémont. After protests from prominent abolitionists such as Douglass and William Lloyd Garrison, as well as a plea from Mrs. Frémont—an abolitionist herself—Lincoln reinstated the general but assigned him to the far West, where he could not impact the war.

Kansas Senator James Lane was another leader who bucked Lincoln on the issue of arming blacks. Lane had been a free-soil partisan in the Kansas dispute that preceded the war and had been close with such militant figures as John Brown. When the war broke out, he organized volunteer regiments to defend Kansas and western Missouri. One of those regiments was an all-black force, launched in August 1862 and dubbed the First Kansas Colored Volunteers. Lane recruited at least five hundred men to join the regiment in just a few weeks, openly defying orders from Lincoln's War Department. Two months later, on October 28, the regiment became the first group of black troops to fight in the Civil War, in a battle near Butler, Missouri.

Both Lane and his First Kansas Volunteers would meet tragic ends. The black regiment was eventually officially mustered into the Union Army and fought most of the war. But in the fall of 1864, the regiment was overpowered by Confederate troops at Poison Spring, Arkansas. As the First Kansas retreated, the rebels massacred the injured stragglers rather than taking prisoners; almost half of the four-hundred-troop regiment was lost.

Following the war, Lane briefly joined the "Radical Republicans" in calling for civil rights for African Americans, but then defected in support of President Andrew Jackson's more moderate vision for Reconstruction. When his old allies harshly criticized him for the switch, Lane committed suicide.

Refugees from southern plantations became known as "contraband" during the war.

FIRST SOUTH CAROLINA VOLUNTEERS

In November 1861, the Union Navy took a group of islands off the coast of South Carolina called the Sea Islands. They were home to several of the region's largest cotton plantations, and as the white owners fled, they left behind not only their land but also thousands of slaves. One of the Union's most difficult logistical issues emerged: refugees. Early in the war, General Benjamin Butler exacerbated the problem when a Confederate officer petitioned him at Fort Monroe in Virginia for the return of escaped slaves. Butler informed the rebel leader that since the slaves were technically used in support of the rebels' insurrection, they were considered "contraband of war" and would not be returned. Slaves began rushing into Fort Monroe and other Union strongholds throughout the South.

As the war dragged on, Union officers would rack their brains about what to do with the thousands of abandoned and escaped slaves that joined their armies

as they crossed Confederate lines. They established what came to be known as "contraband camps." These squalid tent and shack communities were the sight of many of the first contacts between northern whites and southern blacks. It was here that white America was introduced to African American spirituals, dance, and other customs. And it was here that many Americans finally came face-to-face with slavery's brutality, as they learned of the barely livable conditions under which southern blacks toiled. Late in the war, General William Sherman would famously attempt to replace contraband camps with self-sufficient communities. He declared that each emancipated family his army encountered would receive "forty acres of tillable ground" in the Sea Islands or coastal areas of South Carolina, along with an army mule.

But General David Hunter came up with another solution altogether for the over eight thousand refugees he met upon taking the Sea Islands in late 1861. Where others saw contraband, Hunter saw soldiers. Faced with a manpower shortage, in the spring of 1862 Hunter echoed Frémont and declared free all slaves who escaped and joined his army. He then set about recruiting from the Sea Island refugees, in many cases impressing them into service rather than waiting for them to volunteer. Lincoln, of course, was furious and immediately issued a statement nullifying Hunter's emancipation offer and disbanding his black regiment. Lincoln, however, did allow one company of the regiment to stand. By this point, the beleaguered president had begun plotting his own emancipation order and the establishment of a segregated black army. So that summer, the War Department allowed General Rufus Saxton, Hunter's replacement, to move forward with the planned black regiment, starting with the leftover company. He created the First South Carolina Colored Volunteers, the first

As they faced manpower shortages, Union officers began to impress refugee slaves into labor.

The First South Carolina Colored Volunteers, the first black unit recognized by the Union Army.

Contraband camps were the sight of many of the first encounters between northern whites and southern blacks.

Contraband camps were squalid tent cities where the Union Army housed slave refugees. Many refugees worked as servants and cooks in army camps as well.

black unit officially recognized by the Union Army.

By fall of 1862, Saxton had recruited approximately five thousand black troops for the First South Carolina. They were led by white officers and com-

manded by the young Colonel Thomas Wentworth Higginson—a Boston abolitionist who had been one of the "secret six" who financed John Brown's raid on Harpers Ferry. Higginson soon began leading the regiment on missions along the southeastern coast. Impressed with their abilities even without significant training, Higginson wrote proudly of these missions as proof that the Union could win the war if only it rallied the valuable military resource African Americans offered. "Instead of leaving their homes and families to fight," he reasoned, "they are fighting for their homes and families, and they show the resolution and sagacity which a personal purpose gives."

LOUISIANA NATIVE GUARD

While the First South Carolina was the first black unit officially recognized by the Union Army, the regiments of the Louisiana Native Guard were the first actually mustered into its ranks. More important, they fought two of the three battles credited with winning the nation's support for enlisting African Americans.

The Native Guard actually joined the war on behalf of the Confederate Army. When Louisiana seceded from the Union in early 1861, Governor Thomas Moore called for volunteers to help defend the state, and he welcomed free blacks to join the effort. Many African Americans responded, including at least one former member of the historic New Orleans Free Men of Color. Just as they had done before the 1815 Battle of New Orleans, leaders in the free black community raised the Louisiana Native Guard regiments to defend their beloved city. For them, the concern was not whether the Union or the rebels would prevail but whether New Orleans would survive the conflict. So when the Union Navy retook the city in April 1862, the Native Guard refused to retreat with the Confederate forces. Instead, they simply offered their services in defending the city to the incoming Union Army.

General Butler, who had been transferred from the post in Virginia where he created the Union's contraband policy, was smart enough to accept the Native Guard's offer. He put out another call for free blacks to join the group and informed the War Department soon thereafter that he had recruited one thousand soldiers for the Native Guard, including seventy-five black line officers. That fall, he mustered them into the Union Army.

Soon thereafter, in May 1863, the Native Guard gripped the nation's attention with their valor in the battle at Port Hudson. But that was only the beginning. Port Hudson had been a stirring effort, but it ended in defeat. One month later, in the Battle of Milliken's Bend, the Native Guard won the first battle credited to the fighting of black Union soldiers. On June 7, an estimated 3,000 Confederate troops attacked a 1,400-man Native Guard force camped just outside of Vicksburg, Mississippi. The rebels stormed the outnumbered Union troops' camp and engaged them in what is counted as the longest hand-to-hand battle of the Civil War. It dragged on for seven hours, with Confederate troops surrounding the camp and firing on the Union soldiers even as the bayonet fighting continued, until the Union ship *Choctaw* finally arrived and forced the rebels' retreat. The Union lost 652 soldiers, mostly Native Guard members. But their inconceivable effort in holding the camp further solidified the growing sentiment that black troops should be rallied into the war. "The bravery of the blacks in the Battle of Milliken's Bend," remarked Assistant Secretary of War Charles Dana, "completely revolutionized the sentiment of the Army with regard to the employment of Negro troops."

The Louisiana Native Guard secured the first battle victory credited to black troops, a seven-hour, hand-to-hand engagement at Milliken's Bend.

IN THE CONFEDERACY

Ironically, the Confederacy never shared Lincoln's reluctance to use slaves in the war effort. The rebels certainly weren't going to arm the region's African Americans, but they were more than willing to use their labor. Both slaves and free blacks were impressed into service throughout the South,

Jeff Fields traveled with Confederate President Jefferson Davis as his cook.

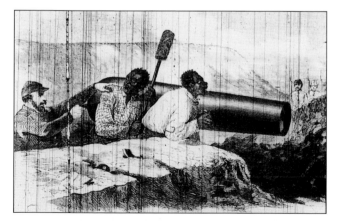

Northern cartoonists mocked the fact that the Confederacy impressed slaves from the war's outset.

building fortifications and performing the same menial duties for the rebel troops as they had done for plantation owners. Confederate President Jefferson Davis, for instance, traveled with his black cook, Jeff Fields. In photographs, Fields even appears to be wearing a Confederate uniform. But while plans for using slaves as soldiers circulated toward the war's end, the Confederacy never mobilized African Americans as part of its combat force.

The U.S. Colored Troops

While Lincoln kept up a stern front against arming black soldiers throughout the war's second year, he secretly spent most of 1862 plotting to recast the war in exactly the terms Douglass and the abolitionists were calling for. By July, he had begun discussing a national emancipation order with his cabinet. New Secretary of War Edwin Stanton was particularly

This 1864 print revolutionized American art's treatment of blacks. Depicting an announcement of the Emancipation Proclamation, it focuses on the freed slaves rather than the soldier reading the document.

Most art memorializing the Emancipation Proclamation lionized Lincoln's benevolence to humble black slaves.

supportive of the idea because it would give his army access to new recruits and foment chaos across the South. In September, just as the Louisiana Native Guard and First South Carolina Volunteers were joining the Union ranks, Lincoln issued a preliminary order warning that slaves would be freed in all states that had not rejoined the Union by the first of the year. Then, on January 1, 1863, he issued his Emancipation Proclamation. The decree was actually more symbolic than anything else. It freed only the slaves in Confederate states, and therefore it actually meant nothing until the Union Army could conquer those territories. But the proclamation changed the nature of the war by both reshaping its goals and opening the army to blacks. And as Douglass predicted, it marked the beginning of the end for slavery and represented the first strike in the struggle to destroy America's racial caste system.

COME AND JOIN US BROTHERS.

The Union Army created posters such as this one to recruit nearly 210,000 African American soldiers for its all-black regiments.

The Emancipation Proclamation also revolutionized the manner in which blacks were depicted in American art. For the first time in American history, following the Emancipation Proclamation and throughout the Civil War, printmakers began depicting African Americans in heroic rather than demeaning portraits. Perhaps the most famous example is an 1864 print published by a Hartford, Connecticut, printmaker titled *Reading the Emancipation Proclamation*. It shows a white Union soldier, who is presumably part of a force occupying a Confederate territory, reading the freedom order to a group of slaves. Unlike all previous prints commemorating Lincoln's proclamation, this one focused on the freed blacks rather than lionizing the freedom-granting whites. It is credited as the first of many future Civil War-era prints to finally begin accurately depicting African Americans.

TO THE FRONT LINES

Things heated up immediately following the Emancipation Proclamation. In March 1863, the South Carolina Volunteers took Jacksonville, Florida, earning still more respect for black soldiers in both the North and South. In May, Stanton's War Department made the Proclamation's military clauses official with General Order 143, which created the United States Colored Troops—a segregated army section for black regiments led by white officers.

Douglass and other abolitionists turned their energies from lobbying Lincoln to helping recruit black fighters. From that point and throughout the war, both free blacks and escaped slaves rushed to join the Union Army and Navy. In all, 209,145 African Americans served in the Civil War, an esti-

"HE DIED FOR ME!"

Between 38,000 and 68,000 black troops died in the war.

mated 174,000 of them former slaves. The 166 USCT regiments that served throughout the war fought in 449 engagements. Somewhere between 38,000 and 68,000 African Americans lost their lives.

Twenty black Civil War soldiers would receive the newly created Congressional Medal of Honor for their service—the nation's highest military honor. (Twenty-one men actually earned the honor, but one was never issued. On January 16, 2001, President

Bill Clinton presented Corporal Andrew Jackson Smith's daughter with the Medal of Honor he earned during the Battle of Honey Hill in November 1864.) One Medal of Honor winner was Sergeant Major Christian Fleetwood from Baltimore, Maryland. The five-foot-four, 125-pound twenty-three-year-old joined the Fourth Regiment, USCT, in 1863 and won his medal for valor during the grueling Battle of Chafin's Farm, Virginia, in September 1864. He and Private Charles Veal saved their Fourth Regiment, USCT, colors along with the American flag, then took over leadership after discovering that all the commissioned officers had been killed. Both received Medals of Honor. Fleetwood was highly literate, and his correspondence with family and newspapers throughout the war has helped historians understand the world

Christian Fleetwood was among twenty-one black Medal of Honor winners.

black soldiers confronted. "I have never been able to understand how Veal and I lived under such a hail of bullets," he wrote in his diary, reflecting on the fight at Chafin's Farm. "Unless it was because we were both such little fellows." Fleetwood left the military at the war's end, declaring that he had joined to abolish slavery and, that accomplished, wanted to join the social and political fight for civil rights.

By the war's end, fully twelve percent of the Union's forces were black. For many of these men, enlistment was not just an opportunity to fight for their own freedom; it was also a chance to immediately improve the lives of their families. They joined in search of housing, education, and income. Often, their wives and children could also work in the army camps as laundresses or in other support roles. Other

Service offered freed slaves a quick route to education, employment, and housing.

Harriet Tubman served as a nurse and spy.

women, such as Underground Railroad conductor Harriet Tubman, served as nurses and spies. The life of a soldier at least held the promise of being a far cut above that of a slave or a refugee. A moving installation at the African American Civil War Museum in Washington, D.C., graphically depicts the army's transformative potential. It presents a photograph of a teenage slave before his enlistment, dressed in tattered rags, and juxtaposes it with the proud portrait of him in the uniform he wore as a drummer in the Union Army. Similarly, a famous series of photographs of a Louisiana enlistee named Peter Godan—reproduced in the July 4, 1863, edition of *Harper's Weekly*—poignantly illustrates the man's journey from battered slave to freedom fighter.

But slaves also joined the Union Army in an effort to find and liberate family members who remained in bondage. Slave economics had ripped apart countless black families by selling spouses and children to different plantations around the South. Once free, people such as Private Spotswood Rice, an escaped slave from Glasgow, Missouri, joined the war hoping to reunite their families. Rice enlisted in February 1864. That September, as his regiment headed toward Glasgow, he sent letters to his daughters telling them that he was on his way. "Be assured that I will have you," he promised Corra and Mary, "if it cost me my life." Rice also put the woman who held his daughters on notice. "I want you to understand Kittey Diggs that where ever you and I meets we are enemies to each other," he wrote. "I offered once to pay you forty dollars for my own child but I am glad now that you did not accept it. Just hold on now as long as you can and the worse it will be for you."

Confederate troops, meanwhile, displayed an equal passion about the prospect of blacks fighting in the Union Army. The same month that Lincoln for-

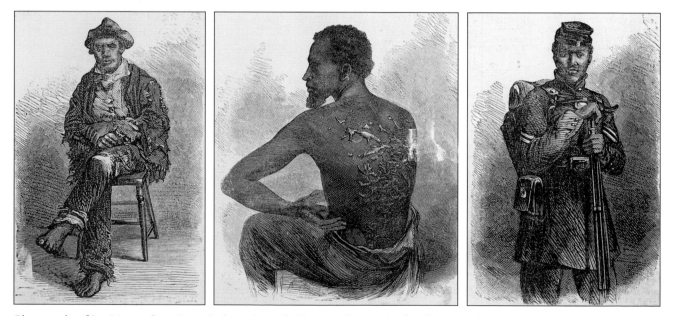

Photographs of Louisiana enlistee Peter Godan poignantly illustrate the typical refugee's journey from slave to soldier.

Southern cartoonists mocked the Union's use of black soldiers, who they depicted as scared to fight.

mally established the USCT, the Confederate Congress passed a law declaring that all white commanders of black troops would be put to death if captured. General Nathan Bedford Forrest offered a soldiers. Meanwhile, black prisoners of war were to be enslaved. Lincoln responded with a similarly ruthless policy. In September 1863 he promised to execute a Confederate prisoner for every Union white officer or black soldier killed while captive. For every black soldier enslaved, he pledged to sentence a Confederate prisoner to a life of hard labor.

General Forrest, however, was undeterred by Lincoln's threats and would later orchestrate one of the Civil War's most galling war crimes. Following an embarrassing defeat in March 1864, Forrest decided to respond with an overwhelming attack on the Union's Fort Pillow in Tennessee. He brought a force of 1,500 men to take the installation, which was manned with fewer than 600 members of the Eleventh USCT and the white Thirteenth Tennessee Cavalry. Forrest's troops stormed Fort Pillow on the morning of April 12, killing 231 Union soldiers, mostly African American, wounding over 100, and taking 226 prisoners—only 58 of whom were black. According to reports from northern witnesses, the rebels rejected black soldiers' surrender and instead massacred them. Some were buried or burned alive, others' corpses were butchered. Black women and children in the camp were slaughtered along with the soldiers. Forrest, who would go on to become the imperial wizard of the Ku Klux Klan, declared in his battle report that the engagement proved black soldiers "cannot cope with Southerners." Forrest would become a Southern hero. Thomas Dixon's 1905 novel *The Clansman*, from which the controversial 1915 movie *Birth of a Nation* was made, was based on Forrest's life.

Fort Pillow became the subject of one of the prints that reflected the era's broadening artistic conception of African Americans. Printmakers Kurz and Allison produced a work depicting the massacre. It was one of a series of wildly popular prints the pair published that featured African Americans in battle

Printmakers Kurz and Allison's popular rendering of the Fort Pillow massacre.

during the Civil War, and it could be found in many homes in black America's slowly emerging professional class at the turn of the century.

BLACK OFFICERS

The logic that black troops required white leaders to succeed persevered throughout the war. There were only just over one hundred black commissioned officers in the Union Army. Almost a third of those were the seventy-five officers of the Louisiana Native Guard, commissioned at the time of its muster by General Butler, before the USCT officially came into existence. The remaining officers were primarily either surgeons or chaplains, rather than battlefield leaders.

The two highest-ranking African American officers during the Civil War were Majors Alexander Augusta and Martin Delany, both surgeons. Major Augusta, the first black officer to be buried in Arlington National Cemetery, was commissioned as a surgeon for the Seventh Regiment, USCT, on April 4, 1863, and thus was the first African American in the U.S. Army to become a field grade officer—the leaders who make up the armed forces' second tier of commanders. At the end of the war, he was made an honorary lieutenant colonel, the highest rank for field officers.

Major Delany, however, was the first African American officially commissioned as a field-grade line officer—or an officer who actually leads troops in combat. Delany, one of the abolition movement's most militant voices, had spent years prodding the country on its problems with race and had helped Douglass found the abolitionist journal *The North Star*. When the Civil War erupted, he was in Liberia scouting out territory for the repatriation of African Americans to West Africa. When Lincoln issued the

Major Martin Delany, the first black staff officer in the Union Army.

Emancipation Proclamation, however, Delany returned home. He then spent much of the war helping recruit black troops and campaigning to have black officers lead the USCT. Those efforts finally paid off on February 27, 1865, when Secretary of War Stanton commissioned him as Major of the 104th Regiment, USCT. Stanton intended to have Delany establish a camp in the South to train other black line officers to lead the USCT, but the war ended shortly thereafter and usurped those plans.

DEMANDING EQUAL PAY

The relative handful of African Americans that were able to win a commission were nonetheless victim to the one form of military discrimination that black

Blacks, regardless of rank, earned $7 a month; whites could earn as much as $100 a month.

soldiers of all rank found most insulting. The lowest-ranking white soldier, from the day of his enlistment, earned $13 a month plus a clothing allowance. As he rose in rank, so did his pay, reaching as high as $100 a month as a chaplain. But due to the lingering effects of the same 1792 Militia Act that had kept African Americans from fighting at the start of the war, no black soldier made more than $10 a month, regardless of rank or time served, with a $3 clothing fee subtracted from that wage. This disparity stemmed from the fact that the legislators who crafted the 1862 law loosening the Militia Act's ban on black service envisioned African Americans as laborers rather than fighters, and they established a pay scale accordingly.

When Lincoln created the USCT, its commanding officer, General Lorenzo Thomas, petitioned for the pay scale to be equalized. Congress, however, ignored him, absurdly citing the salary regulations of the laws that actually forbade the USCT's

existence in the first place. African American soldiers and their civilian supporters were outraged. The abolitionists again refocused their activism, leaving behind recruitment efforts to lobby for equal pay. Within the ranks, some blacks protested by refusing to fight. Sergeant William Walker of the Third South Carolina Colored Volunteers led his colleagues in a work stoppage beginning in November 1863. But the army swiftly responded by dubbing the protest mutiny and executing Walker the following March. Most black regiments instead protested by refusing to accept any pay until it was the same as that of their white counterparts. Many of the white USCT officers joined their men in the protest.

Corporal James Henry Gooding, of the famous Massachusetts Fifty-fourth USCT Regiment, sent dispatches from the front in the *New Bedford Mercury* throughout the war. In September 1863, Corporal Gooding used his column to publish an open letter to the president challenging the unequal pay scale. "Now

A portrait of Company E of the Fourth U.S. Colored Infantry, taken sometime between 1863 and 1865 at Fort Lincoln in Washington, D.C.

the main question is, Are we Soldiers, or are we Labourers?" he asked. "We are fully armed and equipped, have done all the various Duties pertaining to a Soldier's life, have conducted ourselves to the complete satisfaction of General Officers, who were, if anything, prejudiced against us, but who now accord us all the encouragement and honour due us; have shared the perils and Labour of Reducing the first stronghold that flaunted a Traitor Flag; and more, Mr. President. Today the Anglo-Saxon Mother, Wife, or Sister are not alone in tears for departed Sons, Husbands and Brothers. . . . Now your Excellency, we have done a Soldier's Duty. Why can't we have a Soldier's pay?"

Sailor Robert Smalls was one of the war's most acclaimed heroes.

As usual, necessities of war finally moved Congress to alter its policy. As casualties mounted, the Union could ill afford to upset its recruitment efforts. So in June 1864, Congress partially relented. The new regulation allowed for equal pay, but only for soldiers who were free at the war's outset. Moreover, it only provided for payment of back salaries through January 1 of that year. The abolitionists' protests continued, while the USCT officers devised a way to pay the troops who were not free when the rebels attacked Sumter—the men who made up the vast majority of the Union's black soldiers. In what came to be known as the "Quaker Oath," USCT officers simply asked their men to swear that they "owed no man unrequited labor" at the war's outset, accepting the standard affirmative reply without question. Eventually, in March 1865, Congress finally gave up the game and allowed payment of all troops, including back pay to the date of each man's enlistment.

FIGHTING AT SEA

At midnight on March 13, 1862, one of the Civil War's most celebrated black heroes made the first of his many marks on American history. Robert Smalls was the pilot of the Confederate ship *Planter*, docked in Charleston Harbor and loaded down with guns and ammunition to be delivered to Fort Ripley. He'd been quietly awaiting his chance to escape, and when all of the ship's white officers went ashore that night, he knew his time had come. Smalls gathered his seven-man black crew and convinced them to help him steal both the vessel and their freedom. The men slipped off and collected their families, Smalls disguised himself in the overcoat and hat of the ship's white captain, and

The Crew of the gunboat Mendota. Between 10,000 and 30,000 blacks served in the Union Navy aboard integrated vessels.

they set sail. Smalls guided the *Planter* past six Confederate military installations, including the vaulted Forts Sumter and Johnson, before he safely arrived at the Union's offshore blockade.

Smalls's daring deed immediately entered Civil War legend. He was whisked off to meet Lincoln and became a pilot in the Union Navy. After the war, in 1876, he would be elected to represent South Carolina in Congress and would serve five terms, becoming an internationally recognized African American leader. The *Planter* would be used to ferry the South Carolina Colored Volunteers up and down the southeastern coast for their raids into Georgia and Florida. And when the Union retook Fort Sumter in April 1865, Smalls would pilot the *Planter* to the ceremony, carrying two hundred African Americans to join the celebration.

Smalls was one of thousands of African American sailors in the Union Navy. Shortly after the war began, Secretary of the Navy Gideon Welles lifted the five-percent limit on black enlistment that South Carolina Senator John Calhoun had pushed through Congress following the War of 1812. As usual, the nation's manpower needs outweighed its racism. But Welles limited recruitment to free men and restricted their service to support positions such as cooks and assistant gunners. The following spring, however, as disease took its toll on white sailors, Welles again revised the policy, now opening enlistment to contraband as well as allowing blacks to serve in all roles.

The numbers on how many African Americans served in the Union Navy are in dispute. Estimates range from ten thousand, which would have been around thirteen percent of the navy's men, to around twenty-nine thousand, which would have been a quarter of the force. Either way, as had been the case from the navy's inception, black and white sailors served in fully integrated environments. The rigors of sea life have never been hospitable to segregation. Around eight hundred black sailors were killed in battle during the Civil War, and at least another two thousand by disease—which was by far the largest cause of death at sea. Four black navy men won Medals of Honor.

John Lawson was one of four black Naval Medal of Honor winners.

The Massachusetts Fifty-fourth

Of all the Union Army's black units and heroes, none have achieved the notoriety heaped upon the Massachusetts Fifty-fourth Regiment. Its history has been the subject of countless books, both academic and popular, documentaries, and Web sites. In 1989, the regiment's story was told in the Academy Award-winning film *Glory*, featuring some of Hollywood's most acclaimed black actors. The Fifty-fourth perhaps owes its fame to a number of unique circumstances. It was the first black unit recruited in the North and the first to be comprised of almost all freemen. The era's most notable civic figures in both black and white communities were heavily involved in its creation. And, most of all, as with the Louisiana Native Guard, the Fifty-fourth led one of the war's most dramatic battles in which they finally put to rest any misgivings about the use of black troops in the North. The battle also generated the nation's first black Medal of Honor winner.

Immediately following the Emancipation Proclamation, Massachusetts Governor John Andrew, an abolitionist, began petitioning the administration to allow him to raise a black regiment in his state. By the end of January 1863, he had the go-ahead to create two regiments led by white officers. He chose young Robert Gould Shaw, the son of a prominent abolitionist couple, and Norwood P. Hallowell to recruit and lead his Fifty-fourth and Fifty-fifth Regiments. Most of the other white officers were also sons of prominent abolitionists, many of whom were financing the regiments. Only two of the commissioned officers,

**Robert Gould Shaw led the famous Massachusetts
Fifty-fourth Regiment.**

FORT WAGNER

During its first months in the South, the Fifty-fourth found itself largely relegated to noncombat duties. It was a source of immense annoyance for both the black troops and Captain Shaw. They believed General George Strong resented their presence and was deliberately keeping them from battle, and Shaw vocally petitioned for a chance to show his regiment's fighting skills. That opportunity finally came in mid-July. The regiment was part of a massing Union force outside of Charleston, South Carolina, that was preparing for a major assault on the key Confederate city. On July 16, they were sent to an engagement on nearby James Island, where the Tenth Connecticut was being overrun by Confederate troops. The Fifty-fourth rescued the white regiment and helped beat a safe retreat.

After returning to Morris Island on a two-day, nonstop march, Shaw reported to General Strong and received his now infamous orders. The campaign against Charleston was to begin with an assault on the fiercely guarded Fort Wagner, and the Fifty-fourth was assigned to lead the charge. Many historians

William Jackson and Samuel Harrison, were black. Both men were chaplains, and Governor Andrew had to lobby the War Department strenuously for their commission.

Recruitment got off to a slow start. Massachusetts was home to few African Americans, and those there were relatively well-off, middle-class professionals who would not benefit from service in the way that escaped slaves and contraband in the South would. Governor Andrew expanded his recruitment nationally and secured the aid of black leaders such as Douglass and Delany. By that May, the Fifty-fourth had over one thousand members, including Douglass's sons Charles and Lewis. On the twenty-eighth, they marched through Boston headed for the front, with the Fifty-fifth to follow in a few weeks.

The Massachusetts black regiments were the first to enter Charleston when it fell.

Kurz and Allison also recreated the Fifty-fourth's tragically heroic charge on Fort Wagner.

believe General Strong hoped to use the black troops as cannon fodder—sending them on a suicide mission that would draw fire and open cracks that his white regiments could then follow. Whether or not that was the case, Shaw and the men of the Fifty-fourth eagerly accepted their assignment.

At noon on July 18, 1863, after Union cannons had bombarded Wagner all morning, the Fifty-fourth set off down a narrow slip of beach, charging the Confederate fort head-on. Previous Union assaults earlier that week had produced over three hundred casualties, with only twelve Confederate

deaths. Hiding behind sand dunes along the way, the Fifty-fourth nevertheless marched over one thousand yards under fire from not only Wagner but five other nearby Confederate forts as well. Despite massive loss of life, including Shaw's, they successfully charged to Wagner's gates and, during a three-hour bayonet battle, placed the American flag on its parapet. During this charge, Sergeant William Carney earned the first Medal of Honor awarded to an African American.

Carney, a Norfolk, Virginia, native, escaped slavery as a teenager and relocated in New Bedford, Massachusetts, where he joined the Christian ministry.

William Carney was the nation's first black
Medal of Honor winner.

In February 1863, he answered Governor Andrew's recruiting call and enlisted in the Fifty-fourth. As his company charged toward Fort Wagner five months later, he watched as a nearby shell wiped out dozens of his colleagues, including the standard bearer Sergeant John Wall. Carney seized the flag before it hit the ground and raced to the front of his column. He charged ahead of his group and found himself at the fort's entrance alone. There, he hid behind sand dunes and withstood heavy fire while awaiting his men. A half hour later, he spotted what he believed to be his company and ran toward them, only to discover that he was headed into Confederate troops. He turned and fled down the beach, getting shot twice, including once in the head, until he reached the Union lines. When he finally arrived at the rear, still bearing the flag and greeted by cheers, he proudly shouted his famous report, "Boys, the flag never touched the ground!"

But despite Carney and his regiment's bravery, the assault on Fort Wagner ended in a Union massacre. As Corporal Gooding wrote in his dispatch to the *New Bedford Mercury*, "Mortal men could not stand such a fire, and the assault on Wagner was a failure." Over fifteen hundred Union troops were killed, including General Strong. Nearly half of the approximately six hundred members of the Fifty-fourth who fought in the battle died. But, as with the Native Guard at the Battles of Port Hudson and Milliken's Bend, the Fifty-fourth's bravery in the campaign gripped the nation. Black and white Americans alike rallied around the regiment's effort, and, for the time being, debate about whether black troops could measure up in battle effectively came to an end.

After the battle, Frederick Douglass's son Lewis wrote a letter to his fiancée describing the effort. "Not a man flinched," he wrote, "though it was a trying time. Men fell around me. A shell would explode and clear a space of twenty feet. Our men would close up again, but it was no use, we had to retreat. . . . I wish we had a hundred thousand colored troops, we would put an end to this war." When Charleston finally fell in February 1865, the Massachusetts Fifty-fourth and Fifty-fifth were the first Union troops to enter the city. They marched in singing "John Brown's Body."

The Virginia Campaign

As the Union Army closed in on the rebels throughout 1864, the regiments of the USCT helped win major battles all over the South. Black troops excelled from Olustee, Florida, to Nashville, Tennessee. General Ulysses S. Grant was so impressed with his black troops while commanding the Western division that when he was promoted to head the Union Army and transferred to Virginia, he brought twenty thousand black soldiers with him. And of the seventeen Medals of Honor awarded to black army troops during the war, fifteen of them were for valor in Grant's ensuing 1864 Virginia campaign.

Twelve of those medals were awarded to men who fought in the bloody Battle of Chafin's Farm, including Sergeant Major Fleetwood and Private Veal. On September 29, nine Union regiments attacked the Confederate camp at New Market Heights. They were heavily shelled during the assault and suffered over one thousand casualties. But they pressed on through the fire and eventually overtook the rebel fortifications. The first four men to enter the camp were African American soldiers in the New Jersey Thirty-sixth and Thirty-eighth USCT

Regiments. Private James Gardiner of the Thirty-sixth along with the Thirty-eighth's First Sergeant Edward Ratcliff, Sergeant James Harris, and Private William Barnes all received Medals of Honor for their actions.

Meanwhile, on a different front of the battle, the Fourth, Fifth, and Sixth USCT Regiments were struggling through an equally grueling fight. The engagement produced another eight black Medal of Honor winners. Much like Fleetwood and Veal, four members of the Ohio Fifth USCT earned their medals by taking over their companies during the battle after discovering that all of the white commissioned officers had been killed. With over 450 regimental members dead, wounded, or missing, Sergeant Major Milton Holland and First Sergeants Powhatan Beaty, James Bronson, and Robert Pinn seized the lead of their respective companies and guided them through the rest of the day.

Medal of Honor winner Sergeant James Harris.

Medal of Honor winner First Sergeant Powhatan Beaty.

That July, the Pennsylvania Sixth USCT's Sergeant Major Thomas Hawkins had won a Medal of Honor for saving the regimental flag at the Battle of Deep Bottom, Virginia. The same month, Sergeant Decatur Dorsey of the Maryland Thirty ninth USCT won a Medal of Honor for saving the regimental flag during a gruesome engagement at Petersburg. Confederate troops routed the Union forces that day, killing black soldiers and white officers as they retreated. Over 1,300 black soldiers were killed in that battle, which Grant called "the saddest affair I have witnessed in the war." It was the largest single loss of black life during the Civil War.

These hard-fought battles, costly though they may have been in terms of human life, eventually brought the war to a close. On April 2, 1865, Richmond, Virginia, fell into Union hands, essentially signaling the end of the Confederacy. The Massachusetts Fifth USCT Cavalry led the Union forces into the liberated city as most of the remaining black regiments in the area joined Grant in chasing Confederate General Robert E. Lee toward his surrender at Appomattox.

By the war's close, black service members had given the lie to the assertion that African Americans were inferior to whites.

The names of the Union's nearly 210,000 black troops are inscribed on plaques at the African American Civil War Memorial in Washington, D.C.

The End of the War

Two weeks after the war's end, Lincoln was assassinated by John Wilkes Booth, who feared Lincoln would further open society to African Americans.

The Twenty-second USCT were among the soldiers who escorted his coffin during the funeral parade. With the Thirteenth Amendment to the Constitution, which abolished slavery nationwide, on its way, and the first wave of new civil rights laws soon to follow, the war's end was a high watermark for the abolition movement and black America. Black soldiers had given the lie to the assertion that African Americans were inferior to whites in every arena. In at least one aspect of life—one that the relatively young nation placed great value upon   it was now impossible to maintain that deception.

Nevertheless, the hopeful days of early Reconstruction would not last long. The era's civil rights gains would prove meaningless in a South still dominated by white aristocrats whose economic hegemony depended upon exploited black labor and whose political and social power stemmed from a racial caste system. By the century's close, many would feel African Americans living in the South faced just as bad conditions as they did during slavery's era—and in some cases, due to the rampant vigilante "justice" of lynch mobs, much worse. In the North, racism's retrenchment also meant few jobs and little political power for blacks.

Meanwhile, African American soldiers found themselves facing the inconceivable. Having proved themselves on the battlefield in three American wars, they still fought restrictions upon their ability to advance to officer rank. Moreover, they had not faced the last of the charges that they could not be trusted to fight at all. In a June 1865 letter to a former employer, Medal of Honor winner Sergeant Major Fleetwood expressed the sentiments many blacks who had excelled during the war must have felt. Fleetwood had left the army at the war's end and explained his reasoning. "Upon all our record there is not a single blot," he wrote,

and yet no member of this regiment is considered deserving of a commission or if so cannot receive one. I trust you will understand that I speak not of and for myself individually, or that the lack of the pay or honor of a commission induces me to quit the service. Not so by any means, but I see no good that will result to our people by continuing to serve, on the contrary it seems to me that our continuing to act in a subordinate capacity, with no hope of advancement or promotion is an absolute injury to our cause. It is a tacit but telling acknowledgement on our part that we are not fit for promotion, & that we are satisfied to remain in a state of marked and acknowledged subserviency.

A double purpose induced me and others to enlist, to assist in abolishing slavery and to save the country from ruin. Something in furtherance of both objects we have certainly done, and now it strikes me that more could be done for our welfare in the pursuits of civil life. I think that a camp life would be decidedly an injury to our people. No matter how well and faithfully they may perform their duties they will shortly be considered as "lazy nigger sojers"—as drones in the great hive.

CHAPTER

4

BUFFALO
SOLDIERS

*Westward Expansion
and Empire Building*

It was 1889, and a small group of Ninth Cavalry and Twenty-fourth Infantry soldiers were escorting an army payroll wagon through the treacherous landscape of Arizona. It was exactly the kind of work these regiments had been created to do—bring some semblance of order to the wild, freewheeling West. They defended settlers from Native American warriors, rounded up cattle rustlers, and cuffed all manner of bandits—the desert's real predators. The shooting started from a ledge of rocks about fifty feet to the detachment's right flank. The bandits were hunkered down in six stone forts, and their ambush had been well planned. But the troops nevertheless held the desperadoes for over thirty minutes. Though the ideally positioned thieves ultimately made off with $28,000 in army funds, one of the regiment's commanders described the defense his men put up with with breathless praise.

"Sergeant Brown," the commander wrote in his report, "though shot through the abdomen did not quit the field until again wounded, this time through the arm. Private Burge, who was to my immediate right, received a bad wound in the hand, but gallantly held his post, resting his rifle on his forearm and continuing to fire with much coolness, until shot through the thigh and twice through the hat. Private Arrington was shot through the shoulder, while fighting from this same position. Privates Hames, Wheeler, and Harrison were also wounded, to my immediate left, while bravely doing their duty under a murderous cross-fire."

From escorting stagecoaches to rounding up marauding bandits, the all-black Buffalo Soldier regiments were key players in America's fabled taming of the West.

Isaiah Mays won his Medal of Honor in a shootout with bandits that could have been taken from a Hollywood script.

Two members of the Twenty-fourth Infantry, Sergeant Benjamin Brown and Corporal Isaiah Mays, won Medals of Honor for their performance in the battle. Both had been shot at the battle's start while removing the boulder their attackers had set up as a roadblock. Brown continued leading the fight, while Mays set off on a two-mile run for help.

It was the stuff Hollywood's great Westerns were made of except that the heroes were African Americans. And for that reason, the harrowing tale, and countless others like it, would be omitted from America's memory of how "the West was won." In both popular culture and respected scholarship, the men who patrolled the western frontier have been remembered as white. But four of black military history's most accomplished regiments were among the first and last of the soldiers who presided over America's often brutal thirty-year campaign to settle the West. They went on to fight—and win honors—in the Spanish-American War, the Punitive Expedition into Mexico, and the Philippines before being cast aside in undeserved disgrace. They were known as the Buffalo Soldiers.

From Buffalo Bill's dime-store novels to John Wayne's epic films, over the years American culture has deeply romanticized the country's westward expansion. We have molded the era's fictional heroes into vessels for the preservation of those traits deemed representative of our most sacred national values. Such collective mythmaking is a key step in building any nation of people. But the tales omitted from these accumulated western legends perhaps reveal more about America than anything else. Most galling of these omissions is unquestionably the United States' carefully planned genocide of countless Native American nations. The historical gap, however, does not close there. African American contributions—both honorable and dastardly—have been similarly excised from the western landscape.

Following the Civil War, newly emancipated blacks joined their white countrymen in journeying into the rocky western plains in search of new opportunities. Many of the skills they had mastered as slaves translated easily into those needed for survival in rugged, untamed places such as Arizona, New Mexico, and Kansas. By 1890, at least half a million blacks lived in Texas and Oklahoma. Wherever there were settlements, there were black families. Many early cowboys—those who broke wild horses, rustled up cattle, and worked as farmhands—were in fact African American. They achieved both notoriety as rodeo entertainers and infamy as outlaws. Britton Johnson was considered the best shot in Texas in the years following the war. Nat Love, dubbed

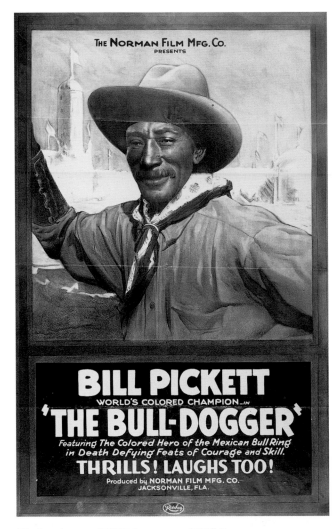

Black rodeo star Bill Pickett counted Will Rogers among his apprentices.

America's western lore are as glaring as that of the Buffalo Soldiers.

In 1866, after the Civil War closed, Congress decided to reshape the army. The feeling in Washington was that the force needed to be smaller, and it needed to be useful in the Indian Wars that erupted as the United States occupied Native America's lands. The reorganizing law reduced the army to ten cavalries, forty-five infantry regiments, five artillery units, and the U.S. Military Academy. Congress disbanded the U.S. Colored Troops and in its place created four all-black regiments: the Ninth and Tenth Cavalries and the Twenty-fourth and

Acclaimed artist Frederick Remington's sketches brought the Buffalo Soldiers to life for East-coasters.

Deadwood Dick, was one of five thousand cowboys who drove cattle from Texas to Kansas for sale in the east. He later penned a boastful autobiography in which he spun classic western tales of his adventures, including his capers with white legends such as Bat Masterson and Billy the Kid. Bill Pickett was a wildly popular rodeo performer throughout the country who counted Will Rogers among his apprentices. But none of these African American exclusions from

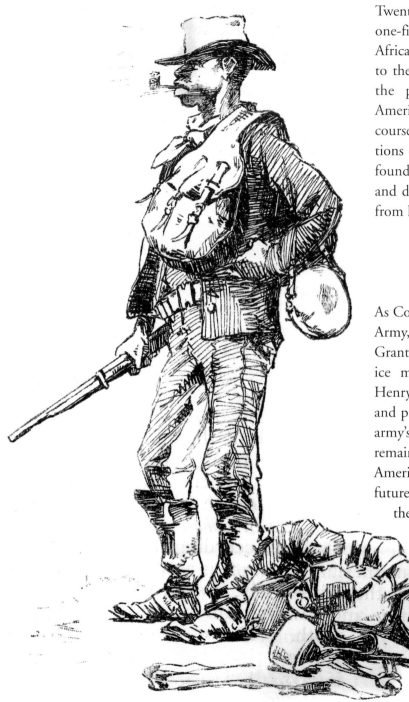

Remington rode with the Buffalo Soldiers during the summer of 1888, filing breathless reports for readers back East.

Twenty-fifth Infantries. Nevertheless, at its outset, one-fifth of the restructured force's soldiers were African Americans. These four units were dispatched to the western territories and charged with keeping the peace between white settlers and Native American tribes. Their primary responsibility, of course, was to harass Indians who left the reservations on which they had been placed. But they also found themselves policing white and black bandits—and defending against violent attacks on their units from hostile white settlers.

The Indian Wars

As Congress went about restructuring the old Union Army, many American leaders, including General Grant, wanted to again close the ranks to black service members. Massachusetts Republican Senator Henry Wilson led the fight against this retrenchment and pushed for blacks to have positions in all of the army's new divisions. But there was, and would remain, widespread opposition to making African Americans artillerymen. Then, and for years into the future, white military leaders believed blacks lacked the intelligence required to operate what was at the time considered complicated machinery. Wilson did prevail, however, in creating four black infantry and two black cavalry regiments. A few years later, in 1869, the army would further shrink and, in the process, consolidate the four black infantry regiments into the Twenty-fourth and Twenty-fifth.

The Native Americans with which these regiments battled gave them the nickname Buffalo

Soldiers. It began with the Tenth Cavalry—probably the most famous of the black western troops—but reports vary on how they won the name. Some say the Cheyenne dubbed the Tenth Cavalry Buffalo Soldiers in 1867 following an incredulous two-day battle near Fort Leavenworth, Kansas. A mere ninety cavalrymen held off eight hundred Cheyenne attackers in that fight, losing only three men in the process. Others say the Tenth earned its nickname during an 1871 campaign against the Comanche. Regardless of when and where the name started, Native Americans used it as a term of respect. Awed by the black soldiers' fierceness, Indian warriors placed a high value on African American troops' scalps, which bore the sort of dark wooly hair that they associated with the revered buffalo's coat. They would eventually apply

A fifth of the post-Civil War army was African American.

Native Americans dubbed black troops Buffalo Soldiers because of the wooly texture of African Americans' hair.

the name to all of the black regiments, but it would remain most closely associated with the Tenth Cavalry, which later added a buffalo figure to the unit insignia.

The respect the black regiments got from Native Americans was in short supply among their army colleagues and the settlers whom they were protecting. Several white officers, including General George Custer, refused assignments leading the black troops. Those who accepted complained about always getting the short end of the stick. Stationed at Fort Leavenworth, the Tenth found itself using second-hand supplies passed down from Custer's Seventh Cavalry. Moreover, the post commander stuck the Tenth's campsite in a muddy bog, and then complained to its leader, Civil War hero General Benjamin Grierson, that his troops were constantly dirty. The post commander then ordered the regiment's members not to come within fifteen yards of a white man.

Throughout their time in the West, the Buffalo Soldiers were regularly sent to the most undesirable posts. The Tenth stood in one of the territory's most contentious zones, between greedy settlers eager for more land and angry Cheyenne, Arapahoe, Comanche, and Kiowa—all tribes eager to avenge betrayals of the reservation treaties they had signed in 1867. The Twenty-fourth Infantry remained in the Southwest the longest, but all of the black regiments spent more time there than white army outfits. Military leaders recognized the burden enough to rotate the regiments' white officers, but argued that African Americans were biologically equipped to live in the grueling heat and that they thus didn't need to be transferred.

Their jobs were further complicated by constant battle with the settlers. Not content to accept the vio-

lent attacks of resentful whites, the men of the Buffalo Soldier regiments responded in kind. One of many incidents occurred in 1881 while several companies of the Tenth were stationed at Fort Concho, Texas. Two soldiers, one black and one white, were killed by a gambler in nearby San Angelo. Just three years previous, a company of the Tenth had engaged in a shoot-out with townspeople there after rioters attacked one of its sergeants. Following this latest affront, soldiers from Fort Concho posted a notice in town, reading,

> We, the soldiers of the United States Army, do hereby warn cowboys, etc., of San Angelo and vicinity, to recognize our rights of way as just and peaceable men. If we do not receive justice and fair play, which we must have, someone will suffer; if not the guilty, the innocent. It has gone too far; justice or death.

A black and a white company then marched into town, arrested the white sheriff, and demanded the jailhouse guards turn over the assailant. General Grierson ultimately convinced them to stand down and return to Fort Concho. In another legendary run-in, after a white man from the town shot a black soldier for sport, a group of Tenth Cavalrymen showed up at a white saloon, had a drink at the bar, and then turned and opened fire, killing everyone there.

The Ninth Cavalry, at Fort Robinson, Nebraska in 1889.

Despite these difficult conditions, all of the Buffalo Soldier regiments were model military units. Not only did they excel in battle, they maintained superb discipline (payback raids on white settlers being the notable exception). The Ninth and Tenth had the lowest desertion rate in the army, with less than a third of that in General Custer's renowned Seventh Cavalry. They were rarely disciplined for inappropriate behavior or drunkenness. And recruitment was not difficult due to unusually high reenlistment rates among the black troops. Many Buffalo Soldiers were Civil War veterans and not far removed from days as slaves. The $13 per month salary that they now received and the opportunity for education were attractive incentives.

ON THE BATTLEFIELD

Stationed on the Rio Grande, the Ninth Cavalry spent an inordinate amount of time policing marauding bandits who raided South Texas settlements and then fled over the Mexican border. But they also fought in countless battles of the region's Indian Wars. The Buffalo Soldiers developed reputations as saviors on the battlefield, as the unit that would arrive just in the nick of time to turn a battle around. In one famous incident, a company of the Ninth rode over one hundred miles and engaged in two battles in little over a day in order to rescue General Custer's pinned-down Seventh. The white company leader, Captain Dodge, won a Medal of

Remington's famous sketch of the Ninth Calvary, entitled *Captain Dodge's Colored Troops to the Rescue.*

Honor, and artist Frederick Remington memorialized the event in his famous drawing *Captain Dodge's Colored Troops to the Rescue*. Remington, who sketched 2,700 drawings and paintings on the western frontier, was the era's most celebrated documentarian of the nation's westward expansion. His stories and drawings awed East-coasters who marveled at the world of frontiersmen. During the summer of 1888, Remington rode with the Tenth Cavalry through Arizona. His reports from that trip challenged racist assumptions about black soldiers' deficiencies that lingered on in white minds despite the now overwhelming proof to the contrary. His vivid drawings, meanwhile, depicted the Buffalo Soldiers in scenes both heroic and mundane.

Starting in the fall of 1879 and stretching throughout 1880 the Ninth Cavalry focused on chasing down Apache Chief Victorio. Also known as the Apache Wolf, Victorio had defiantly led his warriors off the New Mexico reservation to which they had been confined. The Ninth, charged with policing the Apache, set off in pursuit. It touched off a brutal war with skirmishes between the Buffalo Soldiers and Victorio's Apache all over the Southwest. Victorio was fighting for survival. His reservation, as were most, was much too small to sustain his tribe, which was not allowed to hunt elsewhere. As a result, he and his warriors fought fiercely. They began mutilating bodies of dead Buffalo Soldiers in an attempt to intimidate the black troops. After one battle, the soldiers found five of their men staked to the ground. Nevertheless, they continued to pursue Victorio for over a thousand miles before the Tenth Cavalry joined the fight. The Tenth's Colonel Grierson changed the Buffalo Soldiers' strategy. Rather than chase Victorio, he positioned his companies at every mountain pass and watering hole in the area. The tactic paid off, and they ultimately forced the Apache chief and his men to flee into Mexico, where Mexican forces eventually dispatched with them.

Earlier in the decade, beginning in the spring of 1875, nine companies of the Tenth led an expedition with a few companies of the Twenty-fourth and Twenty-fifth Regiments into the great "Staked Plains" of Texas. The territory was previously unexplored by Americans and had been an Indian stronghold. The Buffalo Soldiers trekked over seven hundred

Buffalo Soldiers hunted the defiant Apache Chief Victorio for over a year.

John Denny was one of seventeen Buffalo Soldiers to win a Medal of Honor during the Indian War era.

miles between May and December, mapping out the territory and, toward the end, battling with Native Americans. That July, another six companies of the Tenth, again joined by a few from the Twenty-fourth and Twenty-fifth, set out on a separate expedition through the Staked Plains, further mapping the area. The two missions made it possible for Americans to settle the vast and previously uninhabited stretches of Texas.

These sorts of expeditions were dangerous not only because of the potential battles with Native Americans; the unforgiving desert landscape posed just as grave a threat. In one 1877 foray into the Staked Plains, a company of Tenth Cavalrymen survived without water for nearly four days. They had set out in the dead of summer to track down Apache bandits who had been terrorizing stagecoach stations. Eight days into the journey, they ran out of water and could find no new source. A scout went in search of lake beds and streambeds that the soldiers hoped would hold buried freshwater, but he never returned. The soldiers were driven to drinking urine and horse blood before they finally discovered a lake bed that provided freshwater.

The rugged men of the black regiments continued offering these sorts of unimaginable sacrifices until the United States firmly settled the entire Indian Territory in around 1890. They took part in the capture of western legends ranging from Billy the Kid to Apache renegade Chief Geronimo. They won seventeen Medals of Honor during the Indian Wars. Sergeant Emanuel Stance of the Ninth Cavalry was the first Buffalo Soldier to win a Medal of Honor, for his leadership in a battle with the Kickapoo in which his detachment was outnumbered three to one.

THE SEMINOLE NEGRO INDIAN SCOUTS

Four of the Buffalo Soldiers' Medals of Honor were given to men from a unique group of trackers that have been dubbed the Seminole Negro Indian Scouts. They were of mixed heritage, the descendants of escaped slaves who lived among the Seminole nation in Florida. When President Andrew Jackson forced Native Americans out of the state, on an infamous march across the country now known as the Trail of Tears, many Seminoles migrated to Mexico. There, they allied with the Mexican Army in its wars with Apache and Comanche Indians, until the United States came to recruit from among them in 1870. At that time, with the army in ever growing need of expert scouts for its Indian Wars, General Zenas Bliss offered to pay the black Seminoles a soldier's salary, finance their families' relocation to the United States, and give them each land once there. It was an attractive deal, and Bliss was able to put together a band of fifty black Seminole trackers.

The group was placed under the command of Lieutenant John Bullis, a Quaker who had led U.S. Colored Troops during the Civil War. Lieutenant Bullis earned the deep respect and utmost trust of the black Seminoles, and his unit became known as one of the most effective fighting forces in U.S. military history. In their entire eleven-year career, the Seminole Negro Indian Scouts did not lose one man in battle. Their tracking skills were renowned, as was their bravery in battle. Three of the unit's Medals of Honor were awarded for saving Lieutenant Bullis's life. In 1875, Bullis led Sergeant John Ward, Private Pompey Factor, and trumpeter Isaac Payne on a scouting mission that resulted in the detachment attacking a group of around thirty Comanche.

Former members of the Seminole Negro Indian Scouts.

Retreating from the fray, Bullis was knocked from his horse and almost left behind. But the men rode back into the charging Comanche, where Sergeant Ward gathered their leader as Private Factor and Payne fired away.

But the U.S. government would nonetheless deal just as dishonestly with the black Seminole scouts as it did with other Native Americans. General Bliss's promises of land and pay were not kept, and the United States ultimately claimed they had never even been made. Meanwhile, white settlers were able to do inside their "civilized" towns what no frontier opponent had been able to accomplish on the battlefield: murder three of the black Seminoles, including the fourth Medal of Honor winner, Adam Paine. Following Paine's 1877 murder, Private Pompey and a small group of the trackers returned to Mexico. He never received a pension, as the U.S. government insisted there was no record of his service.

Unwelcome at the Academy

In the years following the Civil War, a handful of representatives known as the Radical Republicans were determined to change the way the nation dealt with African Americans. They not only pushed through Congress new civil rights protections—measures that would, after only a few years, be rendered useless by Jim Crow laws in the South—but they also wrestled with the military establishment to open opportunities for black service members. To that end, Republican members of Congress insisted upon appointing black candidates to the officer training academies of the army and navy. Both schools bowed to the political pressure and accepted blacks in word, but they would keep African American cadets from graduating by applying the same mixture of vigilante violence and official corruption used throughout the South to keep blacks from accessing their newly created rights. Of the twenty-five African Americans appointed to the academies during the nineteenth century, only three would graduate. Half of those appointed either "failed" the entrance examination or lasted only a semester.

There was never any real question about whether blacks would be allowed to become naval officers. The U.S. Naval Academy admitted only five black candidates from the time of its creation until 1949. Only two of those actually attended the school, both of whom were chased out before gradu-

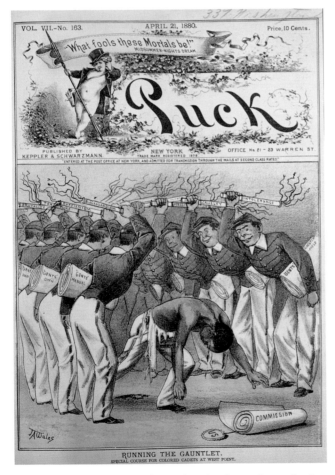

This 1880 drawing depicts the cruel tactics the service academies used to prevent black officer nominees from graduating.

ation. The real battleground for black officers was the army's U.S. Military Academy at West Point. The distinguished institution admitted its first black cadets in 1870—James Smith from South Carolina and Michael Howard of Mississippi. Howard failed his first exam and left, but his roommate, Smith, was determined to beat the system. Smith later wrote to a black newspaper to describe the harassment he endured. He was not allowed to eat in the dining room until all the other cadets had been served, because they objected to using dishes he had touched. Someone poured a slop bucket over his head in his sleep. When his family visited, they were insulted and harassed. All of his complaints to superiors were ignored, and rather than protection he received bogus charges against himself. He underwent two court-martials and one court of inquiry before making it to his final year at the academy. Ultimately, however, he was dismissed before graduation in 1874.

A more egregious case is that of John Chestnut Whittaker, who entered West Point in 1876. As did Smith, Whittaker withstood intense physical and psychological abuse; overcame the corruption of his superiors, his instructors, and his classmates; and made it to his final year. But on April 4, 1880, he was found tied to his bunk, beaten unconscious and bleeding profusely. The commandant declared that Whittaker had faked the attack—despite the fact that he was so securely bound that he had to be cut free when he was found—because he knew that he was going to fail a philosophy class. Whittaker demanded a court of inquiry to set the record straight, and his case became one of a newly emboldened black community's first national political causes. The inquiry supported the commandant's findings. And in June 1881, a legal team that included Harvard's

Henry O. Flipper was the first African American West Point graduate.

first black graduate, Richard Greener, represented Whittaker at a court-martial that also ended in charges that he staged the attack. The following March, President Chester A. Arthur, led by Secretary of War Robert Lincoln (son of President Abraham Lincoln), overturned the ruling. It was too late, however, as the academy had already officially dismissed Whittaker for failing his philosophy course.

THE GRADUATES

The Academy's determination to block Whittaker's matriculation was likely influenced by its failure to stop that of Henry Ossian Flipper. In 1877, just as Whittaker was entering the school, Flipper became West Point's first black graduate. The son of a Georgia slave-turned-entrepreneur and Atlanta University alum, Flipper graduated fifteenth in a class of seventy-six students. He was the seventh black cadet at the academy, which had by then developed a reputation for mistreatment of African Americans. He wrote an autobiography detailing his experience, *The Colored Cadet at West Point*, published the year following his graduation. He described his strategy for success as remaining single-mindedly focused on his studies and downplayed the notion that the academy was intolerable for blacks. He avoided conflict and asserted that only a handful of the white West Pointers were aggressive racists—most simply steered clear of him or, at best, privately offered support (which Flipper took as indicative of "a want of backbone" among his fellow cadets). Rather than complain to his superiors as Smith and Whittaker did, Flipper rejected the notion that he needed protection. "If my manhood cannot stand without a governmental prop, then let it fall," he wrote. "If I am to stand on any other ground than the one white cadets stand upon, then I don't want the cadetship. If I cannot endure prejudice and persecutions, even if they are offered, then I don't deserve the cadetship, and much less the commission of an army officer."

Upon graduation, Flipper was assigned as a lieutenant in the Tenth Cavalry, then stationed at Fort Sill, Oklahoma. He primarily worked as an engineer—a skill for which he developed renown while in the academy—building the army's telegraph line. During the Tenth's 1880 war against Chief Victorio, however, he served as a scout and messenger for Colonel Grierson. But Lieutenant Flipper's career didn't last long. After a courtship with the daughter of a white officer, he was transferred to Fort Davis, Texas. Soon after his arrival, he was accused of embezzling funds from the commissary where he worked. Lieutenant Flipper discovered what he believed to be a plot against him when he noticed money missing from the till. Rather than come immediately forward, he sought to undermine the conspiracy by replacing the funds himself. He was arrested nonetheless and court-martialed. The embezzlement charges did not stand, but he was convicted of "conduct unbecoming an officer" and dishonorably discharged in December 1881. In 1977 the army reversed the ruling, and in 1999 President Bill Clinton finally cleared Lieutenant Flipper's name with a presidential pardon.

Lieutenant Flipper's success at West Point was finally followed ten years later by John Alexander's.

In 1889, Charles Young became the last black graduate or the next fifty years.

John Alexander became the second black West Point graduate fully ten years after Flipper.

Upon graduating in 1887, Alexander served as a second lieutenant in the Ninth Cavalry in Nebraska and Utah. After seven relatively uneventful years—the Indian Wars had largely come to a close—Second Lieutenant Alexander became a military professor at Wilberforce University, one of the country's first historically black colleges, located in Ohio. But he died suddenly from a heart attack in March 1894.

In 1889, Charles Young became the third and last West Point graduate for the next fifty years. Assigned to the Tenth Cavalry, Young would spend thirty years as an officer in the U.S. Army and rise to the rank of colonel. He would lead troops in both the turn of the century Spanish-American War and in America's 1916 battle with Mexican rebel Pancho Villa, earning a reputation as a hero. His famous tenacity was displayed most vividly as the army sought to finally dispatch with him at the start of World War I. With military racism regaining its vigor at the time, there was no place for a black officer in an overseas conflict. Army officials thus told Colonel Young that he was not healthy enough to serve on active duty. To refute it, Colonel Young mounted a horse and rode from Ohio, where he was teaching at Wilberforce as a replacement for Second Lieutenant Alexander, to Washington, D.C., and back again. The feat did nothing to budge the army, and Colonel Young was not allowed to continue serving.

The Spanish-American War

The expansionist fervor that fueled the Indian Wars found a new focus on February 15, 1898. An accident in Cuba that day prompted a nation that had not yet known a prolonged era of peace to manufacture yet another war. The USS *Maine* had been stationed in Havana's harbor as a statement of support for the Cuban revolution against Spain. An acciden-

Members of the Ninth Calvary in 1898.

The Twenty-fifth Infantry's Tampa, Florida camp, en route to fight the Spanish in Cuba.

tal explosion on board the ship killed 260 sailors, 22 of whom were black, and sank the ship. At the time, America eagerly accepted the military's initial assertion that the ship had been hit by an underwater Spanish mine (more recent investigations have proved that it was in fact an on-ship accident). And the brief 113-day war with Spain was on. It would lead to a decisive U.S. victory and mark the beginning of America's imperial aspirations.

The navy launched the war in the Philippines, where black gunner's mate John Jordan led the crew that fired the war's opening shots. But the bulk of the fighting took place in Cuba. All four regiments of Buffalo Soldiers were shipped south to Florida and

Georgia, along with the rest of the army, where they could prepare to invade Cuba and drive the Spanish out. The Twenty-fifth Infantry Regiment was the first U.S. force to arrive. But all of the regiments needed to be brought up to wartime strength, and the War Department set about frantically recruiting three thousand new black troops to quickly be trained. The actual recruitment was left to the states, and eight states offered black volunteer militia units: Alabama, Illinois, Indiana, Kansas, Massachusetts, North Carolina, Ohio, and Virginia. Young, now promoted to major, led the Ohio black militia.

In addition to the new militia recruits, Congress authorized the creation of ten new regiments com-

posed of people considered to be immune to tropical viruses. The army feared the diseases its troops might encounter in Cuba and wanted to have insurance forces. So a batch of recruits were selected from areas where tropical diseases were believed to be most prevalent and from among African America at large—based on the ongoing assumption that blacks, due to African ancestry, were genetically immune to viruses such as yellow fever. Four of the new ten "immune" units were therefore all black: the Seventh, Eighth, Ninth, and Tenth Volunteer Infantry Regiments. Among the Eighth Volunteers was an eighteen-year-old named Benjamin O. Davis. His unit would never see action in the war, but he would eventually become America's first black general.

As the Buffalo Soldiers now finally left the West, the wildly popular new war effort shined upon them just as it did the rest of the armed forces. They departed as loved heroes rather than the hated intruders they had once been considered. But the Buffalo Soldiers and the new black recruits met a much different world when they arrived in the South. Whites, both inside and out of the armed forces, did not want them there and made it known. Local militias refused to accommodate the black units sent from predominantly northern and Midwestern states. And local police aggressively enforced Jim Crow laws in public places, violently harassing black troops.

The army recruited thousands of black troops to augment the Buffalo Soldiers, including the Ninth U.S. Volunteer Regiment pictured here.

THE BUFFALOS AND THE ROUGH RIDERS

The Cuban invasion got off to a spirited start. The cavalry hit the beach at Daiquiri on June 22, and two days later they were storming a Spanish outpost at the village of Las Guasimas. Along with the Ninth

and Tenth, Theodore Roosevelt's famous Rough Riders, the First Volunteer Cavalry, were among the troops there. Over the next few weeks, in hectic battles where divisions were mixed and matched to meet immediate needs, the Rough Riders and Buffalo Soldiers fought side by side in what was likely the most integrated American force thus far. The Rough

This Kurz and Allison print pictures the Tenth Calvary rescuing Roosevelt's "Rough Riders" in the war's opening battle at Las Guasimas.

Riders were the first to storm Las Guasimas and were soon pinned down by Spanish riflemen. The Tenth, augmented by members of the regular white cavalry, played its usual role as rescuers, sweeping in from the woods to take out the Spanish riflemen. The country swooned over the Tenth's heroism, and printmakers Kurz & Allison added the battle to the list of heroic African American–focused works they produced.

After taking Las Guasimas, the cavalry, now joined by the infantry regiments, moved on to the village of El Caney and San Juan Hill and Kettle Hill. The Twenty-fifth Infantry, accompanied by the white Twelfth, stormed El Caney on July 1, opening one of American military history's most acclaimed days of battle. Taking cover in a dry riverbed, the regiments'

snipers were able to force a speedy Spanish surrender. The battle nevertheless took longer than expected, and the Twenty-fifth was not able to immediately join the attacks on San Juan and Kettle Hills as planned. As a result, battle plans changed abruptly, and confusion reigned on both hillsides. Colonel Roosevelt's Rough Riders and companies from all four Buffalo Soldier regiments nevertheless charged forward, convinced they'd be easy targets otherwise. Casualties were still high, with the Tenth alone loosing twenty percent of its men. At one point in the charge, the Twenty-fourth pushed aside several white regiments that were reluctant to move forward, sustaining massive losses. Rough Rider and future Secretary of the Navy Frank Knox would later

The famous charge on San Juan and Kettle Hills was one of America's most integrated battles to date.

remark of the black troops at San Juan and Kettle Hills, "I must say that I never saw braver men anywhere."

By late afternoon on the first, the American forces had taken all three of the day's locations and essentially concluded the war. The Spanish fleet could not evade the U.S. Navy blockade and was soon decimated. A number of printmakers would memorialize the Buffalo Soldiers' heroism at El Caney and San Juan and Kettle Hills, and five Tenth Cavalrymen won Medals of Honor. But the praise, and national memory, primarily went to Roosevelt's Rough Riders.

As the war closed, a brutal yellow fever epidemic opened. The "immune" regiments had never been mobilized in Cuba, and the Twenty-fourth thus drew the job of working at the hospital. When all the white units guarding the hospital refused to serve as volunteer nurses, the Twenty-fourth's members eagerly stepped in. As had happened in the past, the pseudoscientific theories about African American immunity to tropical diseases were proven false. Half of the 471 Twenty-fourth Regiment members who worked at the hospital contracted the virus.

Building an American Empire

The fallout from the fighting in Cuba was seen over the next few years in Puerto Rico and the Philippines. Immediately following Cuba, U.S. forces, including a volunteer militia from Massachusetts with a company of black troops, landed in Puerto Rico. The Spanish surrendered soon thereafter, and Puerto Rico became a U.S. territory. The Philippine rebels, however, had other thoughts.

To them, the Americans were simply the new Spaniards, and their rebellion continued against a fresh enemy.

The country at large did not support a war effort in Asia with the same gusto that it offered for the one in the Caribbean. African Americans were no different, and objections by the black community to the war stressed racial dimensions that black leaders had noticeably ignored in the nation's combat with Native Americans. Even educator and orator Booker T. Washington, considered a friend of the administration, spoke out against launching a war against people of color around the globe when there were still so many social problems to deal with among people of color at home. Nevertheless, President William McKinley authorized the War Department to raise two new black infantry regiments to aid the Philippine effort—the Forty-eighth and Forty-ninth Volunteer Infantries. They recruited both troops and officers from among the volunteer militias that had been raised for the Cuban effort, and those men joined the Buffalo Soldier regiments in rushing to the island chain to aid a vastly outnumbered American force.

Major Young had not fought in Cuba, but he led black troops in the Philippines for an eighteen-month tour of duty beginning in spring of 1901. While there, he developed the nickname Follow Me as a result of his bold leadership against rebel guerrillas fighting unfamiliar jungle warfare. The Twenty-fourth and Twenty-fifth put in similarly, and by now routinely, energetic efforts. They were among the first regular army units to arrive, and the Twenty-fifth engaged the first significant battle of the conflict, taking the town of O'Donnell on Luzon, the rebels' stronghold. As with other early-arriving regiments, the Buffalo Soldiers fought sweltering heat and a dense landscape that they had not encountered in the West or in Cuba, using worn supplies that were left over from previous battles. Some reported marching barefoot and even stripping down to their underwear after crossing rivers and deep mud bogs.

But American troops' heroism during their effort to quell the Philippine insurrection was colored by their officers' documented war crimes. While it was certainly not the first time America's military had committed atrocities during warfare, it was the first conflict in which individuals were charged for those crimes. Officers routinely gave orders to take no prisoners and tortured those who were captured. White officers openly promoted the idea that Filipinos were to be considered "niggers" and treated accordingly. Black officers were no more humane. After rescuing a group of captured American troops, the Twenty-fifth burned the homes of villagers in the town. A Tenth Cavalry officer was court-martialed for the common American torture tactic of flushing water into the nose and mouth of a prisoner until the person drowned. Most of the American officers sentenced for these crimes received light punishments, some of which President Theodore Roosevelt reversed or further lightened.

The Philippine conflict was not unique, however, in that America's enemy sought to exploit its racial divide. As the British had done during the Revolutionary War, the Philippine rebels urged African Americans to abandon the United States. But they went a step further—inventing a tactic that would haunt the U.S. military for the rest of the century—by actively encouraging black troops to defect as well. They circulated broadsides that invoked the specter of prominent African American lynchings and argued that the United States was using blacks as pawns in its racist campaign of imperialism. The appeal largely failed, as no more than five black troops are believed to have defected. Most prominent of these was Corporal David Fagen of the Twenty-fourth. In November 1899, Fagen fled the Twenty-fourth and joined the Philippine rebels. He became a captain and led a rebel squadron for two years in several battles against U.S. forces. Some believed he killed American prisoners, but two members of the Twenty-fourth whom Fagen took captive returned

West Point graduate Young led black troops in the Philippines.

Eight states formed black volunteer militias during the Spanish-American War. The Eighth Illinois (right) would be the most lasting of those.

and professed to humane treatment. Fagen is believed to have been killed in December 1901, when a bounty hunter brought in a decomposed head and proved to the U.S. Army's satisfaction that it was Fagen's.

The End of an Era

The beginning of the twentieth century marked the start of the Buffalo Soldiers' decline. Despite their heroism in the Spanish-American War, only three blacks received commissions at its close. Benjamin O. Davis reenlisted after the volunteer militias were disbanded and was assigned to the Ninth Cavalry. There, he met Major Young, who tutored him for the officers' exam. In 1901 the War Department opened 1,100 new officers' positions, largely to accommodate militiamen who were added to an expanded army designed to facilitate policing of the new territories. That year, Davis, John Green of the Twenty-fourth, and volunteer John Lynch received the last three black commissions until 1948.

Meanwhile, President Roosevelt, who succeeded President McKinley following his 1901 assassination, led the navy even further away from its long-held status as the nation's most integrated military branch. In 1906, concerned about growing Japanese influence, Roosevelt created his Great White Fleet. Composed of sixteen ships painted all white, the fleet sailed the Pacific Ocean as a symbol of the Caucasian race's might. The crew, therefore, needed to be as white as the ships themselves, and blacks were relegated to service roles such as cooks. The fleet was just the crowning point in years of Jim Crow's growth in the navy. Segregation had solidified throughout the United States by the turn of the century, and the

navy was no different. Moreover, the hard sea life that had always prompted labor shortages in the branch had softened considerably with the development of steam engines. The navy now sought young, disciplined, and clean-cut recruits that could show off the nation's white superiority rather than the rough-and-tumble social castaways, white and black, that had always been willing to brave the dangerous life at sea.

A similar process ensued in the new National Guard. The opposition the black volunteer militias encountered when stationed in the South at the Spanish-American War's outset only worsened. By the start of World War I, there were only five thousand African Americans in the National Guard. The overwhelming majority of those troops were in Davis's former Eighth Illinois or the Fifteenth New York Volunteer Regiment.

The armed forces' racist retrenchment was sealed in 1906 with an infamous episode at Brownsville, Texas, involving the Twenty-fifth Infantry. Despite a history of severe racial tension between white militiamen in Texas and black troops, the War Department sent the Twenty-fifth's First Battalion to Brownsville's Fort Brown to train with the Texas National Guard. The black troops were routinely harassed on and off post by both soldiers and local police. One evening a white customs officer pistol-whipped two black privates whom he accused of pushing his wife as they passed on the street. That same evening, another officer threw a black private into a river because he found him drunk. Shortly thereafter, on the night of August 13, someone began firing weapons in town, killing one person and injuring several others. The authorities immediately blamed the men of the Twenty-fifth, citing spent army shells found at the scene and anger

Members of the Twenty-fifth Infantry in full regalia. The legacy of such black frontiersmen did not survive a retrenchment of racism at the turn of the century.

over the recent run-ins with customs officers. When none of the troops would come forward and either admit to the crime or reveal the culprit, the War Department dishonorably discharged all 176 black troops who were present that night.

The incident became a national rallying point for both whites bent on ending black military service and African American political leaders fed up with the fading promise of the Roosevelt administration. Subsequent investigations made it clear that the men of the Twenty-fifth had been framed by someone from the Texas National Guard, but their names were not cleared until 1972, when Democratic Representative Augustus Hawkins led Congress in changing the troops' discharges to honorable.

The Buffalo Soldiers would remain part of the army through World War I, but they would not be allowed to fight in it. Following Brownsville, generations of black military heroism were set aside in favor of the nation's new consensus that African Americans were best left as second-class citizens in all arenas. Historians and the producers of pop culture would spend most of the twentieth century erasing the rich legacy of America's black frontiersmen.

5

SOLDIERS
IN SEARCH OF
AN ARMY

The World War I Era

In early 1917, following the Punitive Expedition into Mexico, in which U.S. troops tracked down Mexican bandits led by Pancho Villa, the Buffalo Soldiers were sent back west. The Twenty-fourth Infantry Regiment's Third Battalion drew an assignment guarding Camp Logan, which the army was building just outside of Houston, Texas. There, they met the same sort of racist harassment from local police and townspeople that black troops had seen at nearly every post since Reconstruction. But the Buffalo Soldiers had suffered through a great deal already. Having fought without recognition from the Indian Wars to Cuba and the Philippines, and having already endured low-intensity conflict between their members and law enforcement in places such as

Florida and South Texas, many of them were likely out of patience. Moreover, the nation's race wars in general were approaching a violent apex. Over twenty-five hundred documented lynchings in just the previous thirty years led the National Association for the Advancement of Colored People (NAACP) to stage a silent march through Harlem in July 1917. A month later, the Twenty-fourth's Third Battalion marched through Houston in protest of violence against black Americans, but they did not do so silently.

The problems began on the morning of August 23, when Private Alonzo Edwards discovered policeman Lee Sparks beating a black woman. The unarmed Private Edwards interfered, so Sparks turned his violence upon the young man as well.

Members of the Twenty-fourth's Third Battalion, on trial for their violent uprising in Houston, Texas.

After beating the private, Sparks jailed him. Soon thereafter, Corporal Charles Baltimore, one of the battalion's military policemen charged with blocking conflicts between the black troops and white locals, inquired about Private Edwards, also approaching the police officer unarmed. Sparks responded by attacking Corporal Baltimore, firing upon him, and ultimately arresting him as well. At this point Third Battalion white officers intervened, freeing both Corporal Baltimore and Private Edwards and securing punishment for Sparks. But to the proud Buffalo Soldier battalion, irreparable damage had been done. Somehow, this incident crossed the line that none of the hundreds before it had.

Fearing trouble, the white officers locked the battalion's guns and ammunition away. But a group of troops broke into the store and, led by eighteen-year-old Sergeant Vida Henry, marched toward the nearest police station intending to do battle. Over the next two hours, a contingent of over one hundred Third Battalion troops killed five police officers and ten townspeople, wounding twelve more. Four of their own men were killed.

Whatever chance remained that the Buffalo Soldier regiments would continue in the U.S. armed forces following Brownsville disappeared with this bloody rampage. The War Department court-martialed sixty-three members of the battalion, sentencing thirteen to hang and forty-one to a life of hard labor. Several others were convicted of lesser crimes at a subsequent court-martial. Fearing African American backlash, President Woodrow Wilson commuted ten of the death sentences but allowed three of the men—those convicted of specific murders—to hang. And his War Department decided to exile most of the remaining Buffalo Soldiers to the sidelines of World War I.

W.E.B. DuBois first championed the war effort and encouraged blacks to enlist.

"This war has disillusioned millions of fighting white men," wrote W. E. B. DuBois of World War I in the June 1919 issue of *The Crisis*, the NAACP journal that he edited, "disillusioned them with its frank truth of dirt, disease, cold, wet and discomfort; murder, maiming and hatred. But the disillusion of the Negro American troops was more than this, or rather it was this and more—the flat, frank realization that however high the ideals of America or however noble her tasks, her great duty as conceived by an astonishing number of able men, brave and good, as well as of other sorts of men, is to hate 'niggers.'"

These were the words of a deeply embittered African American leader, one whose hopes that World War I would bring progress against racism and discrimination had been emphatically dashed. What happened to a group of black infantrymen at the close of the Great War is a testament to how badly American race relations had deteriorated by that point. After loading the USS *Virginia* with coal for its trip from Europe back to the United States, a detachment of 367th Regiment troops were to board the ship and travel home with its crew. But the ship's executive officer refused them entry, citing the fact that no black soldiers had ever disembarked with a U.S. battleship and vowing not to have it happen on his watch. Seemingly ignorant of the navy's rich history of sailing integrated vessels into some of America's most storied battles, he left the black servicemen stranded ashore.

But this sort of slight could have been expected. No one in the U.S. armed forces had feigned to want black troops with them in Europe in the first place—and everyone treated them correspondingly from the war's outset. Not a single African American was awarded a Medal of Honor during World War I, the first conflict in which that was the case since the medal's creation.

From the beginning, many of the burgeoning civil rights movement's leaders struggled to overcome this hostility to black service members. Not the least of these was DuBois, one of the movement's most prominent voices. DuBois championed the war effort, both pushing blacks to enlist and cajoling the War Department to use them more widely. His reasoning was the same as Douglass's during the Civil War, which was the same as his predecessors during the War of 1812 and the Revolutionary War: By joining the nation in this fight, black Americans could strike a fatal blow to the logic that supported the racial caste system. If they could defend their nation's values with the same dedication and heroism as whites, they could prove they were not lesser beings. DuBois had not learned from history that white America was more than willing to simply ignore black soldiers' valor.

A young A. Philip Randolph urged blacks to protest the war from its outset.

Asa Philip Randolph and Chandler Owen, however, had taken that lesson to heart. Editors of the black socialist newspaper *The Messenger*, Randolph and Owen emerged in the 1910s as regular critics of DuBois and the NAACP, arguing that they placed too much stock in the American system's willingness and ability to reform from within. They lashed out at the war effort and urged blacks not to fight. "We are conscripting the Negro into the military and industrial establishments to achieve this end for white democracy four thousand miles away," the radical labor leaders wrote, "while the Negro at home, though bearing the burden in every way, is denied economic, political, educational and civil democracy." Their agitating drew the ire of Attorney General A. Mitchell Palmer, who dubbed Randolph and Owen "the most dangerous Negroes in America" and, in July 1918, imprisoned them under the Espionage Act for interfering with troop recruitment.

The raging battle within the African American community about whether to join the war effort was enough, however, to convince the Republican Wilson administration that some outlet needed to be created for black participation. Unlike Democrats, the northern-based GOP welcomed black voters, and President Wilson was clinging to what black support the party had left following the Roosevelt years. So the War Department created two new black divisions for World War I—conceived as tokens of political necessity rather than valuable military resources. The divisions were built from untrained draftees and black National Guard units originally established during the Spanish-American War. The four existing black regiments—the Buffalo Soldiers—were left scattered about the now irrelevant arenas of Hawaii, the Philippines, Mexico, and the western United States.

Shipped to Europe, Untrained

When the United States decided to enter World War I in early 1917, the navy and marines had no second thoughts about their policy on black troops. The marines continued its absolute ban on African American enlistment, and the navy went on relegating blacks to on-ship service roles such as stewards and menial labor tasks in general. President Wilson's political concession to African Americans would instead be made within the ranks of the army. After

President Wilson created two black divisions to win political points, but intended them to serve as laborers only.

Four hundred thousand blacks were drafted during the war, largely to do labor such as repairing shell-torn fields in France so that they could be farmed.

originally restricting the draft to whites, the army opened its draft to blacks as well in May of 1917, two months after Congress declared war on the Central Powers. Blacks were drafted in large numbers (some speculate in part because all-white southern draft boards were eager to essentially deport their community's African American men) and at significantly higher rates than whites. The nearly four hundred thousand blacks drafted during the war represented thirteen percent of the total.

But the War Department was not yet sure what to do with all of these new black servicemen. Plans to create multiple black regiments were derailed by the Twenty-fourth Infantry's actions in Houston and the logistical concerns caused by Jim Crow—if the department created too many black regiments, their training would have to be integrated with whites'. So instead, the War Department decided to create one

black combat division, consisting of four infantry regiments plus artillery, engineer, and other support units. Training would be kept to a minimum, thus allowing the army to preserve its ever important segregation, and all field and general grade officers would be white. Furthermore, the new Ninety-second Division, formally established in October 1917, would be trained in seven different locations, thereby alleviating concerns about having thousands of armed blacks together at one time. The particulars of the division's training were of little concern, since, official combat designation aside, the units were conceived as laborers. Nevertheless, lest its political point be missed, the Wilson administration insultingly dubbed the Ninety-second his Buffalo Soldier Division.

Most of the remaining black draftees joined the real Buffalo Soldier regiments at their out-of-the-way posts or worked in one of a number of black labor

**Black soldiers sort
shoes in a salvage dump
in France.**

divisions. A contingent of those from South
Carolina, however, was funneled into a second black
combat division hastily created in December of
1917. That division, the Ninety-third, was built from
the black National Guard units still in existence—
primarily the Eighth Illinois and the Fifteenth New
York National Guards—which had been mobilized
as the draft began. The Ninety-third's regiments
received no training in the States and were sent
immediately to France, where they served on detail
under French commanders desperate for replacement
troops. American military leaders had also assumed
these men would simply be used as laborers, but
necessity forced the French to use many of them in
combat. Still, eighty percent of the black troops in
France and ninety percent of all black troops served
as laborers. As DuBois wrote in his *Crisis* essay, "If
American food and materials saved France in the end
from utter exhaustion, it was the Negro stevedore
who made that aid effective."

Another of President Wilson's moves to quell
increasingly vocal black Republican discontent was
to appoint Emmett Scott as Secretary of War
Newton Baker's Special Assistant on Negro Affairs.
As Tuskegee President Booker T. Washington's
executive assistant, Scott had been considered one
of the nation's most influential African Americans.
He was the gatekeeper to the man most of white
America considered the black community's leader.
And this appointment, announced at the same
time the administration created the Ninety-second
Division, now made him the highest-ranking black
government official in history. But, as with
Washington, many African Americans considered
Scott a meaningless token wielded by the Wilson
administration to derail political progress. While
that was almost certainly President Wilson's intent,
Scott did preside over one of the largest expansions
of black officers and service members in military
history.

BLACK JUNIOR OFFICERS

While Scott certainly helped shepherd an initiative that brought 1,250 new black officers into the army during World War I, the plan began at the war's outset, months before his appointment. And it stemmed not from internal initiative but rather from agitating on the part of DuBois and other black intellectuals, including Scott.

When the draft began, Secretary of War Baker suggested that the Army War College train a contingent of black junior officers to help lead the black

Soldiers shooting dice during R&R.

division then still being debated—again citing the political benefits rather than any expectation that they could prove militarily valuable. A primary argument against the use of black officers to this point had been that they lacked the intellect, or at least the educational background, necessary to lead troops in battle. In a preemptive strike against that argument this time, the NAACP organized 1,500 students from Howard University, a historically black college in Washington, D.C., into the Central Committee of Negro College Men. The committee launched a massive national campaign, lobbying Congress to approve the junior officer training program. In his thorough account of black World War I military service, *Scott's Official History of the American Negro in the World War*, Scott summed up the irony of a situation that had now persisted for over a century. "Colored men," he incredulously wrote, "were fighting the government in order to wring from it permission to fight for it."

The baseball team of the 609th Pioneer Infantry playing the white league champs. The 609th won handily.

Absurd as it may have been, the campaign built considerable steam and ultimately succeeded. And in June 1917, the War Department established a black officer's training school at Fort Des Moines, Iowa. The school admitted 250 noncommissioned officers from the four Buffalo Soldier regiments, and a thousand volunteers from the black state militias. On October 14, 639 black junior officers were sworn into the ranks; the remainder of the class was dismissed. Before that afternoon, the army had commissioned six African Americans; the next day it had 369 black first lieutenants, 204 second lieutenants, and 106 captains. The men were assigned to the Ninety-second Division, where they would be closely supervised by superior white officers. At the same time, the army forced Colonel Charles Young, still the last of three African Americans to graduate from the U.S. Military Academy at West Point, into his early retirement. Colonel Young's achievements and resulting rank meant it would be difficult to prevent him from leading white troops in Europe—a scenario the army certainly didn't intend to risk.

A BAD RAP FOR THE NINETY-SECOND

The Ninety-second Division's ill-fated tour began in June of 1918, when it joined the American expeditionary forces in France. Before arriving, the division's four regiments—the 365th, 366th, 367th, and 368th—had received five months of haphazard training. Rather than by Colonel Young, who most blacks felt should have been atop the division, the troops were led by Major General Charles Ballou—a "timid, changeable white man," as DuBois called him, who had already earned his troops' resentment by order-

The 368th Infantry, Ninety-second Division advancing to the front in Marne, France.

The Ninety-second in a gassing drill in France.

ing them to tolerate the indignities of Jim Crow in the cities where they trained. After an incident in Manhattan, Kansas, in which a black sergeant protested when a movie theater manager refused him entry, Major General Ballou issued his "Bulletin No. 35." In it, he repeated an earlier plea that the troops "refrain from going where their presence will be resented" and warned "white men made the Division, and they can break it just as easily if it becomes a trouble maker." The commander's comment was not only paternalistic but also incorrect, since the division was not the result of white largesse but political pressures created by black activists. And although he mainly intended to protect the division from white backlash, his order became an infamous symbol for both civilian and military African Americans of the disrespect the U.S. armed forces showed them. Things had gotten off to a bad start.

"Big Nims" of the 366th Infantry during a gassing drill.

After eight weeks of additional training in France, the Ninety-second moved up to the front line sector of St. Die in August. They arrived shortly after U.S. and French troops had scored a major victory, and the Central Powers were thus on the offensive. But ten companies from all four regiments fought at the front throughout the next month, successfully defending the St. Die sector. During the fighting, Lieutenant Aaron Fisher of the 366th Regiment became the war's first black Distinguished Service Cross winner. Seventeen more troops from the division won crosses during this twenty-eight-day period on the front. In a different fate, First Lieutenant Thomas Bullock earned an unwelcome place in history as the first African American commissioned officer killed in battle.

Despite its impressive performance in the first month, the Ninety-second Division's reputation would be forever stained by accusations of cowardice launched against the 368th Regiment. In September 1918, the entire division moved to join the Allies' major offensive at Meuse-Argonne. Six hundred and fifty thousand American troops participated in the attack, which military planners hoped would break the Germans' line once and for all. The Ninety-second was used largely as a reserve. But battalions of the 368th Regiment ended up at one section of the front, where they saw heavier fighting than they had previously encountered or for which they had ever trained. The regiment lost 450 men in the battle, and Major General Ballou and his outspokenly racist Chief of Staff Colonel Allen Greer declared that the

Germany encouraged black troops to defect, and created propaganda such as this photograph to aid the campaign.

lot had performed timidly and embarrassed the division. They particularly blamed the black junior officers, asserting that their poor performance proved the training experiment at Fort Des Moines a failure. They dismissed thirty officers and sent them home, court-martialing five of them for cowardice. Four of those men had been sentenced to execution and one to life in prison before all were exonerated in a subsequent investigation. It was but the most dramatic in a series of accusations launched by white senior officers against the blacks trained at Fort Des Moines. Throughout the war, white superiors worked—successfully—to discredit the cohort of trainees, forcing many out of their commissions.

Again, these junior officers' treatment became

a rallying point for civilian and military blacks alike, who were increasingly insulted by the army and the War Department's treatment of African American troops. Ultimately, even Major General Ballou admitted that many of the charges of cowardice likely came from white senior officers who focused more on discrediting blacks than anything happening on the battlefield. Nevertheless, white America had already heard what it wanted to hear, and the men of the Ninety-second Division, as well as black soldiers in general, were widely considered failures.

Meanwhile, the German forces picked up on the technique used by the Philippine rebels earlier in the century. During the Ninety-second's stay in the St. Die sector, German troops captured two members of

the 366th Regiment. Shortly thereafter, gas shells began falling on the 367th that contained a weapon the Germans figured to be more potent than chemicals: propaganda attempting to incite black troops' resentment of white America. The German flyers invoked the slights of segregation in the same manner the Philippine rebels had highlighted lynching. "Do you enjoy the same rights as the white people do in America, the land of Freedom and Democracy, or are you rather not treated over there as second-class citizens?" the flyers asked.

Why, then, fight the Germans only for the benefit of the Wall street robbers and to protect the millions they have loaned to the British, French, and Italians? You have been made the tool of the egotistic and rapacious rich in England and in America, there is nothing in the whole game for you but broken bones, horrible wounds, spoiled health, or death. . . . Let those do the fighting who make the profit out of this war. Don't allow them to use you as cannon fodder. To carry a gun in this war is not an honor, but a shame. Throw it away and come over into the German lines. You will find friends who will help you along.

Kathryn Johnson, who taught black troops as a Y-secretary, wrote a book detailing the indignities black troops endured.

The Germans' campaign did not enjoy even the minimal success of the Filipinos'. No black soldiers defected during World War I.

The Germans did not need to remind black soldiers of the absoluteness of their second-class status back in America, because relief agencies that crossed the Atlantic to both care for and provide diversions for armed forces personnel brought Jim Crow with them. The Young Men's Christian Association, or the YMCA, set up "Y-huts," staffed by "Y-secretaries," where soldiers could seek out entertainment, educational programs, and sports. But the huts were strictly segregated. Unlike all other relief agencies, however, the YMCA sought to abide by the nonsensical separate-but-equal logic of segregation and actually employed black volunteers to tend to the black troops. As usual, of course, the separate facilities were nowhere near equal. Addie Hunton and Kathryn Johnson, two of the nineteen women who were among a total of ninety-two black Y-secretaries who served at some point during the war, later wrote a book about their experiences teaching black soldiers to read and write. They also described the aversion most YMCA volunteers had for African American troops, and the mistreatment the soldiers endured as a result.

Despite all of this, the men of the Ninety-second Division still fought bravely from the time of their deployment until the war's last battle. One hundred and three officers and 1,543 enlisted men in the division were killed or wounded in France. Fourteen officers and forty-three enlisted men in total won Distinguished Service Crosses. Several more won the French medal Croix de Guerre, including the entire 367th Regiment for its heroic efforts at Metz, during the war's closing battles on November 11 and 12, 1918.

THE NINETY-THIRD DIVISION UNDER FRENCH COMMAND

On August 6, 1918, as the army continued detailing regiments of the Ninety-third Division to the French forces, General John Pershing's general headquarters in France issued a curious communiqué. The directive contained "Secret Information Concerning Black American Troops" and circulated not only throughout the French army but also to all of the country's local-level civilian leaders. "Although a citizen of the United States, the black man is regarded by the white American as an inferior being with whom relations of business or service only are possible," Pershing's order declared, offering instruction on how French officers were to deal with their African American charges. "The vices of the Negro are a constant menace to the American who has to repress

General Pershing reviews members of the Ninety-second Division, which was unfairly charged with cowardice.

Chicago men line up to enlist in the state's black militia, which became the 370th Regiment and fought in the French army.

them sternly," it continued, later adding, "We must not eat with them, must not shake hands or seek to talk or meet with them outside the requirements of military service. We must not commend too highly the black American troops, particularly in the presence of Americans."

Pershing, assuming the voice of the French commanders, went on to issue a special warning against "spoiling" African Americans or allowing intimate contact between black men and white women. The communiqué revealed the depth of white apprehension about allowing blacks to fight in Europe. Their fears were justified. Black soldiers returned from Europe with a renewed sense of self-worth and—much like the Buffalo Soldiers following their experiences in Cuba and the Philippines—a decidedly reduced tolerance for Jim Crow. This was particularly true for the men of the Ninety-third Division. The war-weary French, in dire need of new soldiers, welcomed the black troops with open arms, both within the military and among the civilian population. The national government, in fact, openly rejected Pershing's desperate instructions on race relations and reportedly even recalled copies of it and had them burnt.

The Ninety-third Division shipped to France in parts and never fought as a whole unit. It consisted of four infantry regiments—the 369th, 370th, 371st, and 372nd—and none of the usual additional artillery or engineering units. The regiments were primarily composed of state national guards—the Eighth Illinois, the Fifteenth New York, and black companies from the National Guard units of Massachusetts, Maryland, Ohio, Tennessee, and Washington, D.C.

The Eighth Illinois held a unique place in the state's history, similar to that of the independent-minded black militias of New Orleans that joined the

American leaders expected France to use the Ninety-third as laborers, but the division fought and won hundreds of service awards.

Army during the wars of the 1800s. Since its inception U.S. Army during the Spanish-American War, the Eighth was largely considered an elite black social club, peopled with some of the city's most educated and respected professionals. This special standing stemmed in part from the fact that, like the New Orleans black militias, it was completely led by African Americans. From corporal to colonel, all of the regiment's officers were black. Colonel Franklin Dennison, a prominent lawyer in Chicago government, commanded the militia, which he had already led into battle during the Punitive Expedition against Pancho Villa in Mexico. Because of this black leadership, the War Department hesitated to send the Eighth to France. Ironically, the Buffalo Soldiers' uprising at Camp Logan in Houston helped relieve the department's apprehension. The Eighth had been deployed to Camp Logan just weeks before the riot, and Colonel Dennison's steady leadership over his men during the tumultuous time comforted white military officials. So, in April 1918, the Eighth deployed to Brest, France, and became the 370th Regiment.

The regiment trained briefly with France's Seventy-second Division, then moved to the front line at St. Mihiel and, later, Argonne, where they fought in French uniforms using all French arms and supplies. After an uneventful first few months, several companies of the 370th joined in the regiment's first offensive action, capturing the German stronghold of Mont des Signes. Sergeant Matthew Jenkins won a Distinguished Service Cross and the French medal Croix de Guerre for leading his platoon in a particularly grueling engagement. After overtaking a large section of the German line, Sergeant Jenkins's platoon held it alone for thirty-six hours, with no food or water, until reinforcement could arrive. Sergeant Jenkins's medals were one of twenty-one

Distinguished Service Crosses and sixty-eight Croix de Guerre awarded to the 370th Regiment.

From September 1918 until the war's end in November, the regiment joined heavy fighting with the French Fifty-ninth Division, earning the nickname Black Devils from their German adversaries. They were among the first Allied troops to break the Hindenburg Line, and the first Americans to enter the French Fort Laon, which had been occupied by the Germans since the war's outset in 1914. They fought in the war's last battle, in Belgium on November 11, capturing a German train and its crew a half hour after the armistice. The 2,200-man regiment suffered twenty percent casualties but had only ninety-five members killed.

But the 370th's companies fought amidst leadership chaos. While the War Department had allowed the regiment to arrive with its six black field

Regardless of race, troops suffered life-altering injuries such as amputations.

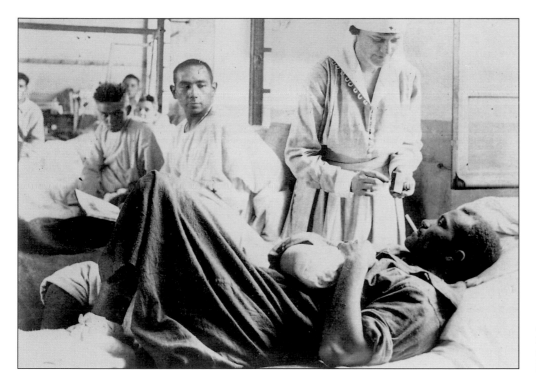

A member of the
371st Infantry receiving
treatment at a Red Cross
hospital.

officers in place, the American expeditionary force's white leadership worked assiduously to poison the French command's faith in those black officers. As a result, Colonel Dennison was sent home shortly after the regiment's arrival and replaced with a white colonel whom the troops openly rejected. Most of the other senior black officers were shipped back to the United States as well. But because of the black troops' backlash, it was widely accepted that the replacement white regimental commanders were merely rulers in name. The remaining black officers in each company ran the regiment.

The 371st Regiment's beginnings were a polar opposite of the 370th's. Composed of black draftees, primarily from South Carolina, the regiment was led entirely by white officers, also primarily southern men. After initial tensions between the troops and officers, however, they developed a relatively trustful relationship. The regiment's members were the first American draftees to begin fighting in France. They arrived in April on the heels of the 370th and fought without rest until the armistice in France's 157th Division.

After three months on the front line in Avocourt and Verrières, the regiment joined the massive Champagne offensive—which opened on September 25 with the largest artillery bombardment in history. Here the regiment won praise from its French colleagues and commanders for taking several towns and shooting down three German airplanes with rifle and machine gun fire. Eighty-nine black enlistees and thirty-four white officers won the Croix de Guerre, while twelve enlistees and ten officers won Distinguished Service Crosses.

This success, however, came at a heavy human price. The 371st lost nearly half of its men. Most of those troops were killed or wounded during the opening three days, as the regiment attempted to enter a German stronghold at which they believed the enemy had already surrendered. The night before the planned attack, a German representative entered the 371st's camp and announced that his men no longer wanted to fight. As the regiment approached the Germans' works the next morning, the Germans climbed from their trenches and raised their hands in apparent surrender. Once the 371st was convinced, the Germans suddenly regained their battle footing and opened fire, slaughtering many of the regiment's members. They fought bitterly over the next three days, however, and ultimately prevailed.

The 371st Infantry was composed of black draftees from South Carolina.

Members of the 371st were the first American draftees to fight in France and stayed there until the armistice.

HARLEM'S OWN

Of all the black regiments who fought or labored in World War I, by far the most famous is the 369th Regiment, which was created from the Fifteenth New York National Guard. Known to the Germans as the Hell Fighters, to the French as the Enfants Perdus (literally, the Lost Children—a reference to their second-class treatment by America), and at home simply as Harlem's Own, the 369th was the most decorated American fighting unit in the Great War. And, perhaps just as significantly, the regiment's band is credited with introducing France to jazz music in particular and black culture in general, inaugurating a mutual fascination between African American and French cultures that peaked in the postwar years but that endures to date.

New York Governor Charles Whitman created the Fifteenth in 1916, responding to years of political campaigning for a black Guard unit. Governor Whitman named Roosevelt Republican Colonel William Hayward commander, who filled out his chain of command with a number of other white Ivy Leaguers from prominent New York families and a handful of African Americans. When it joined the Ninety-third Division, the Fifteenth became the 369th Regiment. It arrived in France on New Year's Day, 1918, and was not only the first black unit to do battle but also one of the first American units to fight in France. The regiment would stay longer on the front line than any other unit in the war, serving a stretch of 191 consecutive days that encompassed the war's most intense fighting.

The regiment's introduction to the U.S. Army was a difficult one. During training in Spartanburg, South Carolina, it ran into the same problems black troops had faced in the South for decades. The men

Private Needham Roberts was the first American to win the French Croix de Guerre.

of the regiment, however, were completely unaccustomed to the region's aggressive enforcement of segregation, and they clashed heatedly with the local community. Similarly, once they arrived in France, the regiment's members found themselves in near combat with southern white U.S. Marines at St. Nazaire, where they were being employed as a labor unit. The tensions were soon eased, however, when the regiment transferred to French command and by April were on the front at Marne.

In May, while defending the Marne sector—which accounted for twenty percent of all territory held by American troops in France at the time—the 369th's Sergeant Henry Johnson and Private Needham Roberts became the first American enlistees to win the French Croix de Guerre. The men were on guard duty when they heard wire cutters in the distance and realized the Germans were raiding. They sounded the alarm and began to face down heavy fire and a shower of German grenades. Sergeant Johnson and Private Roberts, both direly wounded, propped themselves up in the doorway of

a dugout and lobbed enough grenades of their own to slow the enemy advance. As the Germans entered the dugout, forced to come in single file because of the narrow passage, Sergeant Johnson felled them one by one in hand-to-hand combat. The story, soon circulated in the popular press, catapulted the 369th to international fame and earned them the Germans' nickname, Hell Fighters.

The summer of 1918 witnessed a major German push, and with the French army reeling, the 369th was one of a number of American units that swooped in to help the Allies gain footing. The regiment struggled through heavy fighting throughout

James Reese Europe led the 369th band, which introduced jazz to Europe.

The 369th was the most decorated fighting unit in the Great War.

The 369th was created from volunteers for New York's elite black militia.

The 369th spent 191 consecutive days at the front, longer than any other unit in the war.

June and July, fending off some of the most significant German attacks and launching key Allied counteroffensives. Then, in late September, the troops joined so many others in the massive Champagne offensive that turned the war's tide. The 369th's gallantry in these weeks of battle prompted the French command to award a regimental Croix de Guerre. All told, over 170 members of the regiment won individual Croix de Guerre and Distinguished Service Crosses.

But the 369th's fame at home and abroad was as much due to its regimental band as its fighting. Star swing band leader James Reese Europe, whose orchestra had helped spark the early American century's dance mania, volunteered to join the Fifteenth New York in 1916. He was a line officer, but Colonel William Hayward compelled him to put together an impressive band as an additional duty, accurately predicting that this would boost enlistment. Colonel Hayward raised money so that the band could have

French Cross winner Henry Johnson rode in the 369th's homecoming parade.

Over a million people gathered in New York City to watch the 369th march up Fifth Avenue and into Harlem.

forty-four instead of the army standard twenty-eight pieces, and Lieutenant Europe recruited players from around the country. (The Fifteenth's other famous black enlistees included Ziegfeld's *Follies* star Bert Williams and jazz singer/songwriter Noble Sissle.) When the regiment arrived in France, Europe's band set out on a tour through the front to entertain troops and raise the lagging French spirit. It was the country's introduction to jazz music, and soldiers and civilians alike became obsessed with it. In March, the band rejoined the rest of the regiment as it prepared to head to the front for battle, but they again toured in August following Allied military gains.

When the Fifteenth New York left the state for training in South Carolina back in June 1917, Governor Whitman had blocked the regiment's participation in the National Guard farewell parade in New York City. Their return on February 17, 1919, was a different matter altogether. Over a million people gathered to watch the 369th march up Fifth Avenue and into Harlem, led by Europe's band wailing the newly popular wartime jazz tunes.

Black soldiers, emboldened by their European experiences, returned to a rabidly racist nation.

At War in a Time of Peace

The 369th Infantry Regiment may have returned home heroes, but that didn't last long for them or any of the black World War I vets. Seven hundred and fifty African Americans lost their lives in Europe; another five thousand were wounded in battle. While this sacrifice earned breathless praise from French military leaders, America's armed forces officials responded with disdain. To them, and to America at large, the overriding story of black military service in the Great War was that of the Ninety-second—a deliberately constructed myth that African American combat troops, in particular the black officers trained in Iowa, had been cowards and failures.

DuBois's June 1919 *Crisis* essay was one of several thorough reports he penned after an investigative trip to France with the aim of setting the record straight. But his and other black intellectuals' efforts were in vain. American racism was at a peak. The Ku Klux Klan, stomped out of existence decades earlier, reemerged strong as ever. Black tolerance of mistreatment and insult, however, had waned just as dramatically as racism had grown. The hundreds of thousands of returning black soldiers and their families, stoked by angry civil rights leaders, developed a rage that could not be contained. "We are cowards and jackasses," a May 1919 *Crisis* op-ed declared, "if now that the war is over, we do not marshal every ounce of our brain and brawn to fight a sterner, longer, more unbending battle against the forces of hell in our own land."

The collision of this rabid white racism and renewed black defiance, intensified by a suddenly crowded job market, led to one of America's most violent domestic periods. The summer of 1919 has come to be known as Red Summer, as it witnessed deadly race riots in twenty-six urban centers around the country. At least seventy-eight African Americans died after being lynched that summer, eleven of whom were soldiers, some wearing their uniforms. Black and white mobs burned cities to the ground, particularly African American neighborhoods. And the Wilson administration turned a blind eye.

Meanwhile, the armed forces slowly mustered blacks out of the service. The draft and National Guard regiments were demobilized, leaving the withering four Buffalo Soldier regiments as once again the only home for African American service members. As the army expanded its air corps, a unit closed to African Americans, it maintained the branch's overall size by slowly slimming down the black regiments. As members left the service, they were not replaced with new black enlistees. The resulting skeleton units were essentially transformed into full-time labor regiments by the 1930s.

The dissolution of the Buffalo Soldier regiments was engineered by military planners who cut their teeth in Wilson's War Department, many of whom were the same white senior officers that launched false accusations of cowardice against black junior officers during the war. The Ninety-second's Chief of Staff Colonel Greer was among those on a General Staff College committee that sat in 1920 to consider the future use of blacks in the military. The commit-

tee declared African Americans "careless, shiftless, irresponsible and secretive," and warned against future deployments. In 1922, the War Department developed a mobilization plan to be implemented in the case of another war, and it took the committee's recommendations to heart. It made no account for mobilizing any of the black National Guards, and it held that the number of black army enlistees should be in proportion to the African American community's size within America at large. The air corps and marines continued to ban black enlistment altogether, and the navy recruited blacks only as stewards. By the eve of World War II, there were only around four thousand African Americans still in the army, and only six black officers.

Welcome Abroad

Even as the American military pushed African Americans out of its ranks, other nations opened their arms to blacks. During the war, an American expatriate joined the French air force and became the world's first black combat pilot. Eugene Bullard lasted only six months in the French Foreign Legion, however, before having a run-in with his white superiors and leaving. But in the postwar years, small groups of black Americans would also volunteer to help Ethiopia and Spain defend against the burgeoning fascist movement. With a new world focus learned from World War I, and an understanding of fascism as a global form of the racism they endured at home, black Americans found resonance in these nations' struggles.

In October 1935, Italy's Fascist Party Prime Minister Benito Mussolini sent his forces to conquer the East African nation of Ethiopia. African

Americans had recently developed a fascination with the country, ruled by the eccentric Emperor Haile Selassie, Ras Tafari. This was in part due to radical activist Marcus Garvey's popular "Africa for the Africans" movement—which called for black Americans to repatriate to sub-Saharan Africa and lead the continent in shaking off colonialism. And it was in part due to the mystique of Haile Selassie and his kingdom, where Africans were said to live in luxury as did their own rulers. The tiny nation had beaten back Italy's previous assault in 1896 and uniquely remained independent on the continent. And African Americans hoped Selassie could now strike a similar blow against fascism.

Citizens of several other, largely European nations also hoped the bellicose Mussolini would fail in taking Ethiopia. And mercenary groups from many of those places showed up in East Africa to aid

Hubert Julian, "The Black Eagle of Harlem," flew in Ethiopia's mercenary air force fighting Italian encroachment.

Paul Robeson was among hordes of black and Jewish Americans who supported Spain's fight against fascism.

Selassie. No African Americans joined these mercenary groups in ground combat, but two men flew in the Ethiopian air force. One was John Robinson from Chicago, and the other was the flashy Black Eagle of Harlem, Hubert Julian. Julian was one of scores of Caribbean immigrants to New York City in the early twentieth century and was the first black American to obtain a pilot's license. Robinson drew praise for his brief fighting against Italy's air force, but the charismatic Julian got the press. Julian, how-

ever, crashed one of Selassie's only three planes shortly after arriving in the country and abruptly returned home disenchanted. Italy successfully occupied Ethiopia the following May.

In July, Spanish General Francisco Franco led the nation's North African army in attacking the Spanish mainland. The civil war that erupted gripped African Americans' attention even more than Ethiopia's struggle had. Franco drew aid from Italy and Germany and eventually recruited most of the

Spanish military to his cause. Direly outmanned, the Spanish government built an auxiliary army of volunteers from around the world. Dubbed the International Brigades, the force was largely recruited from the international Communist Party's membership. But for African Americans and Jews in the United States, the fight was simply against xenophobic fascism, and they joined the Lincoln Brigade of the international volunteer force in strong numbers. Nearly a third of the brigade was Jewish, but around 100 of the 2,800 volunteers were black, and most of those were World War I veterans.

Salaria Kee, who worked in Harlem Hospital and had helped raise medical supplies to be donated to Ethiopia during its war, joined the brigade as its only black nurse. James Peck and Paul Williams flew in the Republican air force. But the most famous black American to join the Spanish struggle was acclaimed singer and actor Paul Robeson. The master of Negro spirituals traveled to Spain in late 1937, where he studied the conflict against fascism and offered his fame and talents to the cause. Support for the Spanish antifascist cause was one of the largest of Robeson's several controversial political positions throughout his career. Closely allied with the Communist Party, and later the Soviet Union, his activism against what he saw as global forms of racism—and in support of what he saw as international models for equal societies—earned him the suspicion of his own government. During the Red Scare of the 1950s, the State Department would revoke his passport, and constant harassment from the Federal Bureau of Investigation would ruin his storied career.

6

"ELEANOR'S NIGGERS"

World War II

I t was 7:55 A.M. on December 7, 1941, and Mess Attendant Second Class Doris "Dorie" Miller was collecting laundry on board the USS *West Virginia*, docked at Pearl Harbor, Hawaii. So far, it had been just another morning in the life of a black navy man—forced to work belowdecks in a support role rather than take the kind of job that might build useful mechanical skills or allow him to prove his abilities. But the call to assembly that went off just before the eight o'clock hour that morning signaled

the start of one of American history's most significant events. And Miller, a twenty-two-year-old barrel-chested farm boy from Waco, Texas, was about to be thrust into its center.

"The Japs are attacking us!" was the cry that rang through the *West Virginia* shortly after the alarm sounded. It was unthinkable, but two heavy shocks against the port side hull sent the ship into a rapid list and convinced any doubters that an attack was in fact underway. Miller and his crewmates jumped to

The navy tried to conceal the fact that Dorie Miller (left) was World War II's first American hero.

action, quickly assuming their posts. As the ship's heavyweight boxing champion and a former high school football fullback, Miller's strength had earned him the job of carrying injured sailors to safety during battles. So ship communications officer Lieutenant D. C. Johnson grabbed Miller and enlisted his help in attempting to move the ship's mortally wounded captain from the bridge. (In his battle report, Lieutenant Johnson identifies all those he discusses by their names, except Miller, whom he simply refers to as "a colored mess attendant" who was "a very powerfully built individual.") But the captain, suffering a painful and clearly fatal wound, ordered that he be left alone, and Miller instead joined Lieutenant F. H. White on the forward guns.

Miller, as with all black sailors, had never been trained to use this fifty-caliber antiaircraft machine gun—or any ship guns, for that matter. Nevertheless, he shot down between two and four Japanese aircraft (the number is in dispute), unflinchingly working the gun until he ran out of ammunition and was ordered to abandon ship. "It wasn't hard," he later commented. "I just pulled the trigger and she worked fine. I had watched the others with these guns. I guess I fired her for about fifteen minutes. I think I got one of those Jap planes. They were diving pretty close to us."

The attack on the *West Virginia* marked the beginning of U.S. direct involvement in World War II and the permanent end to the nation's steadfastly parochial worldview. Of the 1,541 sailors on board the ship, 130 were killed and 52 were wounded. Miller's remarkable effort to minimize this carnage provided the first hero's tale of the war. But the navy didn't want a black poster boy and instead heavily publicized the death of a white pilot who crashed into a Japanese vessel after a December 9 bombing

mission. In response, the black press focused unceasingly on Miller's exploits, while civil rights organizations demanded that he be awarded a Medal of Honor. That wouldn't happen for Miller or any other black soldier during the conflict, making World War II the second war in a row in which no black soldier received the nation's highest military honor. Over the objection of Secretary of the Navy Frank Knox, Miller did ultimately receive a Navy Cross for his actions at Pearl Harbor.

Born in late 1919, amid the psychic rubble of the summer's race riots, Miller knew nothing of the disappointments World War I brought black soldiers. He enlisted in September of 1939, a peacetime recruit who was in search of nothing more spectacular than extra money for his family and an opportunity to do some traveling. This motivation stood in stark contrast to that of blacks in previous American wars, who often fought in an effort to achieve freedom and respect for both themselves and their community. But for decades into the future, and in many ways still today, this recognition of the military as a viable alternative to the civilian workforce would be the driving force for minority enlistment.

Following Pearl Harbor, Miller served first aboard the USS *Indianapolis* and then the aircraft carrier USS *Liscome Bay*. He died on November 24, 1943, when a Japanese submarine sank the *Liscome Bay*, killing 646 members of its 918-person crew. His body was never recovered.

Fight for the Right to Fight

The 1930s witnessed a dramatic shift in black politics. Since the time of Lincoln and the Radical Republicans of the Reconstruction era, African

FDR's "black cabinet" gave his administration more black political appointees than any previous one.

Americans had stood firmly with the GOP. They had been largely unwanted in the Southern-dominated Democratic Party in the first place. And, despite their repeated failures to follow through on promises, the Republican presidents of the early twentieth century actively courted the black vote. But with the nation reeling from the Great Depression, blacks in the 1930s joined most other Americans in supporting a Democratic president who appeared to have all the answers—Franklin Delano Roosevelt. While blacks were slow to support FDR in his 1932 inaugural bid for the White House, by the end of the decade the New Deal had won them over en masse. And what FDR's domestic social service and job creation programs didn't do to draw black votes, the First Lady did.

Eleanor Roosevelt was the administration's moral, and liberal, voice. Many historians have speculated that FDR encouraged her famous outspoken-

ness and regular disagreements with his administration's policies as a way to balance the electorate. Her activism allowed the couple to play a good cop/bad cop routine (who was good or bad depended on one's perspective) that secured the broad support they needed to hold the White House at such a tumultuous time in our nation's history. For the party's conservative wing, FDR toed the line on Jim Crow and gender issues, for instance, while the First Lady received awards from civil rights and women's groups for her advocacy on their behalf. They employed the same tactic when it came to the question of how African American soldiers would be used in the event of another war.

Eleanor Roosevelt encouraged her husband to open his administration to black leaders, and as a result it had more black political appointees than any previously. He maintained what became known as

Eleanor Roosevelt pushed the administration's door open to civil rights leaders like Mary McCloud Bethune (above), who led FDR's"black cabinet."

his "black cabinet" of advisers on race relations, which educator Mary McLeod Bethune led. Wielding that group's influence, amplified by the First Lady, African Americans won significant involvement in New Deal programs. Moreover, by this time the black press had grown into a powerful voice capable of mobilizing either significant support for or opposition to new policies. So when the administration began planning a wartime military in the late 1930s, black America's political influence was greater than it had ever been, and African American leaders were thus well positioned to advocate for a more substantive commitment than Wilson made during World War I.

A FACE-OFF WITH THE WHITE HOUSE

The civil rights movement's goal was no longer just the right to fight but the right to fight in integrated units. The NAACP was gunning for Jim Crow, and the military stood as a giant target with the prominence necessary to kick-start a national rollback of segregation laws. So NAACP legal counsel Charles Houston, a World War I vet, put the administration on notice, announcing in a 1937 letter to War Secretary H. A. Woodring, "The Negro population will not silently suffer the discrimination and abuse which were heaped upon Negro soldiers and officers in World War I." The War Department developed a plan that same year to boost the number of black service members so that they would represent ten percent of the armed forces, mirroring their percentage of the American population. That plan also reserved junior officer positions in black units for African Americans. But it angered blacks

by reaffirming the need for segregation.

Three years later, in 1940, President Roosevelt signed the Selective Service and Training Act, creating the country's first peacetime draft. The act contained the first nondiscrimination statement in the armed forces, banning bias based on race and color. This antibias clause marked a major victory for the civil rights movement, but it was nevertheless miles from what civil rights activists were seeking: a fully integrated fighting force. A group of the era's most powerful black lobbyists, including the NAACP leadership and Asa Philip Randolph, who was now the head of the nation's first black workers' union, presented the administration with a set of demands focusing on full integration. The White House responded by again giving some ground—opening officer candidate schools, the air corps, the marines, and all other units to blacks—but continued balking at integration.

Black leaders remained unsatisfied, and FDR, with his eyes trained on his not yet certain reelection, decided to offer his most significant concession yet. Privately, he assured them that he would encourage the promotion of black troops through all branches and into all specialties in the armed forces. Publicly, he met three of the black leaders' earlier demands, all of which involved prominent African American military appointments. On October 25, 1940, Roosevelt announced the promotion of Benjamin O. Davis Sr., who had first enlisted with the Eighth Regiment Illinois National Guard during the Spanish-American War, to brigadier general, creating the nation's first black general. On November 1, he followed that announcement by appointing Judge William Hastie, the dean of Howard University Law School who would later become the first black federal court judge, to Emmett Scott's former position as

In 1940, FDR tapped Benjamin O. Davis, Sr. to be the nation's first black general.

Roosevelt to issue executive orders integrating the military and banning discrimination both within the government and in the private defense industry. And his revolutionary solution to forcing the administration's hand was to call a march on Washington, D.C. Today, civic activists gather in the nation's capital to protest and support causes without a second thought. But such a thing had never been done at the time, and Randolph's brazenness earned him still higher reverence among radical and moderate activists alike.

His January 1941 "Call to Negro America" asked that at least ten thousand African Americans come to the National Mall on July 1, promising that "an 'all out' thundering march on Washington, ending in a monster and huge demonstration at Lincoln's Monument will shake up white America." The NAACP and the National Urban League, formed during the first great migration of African Americans to northern cities in the 1910s, both supported the call, which carefully characterized the mass action as one consistent with patriotism and the nation's defense. "But what of national unity?" it asked.

adviser to the war secretary on African American affairs. He also appointed Major Campbell C. Johnson as an assistant to the head of the Selective Service, where he was supposed to make sure the draft dealt with blacks equitably.

These last concessions bought FDR enough goodwill to retain the White House that year, but the black leaders, particularly Randolph, were not finished. Randolph had seen the gap between White House promises and military implementation during the Wilson years. And unlike World War I, when the attorney general could simply jail him to keep him quiet, Randolph was now an influential enough figure to make sure black America walked away with more than a few meaningless gestures. He wanted

We believe in national unity which recognizes equal opportunity of black and white citizens to jobs in national defense and the armed forces, and in all other institutions and endeavors in America. We condemn all dictatorships, Fascist, Nazi and Communist. We are loyal, patriotic Americans, all.

But, if American democracy will not defend its defenders; if American democracy will not protect its protectors; if American democracy will not give jobs to its toilers because of race or color; if

American democracy will not insure equality of opportunity, freedom and justice to its citizens, black and white, it is a hollow mockery and belies the principles for which it stands.

Roosevelt worked all spring to unhinge the march. He called Randolph in for two meetings, hoping to change his mind. He argued that while he supported the march's goals, he could not issue the executive orders because it would create a dangerous precedent. He pleaded that Randolph understand how sensitive the issue was, that it could not be "settled with a sledgehammer." And he even tried to discourage the other, more mainstream civil rights groups from supporting the event. But none of this worked, and Randolph, even though he knew he had nowhere near ten thousand marchers lined up, refused to call off the march. The two leaders were engaged in a dangerous test of wills, with both claiming that forces beyond them made compromise impossible—and both standing to lose a great deal. Roosevelt could ill afford to have thousands of African Americans rallying in protest of his administration, voicing an open defiance of the new war effort triggered by Pearl Harbor. But Randolph and the civil rights movement could no more afford to actually hold the rally if the threatened ten thousand were not going to show.

Finally, on June 25, barely a week before the rally, FDR blinked. He offered his final concession, issuing Executive Order 8802. The order banned race-based bias in defense industry companies contracting with the federal government and established a committee to oversee compliance, but it did not address segregation within the armed forces. Randolph knew Roosevelt had bent as far as he

would or could, and he realized he had better not gamble his political influence on an unlikely impressive showing at the march. So, despite heated criticism from the young radical black activists who formed his support base, Randolph called off the event. He had won America's first employment nondiscrimination policy and moved the nation a giant step toward integrating its armed forces.

A Reluctant Navy and Marine Corps

There were approximately five thousand black sailors on active duty when Dorie Miller manned those guns at Pearl Harbor, all of them toiling in noncombat support roles—usually serving food, washing dishes, or doing laundry. Their situation would not improve dramatically during the war. As the give and take between the Roosevelt administration and civil rights leaders continued, the navy was perhaps the most reluctant of the branches to accept an expanded role for blacks in the military. Secretary of the Navy Knox stood firmly against not only integration but increasing African American recruitment in general. He asserted that the branch had always stood as a uniquely white institution. And he argued that to open the door to significant numbers of blacks would necessitate integration, given the logistical difficulties of segregating a battleship. That was simply unthinkable in such intimate quarters. Knox was apparently just as ignorant of his branch's rich history of sailing integrated vessels as the naval officer who barred black army troops from returning home on his ship following World War I.

As the 1940 presidential elections neared, a group of African American navy enlistees spoke out publicly about their situation. In an open letter to the influential black newspaper the *Pittsburgh Courier,* fifteen black mess men encouraged other African Americans not to enlist. "All they would become is seagoing bellhops, chambermaids and dishwashers," the disenchanted sailors warned. Combined with pressure from the First Lady and civil rights leaders, the letter helped convince FDR that it was time to push the military forward. So as the war geared up in late 1941, he kept his promises to black leaders and

The navy was the most reluctant to accept an expanded role for African Americans. Black navy personnel were largely left as mess attendants during the war.

began pressuring each military branch to step up black enlistment and to use black troops in more combat and specialty roles. In the navy, he ordered officials to recruit five thousand additional African Americans for posts other than mess attendants.

Knox and his colleagues dragged their collective feet. The secretary created a special board to study the issue, and the board returned with a recommendation that the president's order was militarily untenable. Inaugurating an argument the military brass would later use to deflect calls for allowing women and sexual minorities to serve, Knox's board told Roosevelt that the realities of race relations in America made the move impossible. The navy, it argued, could not be responsible for sorting out social ills, and to bring blacks into nonservice jobs would only anger valued white officers and enlisted men. "These concepts may not be truly democratic," the board wrote, "but it is doubtful if the most ardent lovers of democracy will dispute them."

Black Press writers like Pittsburgh Courier war correspondent Ted Stanford (left) stoked the community's outrage over treatment of black troops.

By this point, however, FDR had reached the end of his patience with Knox's navy. He sent the board's report back and again ordered its members to draft a plan to increase black enlistment and to place black sailors in jobs outside of the kitchen. Knox finally realized he had lost the battle and announced on April 7, 1942, that in the next year the navy would recruit fourteen thousand new African American sailors, who would be trained in all variety of posts beyond mess attendants and stewards. Knox did not, however, concede the war. He had no intention of putting any black sailors on board navy vessels in roles other than mess duties.

The following June, the navy began training black enlistees at the segregated Camp Robert Smalls—named after the black Civil War naval hero—located inside Illinois' Great Lakes Naval Training Center. Most of these trainees were later assigned to domestic ammunition depots and construction projects. The remainder were sent to sea as mess attendants, infuriating the civil rights leaders who had hoped progress was finally beginning. Few black recruits showed in the first place, and blacks still made up only around two percent of the navy until early 1943, when Roosevelt forced the branch to begin accepting draftees as well as volunteers. But African Americans still never represented more than five percent of the navy during the World War II era.

Neither did these men resign themselves to their subordinate roles. The discontent expressed by the mess attendants who wrote to the *Pittsburgh Courier* in 1940 spread through new enlistees and occasionally even led to violent clashes between black and white sailors as the war moved on. Blacks working in labor details regularly protested both their assignments and the substandard treatment they received while working.

The incident that drew the most attention, and most angered the African American community at large, occurred in the summer of 1944 at Port Chicago on Mare Island, California. On July 17, the ammunition depot there inexplicably exploded, killing over two hundred black sailors. It was the war's largest loss of life on U.S. soil and accounted for fifteen percent of black naval casualties. These deaths inflamed the enlistees' resentment of being forced to work in supply posts despite their specialty training. The navy pushed things to the brink by denying the black victims leave time given to all of the accident's white survivors. As a result, 258 black ammunition loaders began a work stoppage. Most of those men caved under their superiors' pressure and shortly returned to work. But fifty men refused, and the navy court-martialed them all for mutiny, which is punishable by death. NAACP lawyer Thurgood Marshall, who would become the first black Supreme Court Justice, defended the men for two years before finally winning their reprieve.

GOLDEN THIRTEEN AND V-12 OFFICERS

In July 1943, with the navy's fleet growing exponentially, the branch decided to expedite officer training. Navy planners combined officers' training school with a college education—which was a prerequisite—creating the V-12 program. As usual, civil rights leaders demanded that blacks be among the new wave of officer recruits; and, as usual, Secretary Knox balked. But Roosevelt, in a now familiar role, ordered Knox to find a way to include African Americans.

The modern navy's first black officers, known as the Golden Thirteen, recorded the highest class scores in the history of the reserve officer training school to which they had been sent.

Unlike Knox, Assistant Secretary of the Navy Adlai Stevenson was a strong supporter of the idea, and he came up with a limited plan to train and commission twelve black officers. Expecting several to drop out along the way, the navy selected sixteen candidates from among its top performing black enlistees for an experimental officer training program. In January 1944, these candidates were put on an abbreviated training schedule at the Great Lakes Naval Training Center—a program reduced to half the time allotted for whites. Nevertheless, all sixteen men not only passed but recorded the best class scores ever seen at Great Lakes.

Despite this success, navy officials decided they

could still only commission twelve of the men. They chose ten who had college degrees, and two who had been to technical school, and on March 17, 1944, granted them commissions as ensigns in the naval reserves. A thirteenth graduate, who had not been to college, was appointed a warrant officer, and the rest were sent back to their earlier enlistment duties. However, the modern navy's first black officers, who decades later dubbed themselves the Golden Thirteen, were immediately classified as "limited" and given domestic posts.

Six of the Golden Thirteen remained at Great Lakes to train new black officer recruits. During the first cohort's training, the navy had reluctantly decided that it was too expensive to maintain a segregated training program for so small of a group and began experimenting with training black and white officers together in the V-12 program. The effort was lackluster, to say the least. Only fifty-two African Americans earned commissions in the program, out of a total of more than seventy thousand graduates. As with the Golden Thirteen, these men were all commissioned into the reserves rather than the regular navy, which primarily drew its officers from the U.S. Naval Academy at Annapolis. Not until the war's close did the academy finally accept a black candidate. In June 1945, black New York City Congressman Adam Clayton Powell appointed Wesley Brown to the naval officers' college. Brown endured the same emotional and physical terrorism that his West Point predecessors had endured, and in June of 1949 he became the first black Annapolis graduate.

While the navy's officer training experiments were woefully limited, the war's early years witnessed a sea change in the branch's dealings with African Americans. The navy was finally open to blacks, at least in word, both as officers and enlisted men. And

the main obstacle to further progress was now simply the leadership of Secretary Knox. That obstacle disappeared when Knox passed away in April 1944. His replacement, James Forrestal, could not have been more different. A New York Democrat, Forrestal was a longtime member of the National Urban League and a vocal proponent of naval integration.

BACK AT SEA

The constant tension between black sailors and their white colleagues convinced the navy in August 1943 to create a Special Programs Unit to further study the issue of race relations within the branch and come up with recommendations for improvement. To Secretary Knox, it was just an extended version of the study board that had originally recommended leaving the navy closed to African Americans. Its purpose was to help the administration deflect political pressure by claiming to be doing something about the issue. But the four junior officers named to the unit—all with experience leading or training black personnel—had different plans.

Throughout the war, the Special Programs Unit cranked out studies and recommendations as expected, consistently promoting the greater use of African American service members and making the seemingly revolutionary argument that personnel should be assigned duties based on their skills alone. Most of those reports were simply shelved. But in early 1944, the unit won approval for another limited experiment. On February 23, the navy announced it would man two vessels with black crews led by white officers. The escort destroyer USS *Mason* was commissioned the following month with 160 black crewmen and forty-four whites, including six officers. In April, the submarine chaser USS *PC-1264* launched with fifty-eight crewmen—fifty black and eight white—and five white officers. A year later, in May 1945, Ensign Samuel Gravely joined the *PC-1264* crew as the first black naval officer on board a combat ship. That June, Golden Thirteen alum James Hair joined the officer team on board the *Mason.*

The *Mason* crossed the Atlantic six times as part of convoys escorting supply ships. The *PC-1264* never went abroad but patrolled the east coast of the United States. These crews were, of course, far from the first black Americans to man U.S. warships. But their deployment was a revolutionary development for the modern navy, and it remains unclear why

The USS *Mason* was one of two experimental vessels staffed with black crews led by white officers.

Knox allowed the experiment to proceed. In all like-lihood, the *Mason* and the *PC-1264* owed their existence to the pro-integration Assistant Secretary Stevenson rather than Knox. And when Forrestal took over as the navy's chief in April—just as the black-manned sub chaser was launching its first patrols—Stevenson and the crusading officers of the Special Programs Unit found an ally in their efforts.

Forrestal conceded that integrating navy vessels was too delicate a job to embark upon mid-war, but he wanted more black sailors at sea right away. So in July he integrated advanced training schools—stemming from his belief that segregated training was simply too expensive—and announced plans to integrate a handful of the navy's auxiliary ships, such as

The marines recruited their first batch of black trainees from among navy mess attendants.

ammunition and other cargo carriers. As with officer training, this first step toward integrating ship crews was an incredibly small one. Auxiliary ships represented less than two percent of the fleet. And Forrestal's plan integrated only twenty-five of those vessels, with African American representation on board each capped at ten percent. But it was a start, and the experiment's smooth implementation—particularly compared to the turbulent conditions segregation fostered, highlighted at Port Chicago—proved that the sky would not fall if blacks were allowed to return to general service on navy vessels. By April 1945, Forrestal had integrated all 1,600 auxiliary ships in the fleet, and by June he had integrated naval basic training. The branch that had been Jim Crow's stronghold since Teddy Roosevelt's Great White Fleet was reclaiming its history.

THE MARINES

But while Stevenson, Forrestal, and the Special Programs Unit officers pushed and pulled the navy into a new era, their colleagues in the marines—formally a part of the navy—worked assiduously not to be swept along. Marine Corps Commandant General Thomas Holcomb was not shy about his objections to allowing blacks into his service and urged Knox's 1942 study board to inform the president that to do so would destroy the Corps. The Marine Corps had been exclusively white since its inception in 1798, and General Holcomb intended to keep it that way.

But the Corps was forced to begin accepting blacks at the same time that the navy as a whole boosted its recruitment in 1942. Despite General Holcomb's protest, and at President Roosevelt's insistence, that April Knox ordered the Corps to recruit nine hundred African Americans a month, as part of the navy's effort to sign up fourteen thousand new black service members over the next year. Like the navy, the marines decided to create only a handful of combat units and assign the overwhelming majority of black enlistees to serve as mess attendants and in ammunition and depot companies. Thus, the only black combat units were two battalions designed to defend foreign bases, the Fifty-first and Fifty-second Defense Battalions.

The first batch of black trainees was recruited from among navy mess men and army infantrymen. They went to Camp Lejune's Montford Point, a seg-regated outpost of the larger training facility located in the Sea Islands off the Carolina and Georgia coasts. There, they endured the famously grueling marine boot camp. Suffering the island's swampy cli-mate, they learned everything from Judo to artillery use from white drill instructors who by and large did-n't expect or hope that they would succeed. But as difficult as the white trainers made the course for this first black cohort, subsequent recruits would experi-ence an even more unforgiving boot camp life under the tutelage of black drill instructors determined to produce undeniably qualified black "leathernecks."

The Corps decided in 1942 to create black non-commissioned officers to lead its new black units as junior officers and to replace white drill instructors at Montford Point. Private First Class Edgar Huff, pro-moted in January 1943, was the first black noncom. Huff had stood out among his colleagues at boot camp and had already assumed a leadership role there. By that May, all of Montford's drill instructors were black, led by the feared Sergeant Charles Gilbert "Hashmark" Johnson. Sergeant Johnson was among the first batch of recruits, transferred from his mess attendant post in the navy. At thirty-seven years old,

Gilbert "Hashmark" Johnson was the feared leader of Montford Point's black marine drill instructors.

he had already served sixteen years in the army and navy by the time he arrived at Montford; he drew his nick-name from the navy stripes he had earned in that time. The marines, however, would not commission a black officer until after the war, when Second Lieutenant Frederick Branch became the first black marine to earn a reserve commission in November 1945.

In the fall of 1943, the Fifty-first Defense Battalion began advanced combat training with heavy artillery. The battalion excelled with all of the weaponry it handled, destroying the still lingering myth that African Americans did not possess the intelligence to operate "sophisticated" war technology. And in February 1944, as a result of that per-

Frederick C. Branch became the first black commissioned officer in the Marine Corps after the war's close.

formance, the battalion shipped out to the Pacific theater to defend bases in the Ellice and Marshall Islands—the first black marines to head overseas. They would remain deployed in the Pacific throughout the war, but these islands were securely held by the Allies and never attacked. Thus, the Fifty-first saw no combat. The same was true for the Fifty-second, which began its deployment, also in the Pacific, in October 1944.

The African American marines who did see combat were those in the support units that had not been specifically intended for fighting. The fifty-one black depot companies and twelve ammunition companies all deployed to the Pacific as well, beginning after the Fifty-first Defense Battalion joined the war. In June 1944, three of these units—the Third

Black marine support units were the only to see combat, such as these at Iwo Jima.

Ammunition Company and the Eighteenth and Twentieth Depot Companies—joined the D day fighting at Saipan. Their performance during that battle won the praise of both the popular press and white Corps leaders—including Marine Corps Commandant General Alexander Vandergrift, who declared following the battle that "the Negro Marines are no longer on trial. They are Marines." Saipan also saw the first African American marine killed in battle, a Twentieth Depot Company orderly named Kenneth Tibbs. Later, black ammunition and depot companies joined the hellish fighting on the beach of Iwo Jima, in February and March of 1945, where over six thousand U.S. Marines were killed.

Unlike the navy at large, the marines never integrated during the war. And, perhaps as a result, blacks never represented even a full five percent of the Corps—far from the ten-percent mandate. At the war's end, the Fifty-first and Fifty-second were disbanded.

Timberlate Kirven and Samuel Love, Sr. were among the ammo depot company marines who saw combat at D day Saipan.

Coast guard steward's mates have a rare chance to man guns.

Merchant marine ship captain Hugh Mulzac (third from right) later piloted vessels in Marcus Garvey's famous Black Star Line.

THE WAVES

One of the lines Secretary Knox had drawn in cement was that black women would not serve in the corps of women navy volunteers. The women were intended to help maintain the stateside shore duties that fighting sailors would no longer be able to keep up, and Knox asserted that since he didn't plan to allow black men on board ships as fighters, there was no need to replace them ashore with women. But when Secretary Forrestal took over, he removed this color bar as well, and he declared in July 1944 that blacks would be recruited for the Women Accepted for Volunteer Emergency Service program—more

WAVES Harriet Pickens and Francis Wills were the navy's only two black female officers.

popularly known as the WAVES. Recruitment got off to a slow start, until President Roosevelt's challenger for the 1944 elections, New York Governor Thomas Dewey, made an issue of it in the elections, charging that the administration was shunning black women in the war effort generally. That October, FDR ordered the navy to step things up.

Still, largely due to this belated opening of the ranks, there were only seventy-two black women in the WAVES during the war. They trained in an integrated setting in New York City at an office compound dubbed the USS *Hunter*. The navy's only two black female officers were among the training staff. Lieutenant Harriet Pickens and Ensign Francis Wills graduated in the last class of WAVES officer candidates at New York's Smith College in December 1944. Lieutenant Pickens graduated third in the class and went on to be an active public face for the WAVES—part of FDR's and the navy's effort to promote the unit's newfound inclusiveness.

The Tuskegee Airmen

If the navy and Teddy Roosevelt's Great White Fleet were the symbol of American military might at the century's outset, by World War II the newly expanded air force had become the nation's reason to strut. Even before the war started, aviation had already staked its place as the new frontier, the realm where one could prove his mettle and daring. In the post–World War I era, Hubert Julian wowed black Americans with his aeronautic feats. By the Second World War, Charles Anderson had taken over as the one to watch. In 1932, Anderson flew the first transcontinental flight piloted by an African American. At the end of the decade, he opened a flight school and commercial air service—where he later took Eleanor Roosevelt up in a two-seater plane. And when the military finally opened its pilot training program to blacks, he directed the flagship black program housed at the Tuskegee Institute in Alabama.

From its start, the Air Corps—as it was originally dubbed, in line with its role as a subdivision of the army tasked with defending ground troops—intended to remain as lily white as the Marine Corps had since the nineteenth century. But black civil rights leaders, bolstered by their usual ally in the First Lady, seemed more eagerly determined to integrate the revered air force than they were any other service branch. In the spring of 1939, in an effort to boost the number of pilots available to the air force, which was about to begin producing fifty thousand new planes a year, Congress created a program in which colleges and universities could use federal funds to establish flight training schools, from which the army would recruit in case of war. In a nod to the civil rights lobby, the law required the army to make arrangements with seven black schools—Delaware State, Hampton Institute, Howard University, North Carolina A&T, Tuskegee Institute, University of Missouri, and West Virginia State College—to qualify African Americans for private pilots licenses. Ever ready with a strategy to keep Jim Crow alive, the army declared that the law, which Congress required support civilian pilot training programs at these schools, did not require that their graduates be allowed to enlist in the air force.

The air force continued to refuse blacks until the 1940 Selective Service Act passed with its groundbreaking antibias clause intact, which forbade discrimination based on race or color in military enlistment and training. The air force responded in typical fashion, allowing blacks to enlist finally but assigning them exclusively to labor duties and denying them officer rank. It was only through a lawsuit, filed by Howard University student Yancey Williams, that the air force relented. In January 1941, with Williams filing suit against the War Department for violating the Selective Service Act's bias clause by refusing to consider his application to become a pilot, the army announced it would begin training black pilots and form a segregated black unit, the Ninety-ninth Pursuit Squadron. The single-seat planes used by pursuit squadrons were ideal, as they allowed the army to at least maintain segregation if not a color bar.

THE TUSKEGEE EXPERIMENT

The thirty-three pilots and four hundred support crewmen of the Ninety-ninth Pursuit Squadron trained at the Tuskegee Army Airfield. The first class of this controversial Tuskegee Experiment—consisting of thirteen cadets—arrived on August 25, 1941, and began an eight-month training program. Most prominent among these officer cadets—pilots automatically ranked as officers—was Benjamin O. Davis Jr., son of the man FDR had just made the nation's first black general. Davis transferred to Tuskegee from the Twenty-fourth Infantry Regiment, where he had been stationed after graduating from West Point in 1936. Having aced the aviation training at the academy, he had originally applied for a piloting assignment, but army doctors claimed he had failed the physical. When the air force finally opened, Davis signed up immediately. After the training program, Captain Davis became the commander of the Ninety-ninth, as he was the only commissioned black officer in the air force.

Colonel Benjamin Davis, Jr. rose to be the young, dashing leader of the Tuskegee Airmen.

Davis was promoted to colonel in mid-1942, advancing so quickly that he skipped over major rank and became the face of the Tuskegee airmen—who dubbed themselves the Lonely Eagles, playing on their isolation from the rest of the branch. As with many in his generation, Colonel Davis had wanted to be a pilot from an early age. And as a tall and dashing young man, at thirty-eight years old, he easily embodied the mythic image the nation had of its pilots. His lineage only further amplified his celebrity status, and

that notoriety would pay off in coming years as he led the ongoing campaign to deflect the army's constant effort to undermine its black pilots. But Davis was not the only celebrity at Tuskegee. Lieutenants Lemuel Custis, Charles DeBow, George Roberts, and Mac Ross were the first four to graduate, in March of 1942, and drew the most sustained attention from the press and the black community as a result.

The army slowly allowed the program to grow, and ultimately 992 African Americans trained at

White America derisively dubbed the Ninety-ninth Pursuit Squadron "Eleanor's niggers." The First Lady helped win the squad's combat deployment.

Tuskegee and became pilots in the U.S. Air Force. Several thousand more trained as support crew for the black squadrons these pilots formed. All pilots were college graduates, and the men were by and large brash, confident, and eager to prove themselves. They attacked their training exercises, and soon each added the individualized style and flare that pilots of that era were known for displaying. But they also endured the same indignities black soldiers stationed in the South and West had faced since the Civil War. And much like the Buffalo Soldiers, these twentieth-century frontiersmen did not swallow the insults from both white superiors and local townspeople easily.

Tuskegee saw a parade of white commanders, each with differing approaches to managing Jim

Almost one thousand blacks trained at Tuskegee and became pilots in the U.S. Air Force.

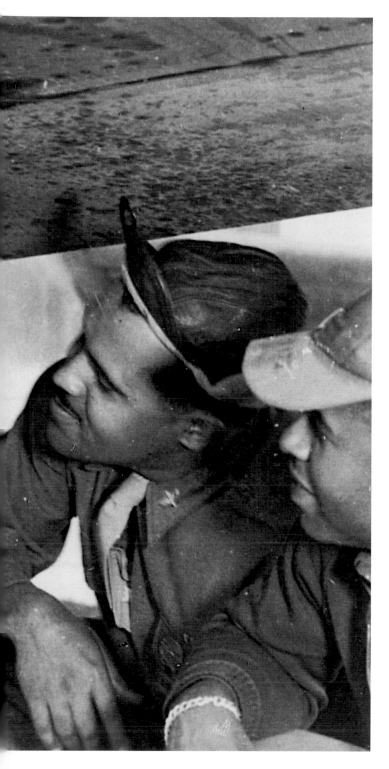

Crow on the base and in the town. At worst, "white only" and "black only" signs went up around the base, while black military police were forbidden from carrying arms; at best, one commander regularly surveyed his troops about the state of race relations on base and developed a close relationship with the airmen as a result. But by the spring of 1943, relations with the white townspeople had deteriorated significantly, and Tuskegee Institute President Frederick Patterson feared an incident such as those that occurred in Houston and Brownsville, Texas, between the Buffalo Soldiers and local law enforcement. Tense relations were compounded by the fact that the airmen had come to believe they would never see combat, that they had been created merely to comply with the letter of the law and score politi-

Crew chiefs helped guide pilots down runways because they could not see in the low-slung P-51 Mustang cockpits.

Captain Arthur McDaniels describes his plane's battle damage to the ground crew.

Trainee Clarence Jamison in his cockpit at Tuskegee.

cal points for FDR. They were, of course, absolutely correct. The issue prompted William Hastie to resign his prominent War Department appointment in protest. And Patterson petitioned Eleanor Roosevelt to yet again intervene and win the Ninety-ninth an overseas assignment.

IN COMBAT

The First Lady did in fact get involved, and on April 5, 1943, the Ninety-ninth Pursuit Squadron —now derisively dubbed "Eleanor's niggers" by white America—deployed to North Africa. They were first stationed in Fez, Morocco, and then moved to Haouaria, Tunisia, where they served

Charles "Buster" Hall was the first black airman to shoot down a German plane.

Davis Jr. and his father, here at a press conference in Washington, D.C., successfully blocked efforts to discredit and disband the Ninety-ninth.

under General Dwight Eisenhower, who led American forces in North Africa. Lieutenant Charles "Buster" Hall, from Indiana, scored the squadron's first kill in a July dogfight with attacking German planes during the campaign to take Sicily.

The men of the Ninety-ninth met a cool welcome in North Africa and received little acclimating help from their white colleagues. This, combined with the limitation of their training at Tuskegee (for instance, they could not fly lengthy training missions because no other air force base would allow them use of the all-white facilities), set the Ninety-ninth off to a bumpy start. White officers, anxious to speed the demise of Tuskegee's training program, sent news to

Washington, D.C., and the national press that the black pilots were not ready for combat and were reluctant to engage the enemy. It was just what the army brass wanted to hear, and discussion soon began about removing the Ninety-ninth from combat and scaling back plans to create a black bomber group. Colonel Davis returned from North Africa and, joined by his father, traveled to Washington, D.C., to ignite a countercampaign that is credited with saving the Tuskegee airmen from extinction. In fact, he not only beat back efforts to end the program but convinced Congress and the air force to expand it.

When the Ninety-ninth participated in a January 1944 invasion of Italy and accounted for the

The success of the Ninety-ninth led to the creation of an entire black fighting group.

most German kills of any unit involved, even the white press began to take notice, and efforts to roll back the air force's opening to black pilots were shelved once and for all. Flying as part of the Seventy-ninth Fighter Group now, the Ninety-ninth was making record numbers of sorties per week. During the two weeks of fighting at Anzio that began in January, the squadron racked up twenty-four confirmed "kills," two of which were at the hands of Lieutenant Hall, who won the Distinguished Flying Cross for his performance.

Having secured the Tuskegee airmen's continued existence and expansion, Colonel Davis returned to the training center in the fall of 1943 to oversee the

Several thousand blacks trained and served as grounds crewmen.

Wendell "Hot Rock" Pruitt, one of the 332nd's ace fliers, always left his lucky ring on the ground with his crew chief.

development of an entire black fighting group, the 332nd. In early 1943, black pilot training had been transferred from Tuskegee to Selfridge Field, Michigan. Leaving the South did nothing to improve the racial tension black pilot trainees dealt with. Segregation on base continued and arguably even heightened as the rabidly racist base commander aggressively enforced Jim Crow rules. Meanwhile, the city of Detroit, which Selfridge Field was located just outside of, faced such dire racial problems that a race riot erupted there in June 1943. As with their predecessors at Tuskegee, the cadets bucked the racism they met, and once again the War Department decided it was just as well that the group

be sent overseas. So in February 1944 the group deployed to Naples, Italy, where the Ninety-ninth Pursuit Squadron joined its ranks as well.

The four-squadron fighter group flew planes with bright red tail wings and thus developed another of its many nicknames, the Red Tails. Throughout the war, it flew bomber escorts—duty rejected by white pilots because it didn't offer as much opportunity to earn kills, and thus praise and promotion—and earned a reputation as the air force's most reliable escort. As both a unit and as individuals, the 332nd became famous within the air force, at home and around the world. Among its most celebrated members was Captain Wendell "Hot Rock" Pruitt, who always left his lucky ring on the ground with his crew chief. Captain Pruitt was probably best known because of his flying flare, such as his habit of performing stunts for the ground crew before he landed. But he also earned respect in combat. He won a Distinguished Flying Cross for exploding a German destroyer in June 1944, along with his similarly popular wingman Lieutenant Lee Archer. Colonel Davis tolerated Captain Pruitt's landing exploits, and perhaps should not have. Having survived the war, Hot Rock Pruitt died in a plane crash back in Tuskegee in April 1945 when he lost control of a victory roll.

All told, the Tuskegee Experiment was an undeniable success and, much like the experiences of the navy and marines in opening the door for blacks during World War II, it set the branch on an irreversible trajectory toward integration. It was simply impossible to continue arguing that African Americans could not fly planes, even in combat. The 332nd flew over 1,500 missions during the war, destroying 261 enemy planes and earning ninety-five Distinguished Flying Crosses.

Approximately 150 members of the unit were killed in combat or during training before the war's end.

Meanwhile, Colonel Davis's career was just beginning. He would go on to become a four-star general in the air force and one of the branch's most acclaimed leaders.

Retrenchment in the Army

During the political tug-of-war between FDR and black leaders at the war's outset, one of the most contentious issues was the treatment blacks received from the draft board. Southern registrars did everything they could to skirt the steady stream of new laws ordering them to enlist blacks—from flunking them in physical exams to simply putting their names at the end of eligibility lists. African Americans were further hindered by the failures of America's farcical "separate but equal" education system. As a result of the substandard education they had received, many

Davis Jr. became an even greater celebrity than his father for his role in leading the Tuskegee Airmen.

African Americans could not pass the military's entry exam on first try, providing prejudiced whites with supposed proof of their inadequacy for the armed forces. But as the war effort ballooned and manpower became a concern, the War Department created special training programs to aid both black and white draftees who failed the exam. Given the educational opportunity they had traditionally been denied, blacks now outperformed whites, graduating from the special program at slightly higher rates than their white classmates.

When African Americans did successfully sign up, they were overwhelmingly assigned to labor positions—nearly eighty-five percent of black draftees served in labor and support battalions during the war. Nevertheless, of the 2.5 million blacks eligible for the draft, half of them were ultimately enlisted. The vast majority of these draftees, fully three quarters, served in the army. There they found a branch that, unlike its navy and air force counterparts, was actively backpedaling on racial equality. The backward slide from the days of integrated combat in the Spanish-American War had begun in World War I and continued into the 1940s. Segregation was a firm reality in the army, as Brigadier General Davis Sr. noted in a 1943 report. "Officers of the War Department General Staff have refused to attempt any remedial action to eliminate Jim Crow," he wrote. "In fact, the Army, by its directions and by actions of commanding officers, has introduced Jim Crow practices in areas, both at home and abroad, where they have not hitherto been practiced."

The state of affairs was perhaps best illustrated by the hoopla that ensued surrounding the December 1944 Battle of the Bulge. White companies had suffered massive casualties fighting off the German offensive at Ardennes, and manpower was quickly becoming an issue. A white army official suggested detailing black labor battalion troops into white combat units in order to fill out the ranks. The army had been at such a crossroads before, most recently at San Juan Hill when the Buffalo Soldiers and Teddy Roosevelt's Rough Riders fought side by side in the chaos of unplanned but nonetheless integrated combat units. Brigadier General Davis Sr. drafted a notice inviting black privates with sufficient training to volunteer for the detail. He announced triumphantly that the volunteers would be assigned "without regard to color or race to the units where assistance is most needed." White politicians and army officials in Washington were incensed. Echoing the protestations of Confederate Army planners who objected to allowing the South's slaves to fight in the final days of the Civil War, opponents' main argument against the plan was that it would give the lie to Jim Crow's intellectual underpinning: the notion that segregation was necessary to maintain a well-ordered society. General Eisenhower, now the commander of the American Expeditionary Forces, intervened. He recrafted Brigadier General Davis Sr.'s announcement to state that the black volunteers were to be placed in all-black platoons. Led by white officers, thirty-seven black platoons were attached to white companies in the First and Seventh Armies. Following the war, the black volunteers were returned to labor platoons, despite General Eisenhower's promise that they would all remain in combat units.

"COMBAT" UNITS

When the war began, the army reactivated the World War I–era all-black Ninety-second and Ninety-third Divisions, this time also folding the still active Twenty-fourth and Twenty-fifth Infantry Regiments

Three quarters of black draftees served in the army, which today still contains more black troops than any other branch.

into the Ninety-third. The War Department also created the Second Cavalry Division, into which it put the old Ninth and Tenth Cavalries. These early moves gave black civil rights leaders and army troops hope that things might actually be different in the Second World War. That flicker of hope was soon snuffed out, as the three black divisions trained and trained while watching a procession of white divisions head off to Europe and the Pacific. It was soon clear that the War Department planned to keep these black combat units on the same out-of-the-way shelf it had kept them on during the first war. The usual lobbying began, and once again it was electoral politics that got things moving. Not until 1944, a campaign year, did FDR begin pushing his War Department to deploy the black divisions.

Once deployed, the regiments of the three black divisions rarely fought as a unit. The only regiment of the Ninety-third Division to see any real combat was the Twenty-fourth Infantry Regiment. The members of the Twenty-fourth joined the black marines at Saipan in the war's final months, where they earned a unit commendation for their efforts. The other regiments of the Ninety-third Division, which was sent to the Pacific theater in early 1944, served on islands the Allies had already secured and thus saw no fighting. Instead, while ostensibly serving as security for the held areas, the division primarily filled labor roles on the islands. The ensuing black political protest of the de facto labor status of a supposed combat division is what ultimately prompted the Twenty-fourth's limited use in battle.

Meanwhile, the Second Cavalry was sent to the Mediterranean, also in early 1944. But by May, the army had decided to disband the entire division, claiming that cavalry troops were not useful in the campaign. Rather than reassigning the men to combat divisions, however, the cavalrymen were sent to

The War Department reactivated the Ninety-second and Ninety-third Divisions, but only a handful of their regiments were allowed to fight.

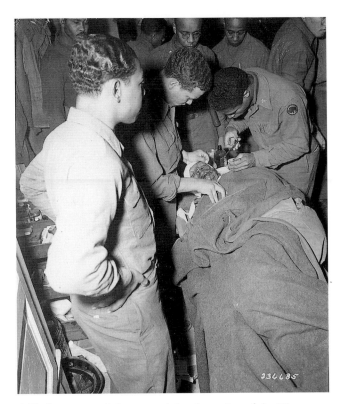

A black surgeon stitches up an injured member of the Ninety-second Division.

The overwhelming majority of black army draftees, eighty percent, were not assigned to these three divisions, but rather to noncombat labor and support units. But they also served in engineering companies and other specialty units. African Americans accounted for three quarters of the famous Red Ball Express, the transportation outfit that ferried supplies around France to the constantly moving Allied troops. The 555th Parachute Infantry Battalion—known as the Triple Nickels—was the first group of black paratroopers, created in 1942 and staffed with black officers. The Triple Nickels never deployed overseas but spent the spring of 1945 secretly battling forest fires that had been ignited in the Pacific Northwest by Japanese firebombs that floated across the Pacific in balloons.

THE 761ST TANK BATTALION

White military planners had always held that blacks were incapable of operating the sophisticated weaponry of modern warfare, and thus had kept artillery and armored battalions particularly off limits to black recruits. When he promoted Brigadier General Davis Sr., FDR had privately assured the civil rights community that this position would change. It did indeed, and the War Department created several smaller-sized all-black specialty units, such as the Triple Nickels. The black unit that saw the most combat during the war was one of these: the still often overlooked 761st Tank Battalion, which served heroically in General George S. Patton Jr.'s Third Army.

In October 1944, General Patton's armored battalions faced the same manpower shortages that would occur two months later at the Battle of the

labor battalions. It was an inglorious end for the famed Ninth and Tenth Cavalry Buffalo Soldiers.

For its part, the Ninety-second Division suffered the same fate it had met during World War I. Deployed to Italy in July 1944, the division saw more combat than the other black divisions. But white officers eager to proclaim it a failure successfully created the impression that the Ninety-second's soldiers were hapless and afraid to fight. From Major General Edward Almond on down, the division's white leaders were southerners with at best spotty records working with black troops. And when the division didn't perform well in its first engagement with the enemy, they immediately declared that their charges had no future as soldiers.

The Triple Nickels, the first black paratroopers, covertly fought forest fires in the Pacific Northwest started by Japanese fire bombs.

The 761st tankers are the forgotten heroes of General Patton's Third Army.

Bulge. At that time, he would refuse to allow integrated combat units in his army. But now, pinned down in France, General Patton needed help. The War Department had created three black armored units, none of which it had deployed. These units were of the same "experimental" nature as the navy's Golden Thirteen and the air force's Tuskegee airmen. One of them was the 761st, which General Patton judged to be the best of the bunch. He requested they join his army in Normandy.

Six days after their arrival, the tankers of the 761st led the Twenty-sixth Division in its D day offensive at the Saar Basin. As the massive Sherman tanks rolled in, the Germans responded furiously, taking control of the early battle and inflicting major casualties on the division's first wave. It was during this period that the 761st lost its first soldier, Private Clifford Adams. But General Patton's army ultimately closed in on the Germans at Metz over the next month of fighting, with the 761st helping to seal off the town. As General Patton pushed forward, the white infantrymen who had helped storm Metz circulated to the rear for rest. The 761st had to stay at the front.

It was Christmas Eve when General Patton received orders to turn around and come to the aid of the First and Seventh Armies besieged at the Battle of the Bulge. They stormed through the snow and arrived in time to finish pushing the German offensive back. Joined by the Eighty-seventh Division, the 761st drove the enemy sixty miles back into Germany in five days of fighting. It was the beginning of the end for Germany, and over the next several months General Patton's army, often led by the 761st, charged into Germany, liberating territory and taking enemy captives by the thousands. At one point, the 761st alone was taking almost three thousand prisoners a day. Its tanks led the army across the Danube on April 27, 1945, and a few weeks later into Austria to rendezvous with the Ukrainian forces—the first meeting between East and West Allied armies. They had driven farther into enemy territory and remained at the front longer than any other armored battalion, and white officers recommended that the battalion receive the same Distinguished Unit Citation awarded to several white units with which the 761st fought. General Eisenhower, however, refused to sign the citation. The 761st thus went unrecognized until 1978, when President Jimmy Carter finally granted the unit its commendation.

THE SIX TRIPLE EIGHT

The army did outpace the other service branches in one aspect of openness during World War II—creating service opportunities for women in general, and black women in particular. In May 1942, FDR authorized the creation of the Women's Army Corps, known as the WAC. (In its first year it was known as the Women's Army Auxiliary Corps, or WAAC, reflecting the belief that women should not be considered fully part of the army.) Keeping with the War

Black tank battalions proved African Americans could operate modern weapons.

Nearly 4,000 black women served in the Women's Army Corps.

Major Charity Adams
reviews the Six Triple Eight
WAC battalion.

Department's overall plan for bringing more African Americans into the armed forces, ten percent of the WAC recruits were to be black. As with the army overall—and every other branch, for that matter— the WAC never approached this goal. No more than six percent of the Corps' members were African American. Nevertheless, almost four thousand black female officers and enlisted personnel served in the WAC during World War II.

The army, however, was no more eager to send its black female recruits overseas than was the navy. And the black WAVES were actually deployed before the WAC. By and large, black WACs found themselves doing the same menial jobs as the black infantrymen they were filling in for on stateside duties—cooking, cleaning, and waiting on whites. Ultimately, only one battalion of African American WACs shipped out to Europe, and then only late in the war and following the usual domestic black protests against the failure to deploy black troops.

But that group, the 6888th Central Postal Directory Battalion, known affectionately as the Six Triple Eight, drew far more attention than the WAVES had, or than most other battalions had, for that matter. This attention was in part due to its uniquely visible duty as coordinators of V-Mail between soldiers and their families and friends back home. But it was also due to the celebrity of the battalion's striking and brash young leader, Major Charity Adams.

Major Adams was among the first African Americans to graduate from the WAC officer training program at Fort Des Moines, Iowa, where she joined the first WAC class in June 1942. In her later autobiography, Major Adams reported that the problems she faced at Iowa had more to do with her gender than her race, as the male staff tasked with training them resented the assignment of working with women. That August, the WAC commissioned forty black officers among its 440 graduates. The WAC would commission 120 black officers during the course of the war.

After graduation, the black WACs were grouped into two companies, one of which was tasked with leading basic training for subsequent black recruits. Major Adams was placed in command of that company, where she, like other WAC officers, was forced to serve underneath male regimental superiors. The tenacious young woman would become known for regularly standing up to these white male overseers when they attempted to regulate her Six Triple Eight. In one famous incident, a general chastised her during a troop review and said he would send a white second lieutenant to teach her how things should be done. Her response was, "Over my dead body."

When the general threatened court-martial, Major Adams threatened one right back, citing War Department directives warning commanders to avoid emphasizing racial differences. The general—more impressed with her will than the nonexistent possibility that the directive would be enforced—backed down.

African American women were also able to serve in the Army Nurse Corps, but far fewer than were qualified and willing to do so. As with everything else, the Nurse Corps only opened its doors to black recruits after significant public and political pressure to do so. It responded by enlisting a typically token

The army reluctantly opened its nurse corps to black women only after political protests.

Only 479 of the quarter million registered black nurses in the country were allowed into the army.

number of black women, less than a percentage point of the total force. Of the approximately quarter of a million registered black female nurses in the United States during World War II, only 479 of them made it into the Army Nurse Corps.

The Beginning of the End

Ultimately, black soldiers in the Second World War faced many of the same problems they confronted during World War I. But there was a qualitative difference. The civil rights movement, powered in

Crew members of the USS *Ticonderoga* celebrate Japan's surrender. By war's end, almost a million African Americans were enlisted in the armed forces.

part by the energy and anger of World War I vets, had grown in strength and political influence. The concessions the armed forces' leadership made would not be as easily reversed at the war's end as they had three decades earlier.

Moreover, black representation in the armed forces had exploded in both number and breadth. At the end of the 1930s, just over four thousand African Americans served in the military. By the war's end, at least nine hundred thousand blacks were enlisted in the armed forces, including four thousand women, serving in all branches and specialties. The military had five black officers, commissioned or otherwise, at the beginning of the conflict. By war's end, there were 7,768 black officers. While this was a paltry percentage of the overall enlisted personnel and officer corps, it nevertheless reflected a sharp

With the Cold War coming, the military wouldn't have time to muster blacks back out of service as they had after previous wars.

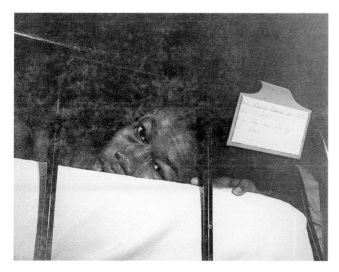

Navy man Charlie Dunston was among thousands of blacks who were injured or killed in the war effort.

growth. And as the war closed, America was about to enter a different kind of peace than it had seen before. While fighting would end, the Cold War would begin. The military, in need of just as large and flexible a force as it had mobilized during the war, would not be able to simply muster talented and ambitious African Americans back out of its ranks.

CHAPTER

7

"THE HIGHEST
STANDARDS OF
DEMOCRACY"

*Korea and the
Cold War*

With World War II coming to an end, many African American soldiers had become fed up with the fact that they were still corralled into segregated units, toiling in menial jobs below their training and living in substandard conditions. They were often housed in run-down barracks, given secondhand equipment, and even forced to sleep on wooden crates while white soldiers bunked in standard metal and mattress cots.

Throughout the military, African Americans were now voicing their displeasure with this state of affairs, often leading to violent clashes and even full-scale race riots. But it comes as no surprise that the most dramatic protest, and the one that drew the most public attention, was staged by the hotshot black recruits of the army air force.

When Colonel Benjamin Davis Jr. beat back attempts to remove his 332nd Fighter Group from

Truman Gibson, the War Department's advisor on racial issues (second from left), tried to defuse conflict between black air force trainees and their white commanders.

combat, he also secured the expansion of the Tuskegee Experiment with training black pilots. That expansion came in the form of the 477th Bombardment Group, which trained at Selfridge Field just outside of Detroit, Michigan. The tension between the 477th's black trainees and white officers began there, when the white base commander Colonel William Boyd held an iron fist around Jim Crow policies. Not content to simply enforce the existing segregation, Colonel Boyd worked to remind his black trainees of their second-class status at every turn. In a particularly egregious example, Colonel Boyd ordered all white members of the Women's Army Corps training at Selfridge to travel with armed guards while on base, ostensibly to prevent the black men from attacking them. Colonel Boyd also insisted on maintaining segregated officers' clubs, in direct violation of a 1940 War Department directive that integrated entertainment and recreational facilities. It was this issue that pushed the 477th's members to the brink.

Truman Gibson had replaced William Hastie as the War Department's adviser on African American affairs. When he got word of the segregated officers' clubs at Selfridge Field, he intervened. He secured Colonel Boyd's transfer from command, and the 477th subsequently relocated to Freeman Field in Indiana. But the army air force's reservations about its new black troops went far higher up the chain of command than Colonel Boyd. His superiors had encouraged his actions, and they did the same for his replacement at Freeman Field. There, Colonel Robert Selway Jr. came up with a way around Gibson's meddling. The officers' quarters would still be segregated, but the divide would be between trainees on one hand and the facility's trainers and permanent base staff on the other. Since all of the

477th's members were black, and all of the trainers were white, this allowed Colonel Selway to keep Jim Crow intact without using the language that would get him in trouble. The army's white leaders found the plan so ingenious that they set about putting it in place throughout the air force.

But the men of the 477th decided to force the air force's hand. They consulted with NAACP lawyers to figure out a way to protest without violating military code. They'd seen the fate of black protesters before, who were usually court-martialed for mutiny, and were smart enough to realize success would mean using the current system of discipline against itself. So on April 5, 1945, four black officers approached the "trainers only" club and were met by military police who barred their entry. They returned with nineteen more officers, who all stayed until the MPs arrested them. By the night's end, 101 black 477th members had been jailed and drawn for court-martial. Again Gibson intervened, this time along with Assistant Secretary of War John McCloy, who led the War Department's advisory council on racial issues. The protesters' preparation paid off. McCloy and Gibson found the Freeman Field policy to be obviously intended as a form of racial segregation and thus in violation of the 1940 directive. On April 26, the department ordered the air force to release the "Freeman 101" and drop the court-martial proceedings for all but three of them, who had actually tried to force their way into the club. Ironically, those three men turned out to be permanent maintenance staff at the base, and thus, according to Colonel Selway's policy, qualified to enter the club. Two of them won acquittals, and the third was charged a $150 fine for shoving the base provost marshal.

The incident was yet another that gripped the attention of the black community, and again the civil rights leadership dutifully exploited it to gain more ground for African American soldiers. Colonel Selway and his staff were removed from Freeman Field and replaced by an all-black staff led by Colonel Davis. It was the first time a black officer had commanded an entire army base. Colonel Davis quickly began trying to prepare the 477th to enter the final stages of the war in the Pacific, but Japan surrendered before the group could deploy.

The saga reveals the sea change that occurred in America's armed forces between the beginning and end of the war. White segregationists were now on the retreat, grasping for new ways to maintain a color bar in all fields and scrambling to defend those tactics when they were challenged. Civil rights leaders and their supporters within the military were meanwhile building steam, and hoped to finally break through and integrate the military during its postwar realignment. But they would find that the racists were not yet out of maneuvers. Politics and protest could only move things so far. Ultimately, it would take an unexpected military crisis in a remote corner of Asia to kill Jim Crow.

Peacetime Reorganization

Among Assistant Secretary McCloy's first acts as chair of the War Department's race advisory board was to order a study of black troops' performance during the war. He asked white army officers, now spread out around Europe, North Africa, and the Pacific, to evaluate the African American soldiers in their charge and make recommendations for their future role. Not surprisingly, the response was largely negative: Blacks were judged too scared to fight and too ignorant to succeed at specialty jobs involv-

ing supposedly complicated machinery.

Armed with these survey results, the army, in which more blacks served than in any other military branch, set up a board to craft future policy on black troops. Led by General Alvan Gillem Jr., the board produced its Utilization of Negro Manpower in the Postwar Army Policy in April 1946. It amounted to much ado about nothing. FDR and a handful of integrationist military leaders had nudged the armed forces forward during the war, but that progress had been made in stutter steps and through seemingly untenable compromises. As a result, the military was stuck in transition, having opened its ranks to massive numbers of well-trained and ambitious black service members, but refusing to allow them to become full participants. The Gillem report essentially called for maintaining this awkward status quo. It reaffirmed the (still unrealized) goal of fixing black enlistment at ten percent, and it judged the experiment with mixed companies at the Battle of the Bulge a success. Henceforth, there would be no more all-black divisions and regiments, but smaller black platoons that would serve within larger white units. This brand of "integration," however, was not to extend to off-duty life. The policy stated that blacks would continue eating and living in segregated facilities.

The Gillem report of course drew intense reaction from the black community. That reaction, however, was certainly not uniform. Some felt it was actual progress, and proof that the new administration of President Harry S. Truman was going to keep the integration ball rolling. Others, such as the NAACP's *Crisis* editor Roy Wilkins, felt the new policy represented not only a cop-out but a step backward. Command opportunities, for instance, would surely shrink for black officers in this system, as the idea of blacks giving orders to white enlisted troops

Black troops stationed
in Europe slowly gained
educational and training
opportunities open to
whites in post-war years.

Most opportunities, such
as training to be military
policemen in Europe,
were slow in coming.

was still unthinkable. Moreover, a few months after the Gillem report's release, a group of black publishers toured European military installations and found that its impact had been nil. There were no new black platoons integrated into white companies, and senior white officers expressed no plans to create them. In fact, Europe-based officers actively fought having black soldiers assigned to their command.

While the army was fussing over minute differences in its policy, the navy continued its relatively rapid expansion of opportunities for black sailors. Secretary James Forrestal's embrace of integration was perhaps more intense than any of the nation's leaders, military or political. He had delayed full

Defense Secretary Forrestal had the will but lacked the temperament to force integration on the branches.

integration in recognition of the complications it may have presented to the war effort. But with the country back at peace, he turned up the heat. He ordered his own study of race relations in the forces and dispatched his newly appointed adviser on race issues, the National Urban League's Lester Granger, to survey both black and white sailors about the state of affairs. Granger reported back that wherever a unit faced low morale or failed to meet its potential, segregation was the primary agent of trouble. So in February 1946, Forrestal took the initiative the War Department still would not. "Effective immediately," he declared, "all restrictions governing the types of assignments for which Negro naval personnel are eligible are hereby lifted." All facilities, from battleships to bunks to mess halls, were to be fully integrated. Actual change, of course, would come slow, as white officers only reluctantly carried out the order. Moreover, the new policy maintained the ten-percent cap on black enlistment. As a result, there developed a conspicuous gap between the branch's trailblazing policies and the entrenched realities of segregation in America.

Meanwhile, the Marine Corps made no pretense of its feeling that the navy's rush to integrate the postwar force was too hasty. Despite the fact that the marines were formally under the control of Forrestal's navy, the Corps maintained an independent policy-making arm. Led by Brigadier General Gerald Thomas, the agency minced few words in its May 1946 recommendation on what to do with black corpsmen.

Brigadier General Thomas clearly resented the way FDR and civil rights leaders had conspired to force the military onto the front lines of America's race war. "The Negro question is a national issue which grows more controversial yet is more evaded as time goes by," he complained. "During the past war,

Black army recruits sign up for integrated training at Fort Jackson, South Carolina.

the services were forced to bear the responsibilities of the problem." Brigadier General Thomas went on to acknowledge the real need to fully integrate the armed forces and to remove enlistment ceilings for African Americans. But he argued that the military should not be silly enough to attempt to do what the rest of the nation still could not. And he concluded that the Marine Corps should thus avoid "radical" system created during the war, in which it allowed limited black enlistment in small segregated units largely assigned to support and labor duties. "It certainly appears that until the matter is settled on a higher level," Brigadier General Thomas wrote, "the services are not required to go further than that which is already custom." His recommendation became policy the following September, and it foreshadowed the coming conventional wisdom on personnel debates. As the century wore on and women and sexual minorities began to advocate for the right to serve, most opponents within the armed forces would parrot Brigadier General Thomas's logic.

Cautionary words such as those offered by Brigadier General Thomas were strengthened by rapid changes under way in the peacetime military, having nothing to do with race. In 1947, the armed forces underwent a complete reorganization as a new Department of Defense replaced the War Department. The air force peeled away from the army and formed an independent third branch. And Forrestal advanced to the new secretary of defense position. The tumult left little time for enforcing new policies created by the army's Gillem report or the navy's 1946 integration order.

African American enlistment still had not even risen to the mandated ten percent in any branch. In the air force, all black pilots were consolidated into Colonel Benjamin Davis Jr.'s 332nd Fighter Group, and all black airmen represented only six percent of the branch's active duty personnel. Despite the navy's "radical" new policies, black representation among active sailors dropped to less than five percent, and sixty percent of those were still serving in the stewards' branch. The Marine Corps was worse still, with black corpsmen representing less than three percent of its personnel. The army, which remained the primary service branch for African Americans, had made the most progress. But integration of the segregated smaller black units into larger white ones moved slowly, and not at all in Europe. Where African American units had joined white bases, they still largely served as laborers and ultimately represented less than nine percent of active duty soldiers.

EXECUTIVE ORDER 9981

The civil rights movement, of course, did not sit idly as the new military policies buckled under the weight of racism's and Jim Crow's realities. Black politicos and the black press had learned much from dealing with FDR—most importantly that if you demand nothing you'll get just that. The northern black vote was now relevant to both the Democratic and Republican Parties, and civil rights leaders were determined to get the best deal possible for their endorsements. A. Philip Randolph once again took the most aggressive action, creating the League for Non-Violent Civil Disobedience Against Military Segregation.

After consulting with other major civil rights groups, Randolph's league began urging African Americans to refuse to register with Selective Service and vowed to aid them in resisting any subsequent draft as long as military segregation persisted. Other black leaders joined Randolph's cause, and President Truman decided to become proactive. He wanted to expand FDR's Fair Employment Practices Commission, created to monitor defense industry compliance with the 1941 antibias executive order, but he was rebuffed by Congress. Instead, he commissioned another study board, this time tasked with coming up with recommendations for solving the full range of America's race problems.

Truman's Committee on Civil Rights, led by General Electric President Charles Wilson and composed of prominent black and white civilians, was to look at everything from housing to military service. Its May 1947 report, entitled *To Secure These Rights*, was a groundbreaking document that went further than any government study or recommendation had previously even conceived. It echoed the NAACP's ongoing demands for a federal antilynching law, it declared the need for a permanent civil rights division of the Justice Department, and even called for statehood for the heavily African American District of Columbia—a contentious issue into which most politicians are unwilling to be dragged even today. On the military issue, the report called for an unequivocal end to segregation and any kind of policy making based on race. Its language provided what may be history's most cogent damnation of the American military's previous 170 years of bigotry:

> **Underlying the theory of compulsory wartime military service in a democratic state is the principle that every citizen, regardless of his station in life, must assist in the defense of the nation when its security is threatened. Despite the discrimination which they encounter in so many fields, minority group members have time and again met this responsibility. Moreover, since equality in military service assumes great importance as a symbol of democratic goals, minorities have regarded it as not only a duty but as a right.**

> **Yet the record shows that the members of several minorities, fighting and dying for the survival of the nation in which they met bitter prejudice, found that there was discrimination against them even as they fell in battle. Prejudice in any area is an ugly, undemocratic phenomenon; in the armed services, where all men run the risk of death, it is particularly repugnant.**

The President's Committee on Civil Rights and its report were part of what was becoming a real commitment on the part of President Truman to improve the lives of African Americans. He was the first president to address a meeting of the NAACP in person, and in February 1948 sent Congress its first Civil Rights Message, in which he formally proposed many of the recommendations detailed in *To Secure These Rights*. His personal perspective on race was complicated, though similar to many white liberals at the time. Perhaps inevitably, given his Jim Crow–Missouri background, Truman's worldview bought into the logic of white supremacy. But he was also profoundly disturbed by the fervent antiblack violence perpetrated by white Americans of his generation. He watched with horror as the Ku Klux Klan swaggered through not only the South but the north as well, lynching black families in its effort to protect an ultimately cumbersome and inefficient system of racial segregation.

Historians believe Truman was particularly shocked by the 1946 beating of World War II veteran Sergeant Isaac Woodard, who had served in the Pacific for three years. En route from Fort Gordon, Georgia, to his home in North Carolina, and still wearing his army uniform, Sergeant Woodard was accosted by the driver of his bus. The bus driver believed he took too long using the bathroom at a rest stop and began to berate him. At the next town, in South Carolina, the driver called a local sheriff to arrest Sergeant Woodard, randomly charging him with drunkenness. In the process of taking the soldier into custody, the local sheriff beat him mercilessly, slamming his baton into Sergeant Woodard's eyes. After spending the night in jail with no medical care, the young man made his way to a nearby army hospital and discovered that he had been permanently blinded. The NAACP seized upon the incident to draw attention to both the treatment black soldiers received in the military and the ongoing lynching epidemic that all blacks faced. Much of white America, including the president, was shocked by the news of Sergeant Woodard's attack. But there was no reason to be; sadly, the attack was relatively minor. That summer, a group of white men in Monroe, Georgia, dragged two black veterans and their wives from their car and shot them sixty times. The couples had dared to vote in the state's primary elections.

But President Truman's aggressive pro–civil rights stance was also born from political wisdom. As the 1948 presidential elections neared, Truman and the Democratic Party were in trouble. He'd ascended to the office after FDR's 1945 death, and many fellow Democrats didn't believe he could beat the GOP's popular candidate, New York Governor Thomas Dewey. The party had fallen into competing factions. Henry Wallace had formed his Progressive Party, taking large numbers of the most liberal Democrats with him. Meanwhile, then South Carolina Governor Strom Thurmond took the party's conservative southerners, angry over a pro–civil rights platform adopted during the Democratic convention, and formed the States Rights Democratic Party. Dubbed the Dixiecrats, Governor Thurmond's faction stood on a platform committed to keeping America's races in their assigned castes.

With Dewey and the GOP actively courting the black vote—their platform explicitly called for integrating the armed forces—Truman knew he'd have to choose sides and either support or fight civil rights. He chose support and heeded adviser Clark Clifford's urging that he take some dramatic action to demonstrate that decision. Most of the civil rights policies proposed in the party platform required congressional action. But the president could affect military policy by fiat. As defense secretary, Forrestal had backed

off his aggressive push for segregation, occupying himself instead with managing tensions among three newly competing branches of the military. As a result, the postwar promise of military reform had rapidly deteriorated into another disappointment for black soldiers. So on July 28, 1948, President Truman signed Executive Order 9981, permanently ending racial segregation in the United States Armed Forces. It was the most significant development in America's battle over race since Reconstruction's Civil Rights Amendments, and it would forever change American politics by solidifying the Democratic Party's association with the Civil Rights Movement. "Whereas it is essential that there be maintained in the armed forces of the United States the highest standards of democracy," the order began,

> **with equality of treatment and opportunity for all those who serve in our country's defense: . . . It is hereby declared to be the policy of the President that there shall be equality of treatment and opportunity for all persons without regard to race, color, religion or national origin. This policy shall be put into effect as rapidly as possible, having due regard to the time required to effectuate any necessary changes without impairing efficiency or morale.**

Asked by reporters if this meant an end to segregation, Truman declared simply and emphatically, "Yes."

His bold move paid off. Leaning on two populations that would make up the Democrats' core constituency for decades to come—labor unions and African Americans—he narrowly upset Dewey to win a second term.

THE BATTLE
OVER IMPLEMENTATION

President Truman's executive order also created a monitoring committee to oversee the order's implementation. The President's Committee on Equality of Treatment and Opportunity in the Armed Services—known as the Fahy Committee, after its chair, Charles Fahy—was endowed with actual power. All departments and agencies of the federal government were directed to cooperate with the committee, and its seven members—all appointed by, and thus beholden to, Truman—could call anyone in the armed forces to testify and demand "such documents and other information as the Committee may require."

The committee would need all of that power, and the active backing of the president, to accomplish its mission. All three branches of the military had been consulted about the executive order in advance of its release, and all promised to dutifully implement the changes it mandated. But the ink had barely dried before they began to backtrack. The same debates that had raged within each branch on if and how to create more opportunities for African Americans kept going.

The navy and the air force were already further along in this conversation and thus took less prodding from the Fahy Committee. The navy had Forrestal's order from two years previous. And the air force, motivated by headaches such as the 1945 protest at Freeman Field, had quietly prepared a plan for implementation in the event of desegregation, which the committee approved. But historic inequities and less than enthusiastic efforts by white officers to promote blacks kept the number of African American recruits for both branches dis-

turbingly low and thus slowed the process of moving them into more specialized positions. Nevertheless, the top ranks of both branches accepted the Fahy Committee's recommendations on how to improve the situation and, in design at least, set about the long process of attempting to right past wrongs.

The Fahy Committee's real fights were with the army and the Marine Corps. Corps Commandant General Clifton Gates echoed Brigadier General Thomas's earlier argument that the military could not successfully accomplish what the rest of the nation still feared attempting. The army brass, with General Dwight Eisenhower among its leading voices, defended its Gillem Board policies as the most appropriate way to deal with race for now, and they vowed to stay the course regardless of the president's supposed order. Meanwhile, Army Chief of Staff General Omar Bradley announced the widespread apprehension among white officers about enlisting massive numbers of poorly educated blacks, circularly arguing for continued segregation by asserting that the "separate but equal" civilian school system couldn't adequately prepare African Americans for military service beyond manual labor.

The State National Guards were similarly recalcitrant. Technically under the control of state governments, the reserves had dealt with the changes in racial policy in recent years in different ways. By and large, southern states maintained either harshly segregated or all-white militias. But several northern states had begun demanding that the army allow them to integrate. As early as February 1947, Connecticut Governor James McConnaughy and the army's racial policy advisor Marcus Ray began making the states' rights argument against a War Department policy that denied federal recognition to reserve units that integrated the races at the platoon level, in accord with the Gillem Board policy for the regular army. The army board charged with watching over National Guard policies rejected Ray and Governor McConnaughy's logic, and essentially ruled that this apparent federal intrusion into a state decision was appropriate. But in order to stave off pressure from northern states where integration was moving apace, the army began issuing exemptions from the Gillem Board policy to the most vocal states. It would continue to handle the question of racial policy in the reserves in this manner until the 1960s.

As the battle between the Fahy Committee and the service branches geared up, Secretary Forrestal set about ensuring that the Defense Department was not ceding policy-making ground to Truman's advisory board. He tried to hammer out a service-wide policy to put forward once the committee made its recommendations. But Forrestal handicapped his effort with his insistence on allowing the branches—which he was actively working to balance vis-à-vis one another in the new national security structure—to maintain veto powers over aspects of the new policy. His ailing health also weakened his hand, and in early March 1949 he retired. Ironically, while Forrestal's replacement Louis Johnson did not share the outgoing secretary's long commitment to integration, he proved far more effective in creating a service-wide integration policy. While Forrestal saw his role in managing the three branches as traffic cop and mediator, Secretary Johnson understood himself to be the boss. Moreover, he understood that his cachet within the Truman administration would go up in direct proportion to how much he helped promote one of the president's signature initiatives. The Fahy Committee, meanwhile, backed by a president who had made a clear decision about which side of the civil rights debate he stood on, similarly considered

itself to be more than a public relations board. It was an implementation committee, and its members intended to see EO 9981 carried out. The stage was set for a showdown.

War Finishes What Politics Started

After wrangling with the three branches for several months, Secretary Johnson and the Fahy Committee had set May 1, 1949, as the deadline by which each would have to report their plans for implementing the president's executive order. By the end of May, the navy reached agreement with the committee on ways to boost black recruitment—for example, by integrating the stewards' branch and bringing black reserve officers onto active duty to help with recruitment—and it was time for the marines to fall in line. Corps Commandant General Gates relented and announced that for the first time in its history, all marine assignments would be open to everyone regardless of race. The historic Montford Point training center for blacks was closed, and integration, in name, was on its way.

The army, however, still clung to its Gillem Board policies, now arguing that these plans were in fact already in compliance with Truman's order. The tug-of-war between the Fahy Committee and the army continued throughout the year and into 1950. When Secretary Johnson appeared ready to cave, Fahy pulled the president himself into the fight. The army insisted the Gillem Board's approach was the best answer because enlistment caps and small segregated units prevented unqualified blacks from turning the entire infantry into the mess that the Ninety-second Division supposedly was during the World Wars. Until the army could be assured its black recruits were up to snuff, they needed to be quarantined so that they wouldn't pull white regiments down to their level.

Finally, Fahy, Truman, and Secretary of the Army Gordan Gray developed a compromise. In March 1950, the army agreed to abandon its racial quota and to assign troops to duties without consideration of race. In turn, it would also significantly raise the bar on its qualification exam, weeding out unqualified recruits of any race. Secretary Gray warned the president that he considered the plan a trial. Neither man knew that all bets were about to be called off, as they would soon once again need massive numbers of new recruits, particularly for the army and marines.

NORTH KOREA INVADES

While Truman's Democratic Party turned inward to deal with the nation's burgeoning civil rights debate following World War II, many in the Republican Party—particularly in Congress, which the GOP controlled—turned their attention to Winston Churchill's Iron Curtain of Communism. These folks were convinced of a Soviet Union–led effort to re-create the problems caused by Nazi Germany's imperialist zeal. And they chafed as Secretary Johnson became the administration's poster boy for cutting military spending and trimming down the force. So when Mao Tse-tung's Communist rebels finally took control of China in 1949, those who wanted to take a more aggressive stance against the "Communist menaces" of the world began hurling mud at the administration, blaming Truman for "losing China."

On June 25, 1950, this debate over military and diplomatic posture vis-à-vis Communism stumbled into a landmine. On that morning, the hundred thousand troops of the North Korean People's Army marched across the Thirty-eighth parallel that divided it and the Republic of South Korea in an attempt to unify the two states under the banner of Communism. Secretary of State Dean Acheson had just months earlier dismissed Korea as outside of the United States' perimeter of military concern, and Republicans now blasted the administration for in essence inviting the North Koreans to attack.

Few Americans, least of all a downsized military that was concentrated in Europe and Japan, were eager to return to war, certainly not in Korea. But Truman couldn't afford to sit idle. Moreover, he was by now a disciple of the theory that held that the only way to avoid World War III, which would this time probably involve nuclear warfare, was to fight smaller battles through the emerging superpowers' proxies. So, acting under the auspices of a United Nations directive, he mobilized air support for South Korea's troops and moved the navy's Seventh Fleet to the Straits of Taiwan—sending a bellicose message to Mao Tse-tung about the cost of his overt involvement in the dispute. Within weeks, four infantry divisions and a marine brigade had shipped from the Pacific to Korea as well. The Korean conflict had begun.

THE CHAOS OF WAR

Even before the war began, as the policy makers continued hammering out their agreements on integration and expanded opportunities for blacks, some white commanders were taking the initiative them-

Having already been pushed forward by Secretary Forrestal, the navy responded easily to Truman's integration order.

selves. Brigadier General Frank McConnell integrated training at the army's Fort Jackson, South Carolina, facility as early as January of 1950. He had found the headaches of segregation too great and simply moved on his own to solve them. Rapid recruitment for the new war created similar headaches throughout the army. When the fighting began in Korea, all branches found themselves over-whelmed by the sudden and unexpected influx of new troops to train. The resulting chaos, when added to the pressure coming from Washington, convinced most white army officers to embrace Secretary Gray's compromise with the administration, and by year's end all of the army's training was fully integrated.

Similar pressures existed in the field. The troops that shipped to Korea from Japan were as caught off guard by the new war as America's politicians had been. The peacetime Eighth Army stationed in the Pacific, under General Douglas MacArthur, lived a relatively charmed life. The Second World War was over, and the occupying forces faced no real threat. So readiness had not been atop General MacArthur's plan and his troops had not been held to the typically grueling agenda of an overseas post. And in any case, military planners expected only a brief deployment. That, of course, was a massive miscalculation. The first shipment of troops stayed on the front line, undermanned and with inadequate supplies, for well over a year. They lumbered through the winter of 1950 in conditions reminiscent of Washington's army at Valley Forge. In the end, over thirty-two thousand Americans would die in Korea.

From the outset, MacArthur's Eighth Army met a determined enemy. As a result, it suffered heavy losses in the war's early days. General MacArthur and his Chief of Staff Lieutenant General Edward

Almond had been outspoken opponents of integrating the armed forces and they continued to drag their feet on implementing reforms coming out of Washington. So the Eighth Army's July 1950 Korean deployment included four all-black units: the still alive Twenty-fourth Infantry Regiment, the Seventy-seventh Engineer Combat Company, the 159th Field Artillery Battalion, and the 512th Military Police Company. Subsequent units contained smaller all-black units within the larger white ones, in accordance with the Gillem Board's recommendations. But as casualties mounted in the opening days, with replacements slow in coming, field commanders were forced to make do with what they had on the ground. Again, the resulting confusion encouraged these commanders to embrace an integration plan that appeared to be inevitable, anyway. They began moving black troops into the white regiments as sorely needed replacements.

Neither General MacArthur nor Lieutenant

North Korea's invasion created a sudden demand for troops that overtook lingering reluctance to integrate in the army.

General Almond approved of this process. Both preferred actually weaving South Korean troops into the ranks of faltering U.S. divisions to moving in their own black soldiers. The commanders, particularly Lieutenant General Almond, who had led the tarnished Ninety-second Division during World War II, truly believed that black troops would weaken their white battalions. Lieutenant General Almond went so far as to demand that field commanders rotate the black troops they had already integrated back out of their battalions as soon as white replacements arrived.

But in the final analysis the same brash independence and refusal to subordinate himself to superiors that empowered General MacArthur to buck integration would be his unmaking—and would drive the nail in Jim Crow's army coffin. MacArthur clashed intensely with President Truman over prosecution of the war, which Truman insisted on characterizing as a "police action." The general longed for a far more aggressive posture than Truman envisioned, and by the fall of 1950 he was openly suggesting that his army's string of embarrassing defeats was actually the fault of his civilian leaders who refused to allow him to take the war into the north and, further, to China. He was emboldened by his rousing and improbable victory that September at Inchon, near the South Korean capital of Seoul, which earned him widespread acclaim in the American press and solidified his image as a John Wayne–style hero. Inchon, he suggested, was what he would offer America more of if Truman would just take off the handcuffs. It was enough to convince the president to at least expand the overall mission, broadening his goals from just beating back the North Korean attack to reuniting the two states under a democratic flag.

By October the North Korean People's Army had fled back into the north, and General MacArthur had sent the Twenty-fifth Division, along with its four black units, in pursuit. Despite Truman's explicit orders to the contrary, the Twenty-fifth advanced all the way to the Chinese border, near the Chongchon River. There, however, they faced a surprise attack from well-trained and battle-hardened Chinese army troops. One of America's most ignoble retreats ensued, ending with the Chinese forces' reoccupation of Seoul in South Korea.

The long winter of 1950–51 began, and when it finally thawed that spring, relations between General MacArthur and President Truman had reached the breaking point. Truman dismissed the recalcitrant general from his Far East Command in April 1951. He chose as MacArthur's replacement General Matthew Ridgway, who declared segregation as a whole to be "un-American and un-Christian."

General Ridgway acted swiftly and decisively to finally end the segregation debate. He immediately ordered that as rotations ended, new individual deployments were to deliberately integrate blacks into white units. From combat to support units, in both the regular army and the reserves, he ordered blacks and whites serving in the Far East mixed together. That summer, he disbanded the Eighth Army's remaining all-black units and mixed their members into other battalions. At the same time, the army's Washington policy makers contracted with Johns Hopkins University to study the effects of integration in its Korean and U.S.-based units. The results, reported in November 1951, were unequivocal. The study found that almost ninety percent of soldiers interviewed felt that black enlistees and officers alike performed as well as whites. Overall, the study declared, integration had increased effectiveness in all units.

Facing mounting casualties among the ill-prepared troops who first arrived in Korea, commanders defied MacArthur and put black recruits in whatever unit needed them, regardless of race.

EUROPEAN COMMAND AND THE MARINES

Armed with its success in Korea, the army brass set about convincing its European commanders to finally move forward on the president's now two-year-old executive order as well. To some extent, white Europe-based officers faced the same chaotic pressures as those in the Far East Command confronted. Truman and his advisers were certain that the Chinese aggression in Korea was part of a larger Soviet plan of attack for Europe. By distracting the U.S. forces with Asia, the theory went, the Soviets would improve their chances of success in a surprise offensive. As a result, the army funneled thousands of new recruits into its European operations, tripling its force in the course of 1951. The number of black troops stationed there skyrocketed from 9,000 to 27,000, while the overall manpower jumped to nearly

235,000 troops. Under such conditions, segregation again proved unmanageable.

Training was the first to integrate, and the Women's Army Corps followed. But General Thomas Handy, European commander, was no more eager than MacArthur to embrace this new reality. Both combat and support units remained largely segregated until the spring of 1952. At that point, pressure from the top finally convinced General Thomas to crack the door open. He planned to integrate but hoped to maintain a one-to-ten ratio of black to white troops in each unit. However, the influx of new troops, black and white, simply overwhelmed him and his fellow European commanders. By 1953, blacks were fifteen percent of the European Command's troops, and Handy's ratio had been completely discarded.

A similar process unfolded in the Marine Corps. The reluctance marine commanders displayed at the

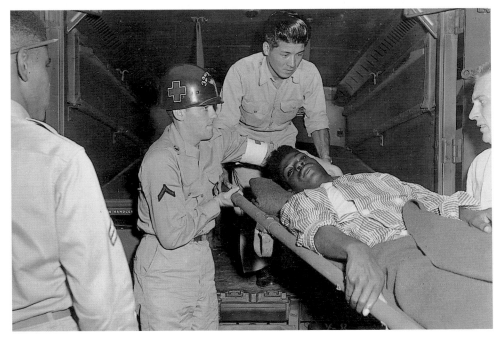

The winter of 1950-51 was a low point for the American forces in Korea, as the number of casualties and those missing-in-action mounted.

After Truman fired MacArthur, his replacement ordered deliberate integration of fighting units in Korea.

A 1951 Johns Hopkins University study, commissioned by the army, found integration had increased force effectiveness.

war's outset was soon overtaken by manpower needs. From the time Corps Commandant General Gates relented to Truman's executive order in May 1949, the Corps had honored its commitment to desegregate. Black units were abolished, and some African American corpsmen began to get combat and specialty assignments. Those assignments, however, were still far outweighed by the number relegated to mess duties. But the recruitment rush sparked by the war proved a boon for black marines. Their number grew from just over a thousand in 1950 to nearly fifteen thousand by the conflict's end in 1953. More dramatically, in 1950 nearly half of the black marines were in the stewards' branch; by the war's end, over eighty-five percent were in the Corps' general service.

The Last Buffalo Soldiers

The Twenty-fourth Infantry Regiment was the American military's last all-black unit. Its history stretched all the way back to the Indian Wars, spanning the young nation's most defining military moments. It had been one of few black regiments to see combat during World War II. And, along with the other Buffalo Soldier regiments, it had survived difficult times. Following the 1917 Houston uprising, it was largely exiled to the army's sidelines. From the post–Civil War era until 1950, the law required the armed forces to maintain four active-duty black regiments. That fact thwarted white military planners' desire to disband the Twenty-fourth and other Buffaloes, so instead they hid the regiments in out-of-the-way posts where no one would have to deal with them. When North Korea invaded its southern neighbor, the Twenty-fourth was at just such a post.

During the peacetime occupation of Japan, General MacArthur and Lieutenant General Almond tasked the Twenty-fourth with guarding military bases at Gifu and Kobe. The regiment received little if any combat training, was undersized with only three battalions, and was led by the most inexperienced white officers, since qualified white senior officers refused what was considered to be a career-ending assignment. If the Eighth Army as a whole was unprepared for its duties in Korea, the Twenty-fourth Infantry never stood a chance. As a result, its final deployment marred the regiment's once proud history. Ironically, however, the unjust reputation for cowardice that the Twenty-fourth developed actually helped push reluctant army officers into embracing integration during the Korean conflict.

The Twenty-fourth, along with three black support units, joined the Twenty-fifth Infantry Division in Korea on July 17, 1950. The whole division received baptism by fire. Regiments throughout the Eighth Army fled the front line in opening battles, officers failed to gain control of their units, and the whole army found itself on the defensive rather than coming to the South Koreans' rescue. But it was the Twenty-fourth that, like the Ninety-second Division during World War II, acquired a permanent reputation

Members of the Twenty-fourth Infantry check foxholes on the west central front. The Twenty-fourth was the last all-black unit in the U.S. Armed Forces.

The Twenty-fourth Infantry troops hold church service at the front under a watchful guard.

Like World War I's Ninety-second Division, the ill-prepared Twenty-fourth was unfairly charged with cowardice.

as the Bugout Brigade—a derisive term pinned on soldiers who flee in battle.

This was in part a result of the simple racism of both the military's white leaders and America's white press, who were eager to find a black scapegoat for the military's embarrassing string of defeats. But it was also because the Twenty-fourth's performance took the longest to correct. Late-twentieth-century army studies (initiated by then Lieutenant Colonel Colin Powell), intended to settle the debate over the Twenty-fourth's performance, concluded that the regiment indeed had its low moments. Individual troops and entire units had fled battle or surrendered. Worse, the study tied the Twenty-fourth to a number of horrifying war crimes—something countless American fighting units in every war have unfortunately been guilty of. These problems persisted because of the same neglect that put a completely untrained black regiment on the front line in the first place. As the war progressed, new officers and recruits rotated into the white regiments. But since the army was still haggling over its use of black com-

Private First Class Vincent Marsh practices his Korean.

Subsequent studies found the Twenty-fourth had in fact performed poorly, but that it was not trained for the warfare it confronted.

bat troops, and General MacArthur was standing in defiant opposition to hosting more of them, the Twenty-fourth's black junior officers and enlisted men saw no relief. This had the doubly negative impact of wearing down the effective troops while preventing the ineffective ones from being replaced.

Despite these hurdles, the regiment often managed to defeat the odds through intense collective sacrifice and individual acts of heroism. The Twenty-fourth won the American forces' first battle victory in Korea. Three days after their arrival, the regiment, joined by the black Seventy-seventh Engineers and

West Pointer David Carlisle (far left) was the first black Army Corps of Engineers officer.

Black army engineers lay wire
near the front.

159th Field Artillery, attempted to retake the South Korean town of Yechon. Although it was the first battlefield engagement for most of the troops involved, they took and secured the town over a sixteen-hour fight before handing it over to South Korean troops. Even the white press hailed the achievement, and the regiment was briefly America's darling.

Weeks later, Private First Class William Thompson became the first American soldier to earn a Medal of Honor in Korea. He was also the first African American allowed to receive the award since the Spanish-American War. Private First Class Thompson unfortunately did not live to collect his recognition. His company was hit by a surprise night attack. Outnumbered and inexperienced, the men retreated in chaos. Private First Class Thompson manned a machine gun to provide cover for the troops as they fell back. Despite suffering multiple wounds, he stayed at the gun until the last company member had moved to safety. He died after being hit by an enemy grenade before he could evacuate himself. His commander waited five months before finally deciding to recommend the soldier for the nation's highest military honor.

The following June, Sergeant Cornelius Charlton of Company C won the Twenty-fourth's second Medal of Honor. During a battle at Chipo-ri, Sergeant Charlton took control of his platoon after the white commanding officer was wounded. He led his men on two separate charges up the hill they had been tasked with taking. When they finally reached the top on the second charge, Sergeant Carlton, suffering several significant wounds, single-handedly subdued the remaining enemy troops.

But this sort of heroism faded from the American memory, while the Bugout Brigade label endured. The regiment's detractors, then and now, pointed in particular to the much disputed story of Battle Mountain. The official military account, buttressed by contemporary white historians, stands in stark contrast to that offered by black veterans who participated in the engagement. On August 31, 1950, the Twenty-fourth participated in an assault on Hill 625, then occupied by the North Korean People's Army. The attack went horribly, and the American forces were driven back. White officers dumped the blame on the Twenty-fourth, arguing that its enlisted men fled in pandemonium despite orders to the contrary from their commanders. Black vets claim that the soldiers simply followed the often frantic orders of their white officers, who were the ones beating a hasty and poorly organized retreat. One way or the other, the battle dragged on for forty-five days, as the American and North Korean forces took turns occupying and losing the hill. Ultimately,

the North Koreans retained control of Hill 625. And the army blamed the Twenty-fourth Regiment.

The regiment's reputation never recovered from Battle Mountain. The following spring, when General Ridgway assumed control of the Far East Command, the Twenty-fourth's supposedly poor performance throughout the war drove many white officers to accept integration. Their reasoning was unfortunate. Segregation, they concluded, served only to concentrate ill-equipped soldiers in one place. Better to spread them out in different units while simultaneously raising the bar for enlistment. So on October 1, 1951, with the army now fully integrated, the historic Twenty-fourth Infantry Regiment, the last of the Buffalo Soldiers, was deactivated.

"Chappie" James

The air force was the first of the branches to embrace President Truman's Executive Order 9981. While, like the navy, it faced recruitment hurdles created by a history of limiting opportunities for blacks, the branch launched an aggressive program to bring more black airmen into its fold. Among those moves was the dissolution of the all-black 332nd Fighter Group in 1949. Its members were spread out around the forces in fully integrated units.

Daniel "Chappie" James Jr. was among the members reassigned following the 332nd's breakup. James had wanted to fly ever since his days growing up near a navy air base in Pensacola, Florida, and after a long wait he finally got his chance during the Tuskegee Experiment of World War II. He earned his pilot's commission in July 1943 and was assigned to the 477th Bombardment Group. There, he joined the protesters at Freeman Field who successfully

Former Tuskegee Airman Daniel "Chappie" James drew public attention from both blacks and whites for his meteoric rise through the air force's ranks.

In 1975, James became the first black four-star general.

North Korean troops and infrastructure. He flew 101 missions during the Korean conflict before being shot down during an unarmed reconnaissance mission. Rescued by marines, the "Black Leader" was reassigned to the Philippines to train new recruits.

In October 1950, Lieutenant James earned a Distinguished Flying Cross for his efforts and received the first of what would be many rapid promotions. In an air force determined to recruit more African Americans, Captain James was held up as proof of the branch's successful integration program. The air force did not shy away from pushing its star black pilot into the public eye, and James, a natural public speaker, readily accepted the additional duties. Some historians and white officers have resentfully argued that his meteoric rise through the ranks was due more to this public relations role than his skills. Blacks who admired him, on the other hand, understood James as but one example of the many talented and dedicated African American soldiers who, when given the same opportunities as whites, could prove their worth. If the air force chose to publicize this, so be it.

By 1952, James had climbed to the rank of major. Stationed at Otis Air Force Base in Massachusetts, he eventually became the first African American to lead an integrated fighter squadron in the United States. He went on to fly seventy-eight combat missions in Vietnam and hold several leadership positions throughout the air force and around the world. By September 1975, he had climbed all the way to the top and become the nation's first black four-star general, placed in charge of the North American Air Defense Command—meaning he was the operational leader for all of the U.S. and Canadian airspace defense forces. It was a remarkable achievement for a man whose military

fought the air force's attempt to maintain segregated officers' clubs. Like the rest of the group, however, he never saw combat in the Second World War.

After the air force integrated, it sent Lieutenant James to the Philippines in September 1949 to become flight leader of the Twelfth Fighter-Bomber Squadron. At six feet four and 250 pounds, the striking major wowed his initially distant white colleagues by not only besting them in every flying category but also disarming them with his surprisingly gregarious personality. The following July, he joined the first cohort of American soldiers that headed for Korea. The air force formed the American contingent's front line, arriving early on to provide ground support first for South Korean troops and later for the U.S. Army and Marine divisions that joined the fighting. Lieutenant James and others manned dangerously low-flying missions in which they strafed advancing career began with sit-ins to demand his right to eat at the officers' club.

General Daniel "Chappie" James Jr. retired in January 1978. One month later, he died of a heart attack.

A New Horizon

On July 27, 1953, a cease-fire brought an end to the Korean conflict, with the disputed boundary in the same spot it had been at the war's beginning. The American military, however, had moved an immeasurable distance. Black enlistment had ballooned in every branch, and those soldiers served in every capacity. The once reluctant army now boasted thirteen percent African American representation, with ninety-five percent of those troops serving in fully integrated units. But the numbers alone don't begin to tell the story. The change is perhaps best illustrated by the posture of General Eisenhower before and after Korea. As president in 1954, the same man who had refused to sign the 761st Tank Battalion's unit

Black and white reservists take preliminary exams for West Point.

commendation during World War II bragged that he had been responsible for the first integration experiment, during the Battle of the Bulge.

Eisenhower's disingenuous rhetoric aside, the military had moved through a debate over race that the rest of America was only just beginning. For the next several decades, it would stand as an island of racial integration within a nation torn apart by questions with which it had already wrestled. The 1948 Women's Armed Forces Integration Act had even inaugurated the military's discussion about gender equity—another topic the rest of the nation was decades away from substantively confronting. The policy opened the forces to women as permanent enlistees. They remained largely tokens—particularly black women—relegated to clerical and nursing positions, but the conversation had begun.

The U.S. Military Academy, meanwhile, appeared to finally be coming around to the idea of commissioning black officers as well. Since Colonel Benjamin Davis Jr.'s 1936 graduation, West Point had accepted and graduated a slow but steady stream of African American cadets. Lieutenants David Carlisle and John Green, classmates who graduated together in 1950, became the first black Army Corps of Engineers officers commissioned at the academy. The following year, Roscoe Robinson Jr. graduated from West Point. He would go on to become the army's first black four-star general, seven years after General James earned his fourth star in the air force.

And so, as America's domestic race wars heated up during the 1950s, service in the peacetime military became an attractive alternative to the limitations of civilian life for African Americans, particularly in the South. Stationed in Europe, blacks could get an education, rise to positions of authority, and live a relatively comfortable life in the absence of Jim Crow.

An integrated service club in Japan.

Even domestic bases literally stood as oases in the desert of America's racial landscape, places where African Americans could lead an entirely different life than that thrust upon them outside of camp walls.

Black soldiers, however, still faced significant bigotry, both from individuals and the military institution as a whole. One particular problem—still evident today—was that African Americans found themselves the disproportionate recipients of severe punishment for code violations. Twice as many African Americans as whites were court-martialed in Korea. A group of Twenty-fourth Infantrymen petitioned the NAACP to look into the matter, and in 1950 the army allowed NAACP legal counsel

Thurgood Marshall to travel to Korea and bases in Japan to investigate. Marshall's study, published in the May 1951 issue of *The Crisis*, found the military's justice system to be rife with prejudice. Blacks were not only brought before tribunals at a strikingly high rate (twice as many black soldiers were court-martialed as whites in Korea), but once there they received cursory trials at best. One soldier had been given a life sentence after a mere forty-two minute trial—a travesty Marshall proclaimed worse than any he had witnessed in the Deep South. Blacks rarely sat on court-martial boards, and no African American served in either the Inspector General's Office or the Office of the Judge Advocate. The result was an unfair system of prosecution followed by an uneven administration of punishments.

While segregation was gone, this sort of institutionalized discrimination persisted in the armed forces for decades longer. Blacks now had vastly greater opportunities open to them, and a select few were rapidly climbing to positions of great authority. But the perception of the majority who remained at the bottom would eventually be that those opportunities were limited in reality if not by policy. By the late 1960s, with America again at war and the military again finding itself host to a large number of new recruits, that perception would become widespread among black troops. And the racial tensions that the armed forces had stood above for a period once again entered its ranks.

CHAPTER

8

"I AIN'T GOT
NO QUARREL
WITH THEM
VIETCONG"

*Vietnam and Its
Aftermath*

It covers less than fifteen years, but from a civil rights perspective, in particular, the period of American history that stretches from the Korean War's close to 1966 might as well be an eternity. In 1953, black America was celebrating the end of its nearly 180-year struggle for the right to stand as equals in the nation's armed forces. By the fall of 1966, a brash new group was introducing a pointedly different agenda that resonated with the country's black urban youth in ways the civil rights movement never had. On October 15, the Black Panther Party for Self-Defense announced its party platform, containing a list of ten demands its members intended to make of the U.S. government. To those who had tirelessly campaigned for President Truman's 1948 executive order, demand number six may have seemed incomprehensible. "We want all black men to be exempt from military service," the document declared.

H. Rap Brown was among a new generation of black leaders who fought against rather than for military service.

We believe that Black people should not be forced to fight in the military service to defend a racist government that does not protect us. We will not fight and kill other people of color in the world who, like black people, are being victimized by the white racist government of America. We will protect ourselves from the force and violence of the racist police and the racist military, by whatever means necessary.

In less than a year, Dr. Martin Luther King Jr. would similarly call upon both black and white youth to denounce the American military's presence in Vietnam. And within a year from that point, only the most traditionalist black leaders refused to join both King and the Panthers in characterizing the conflict as a civil rights problem—and then only because they disliked the idea of criticizing a president who had shepherded two groundbreaking civil rights laws through a hostile Congress.

The problem was that young black men were being shipped off to and dying in Vietnam in numbers that far outstripped their representation in society at large. By 1966, as much as twenty-three percent of American casualties in Vietnam were black. African Americans were being drafted at a rate almost twice that of whites. And individual black families around the nation had long realized they were carrying the burden of a far-off war to which they bore no relation. Moreover, while the twentieth century's black leaders had thus far been unanimous in their goal to win equity for blacks at the front lines, the community had a long history of ambivalence about African

North Vietnamese had been fighting for control of the island for over twenty-five years by the time the defense department acknowledged U.S. military involvement in 1962.

Vietnam was the first American war since the Revolution to open with an integrated fighting force.

Americans dying to protect a country that so clearly devalued their lives. As one nineteenth-century black correspondent wrote when commenting on dying for patriotism in the Civil War, "What do we enjoy, that should inspire us with those feelings?" This was the sentiment that had returned and begun to dominate black America's thinking during the 1960s.

What brought about this radical change in perspective on military service? It was largely the same factor that tarnished the armed forces in the eyes of many white Americans as well: the widespread belief that the conflict in Vietnam was at best a poorly planned debacle and at worst an immoral blight on America's values.

Entering France's "Dirty War"

We could mark the American military entrance into Vietnam's civil war anywhere between 1941 and 1964. Perhaps the best place to begin, however, would be April 1962, when the Department of Defense finally acknowledged that small numbers of U.S. troops—ostensibly military "advisers"—were engaging Vietcong in battle. By that time, the North Vietnamese forces under Ho Chi Minh had been fighting for control of the out-of-the-way Southeast Asian island for over twenty-five years. This is why President John F. Kennedy, who approved the ongoing escalations of American commitment in the early 1960s, had himself warned as early as 1954 against any intervention in Vietnam, declaring, "It seems to me that it would be a hopeless situation."

But the Cold War–era logic that drove Truman to act in Korea had solidified as doctrine in American foreign policy by the time Kennedy took office. The reigning theory was that the only way to contain the Soviet Union and China without triggering a nuclear conflict was to fight smaller wars through proxies. If any state, no matter how seemingly insignificant, joined the Communist block of nations, it represented a loss for democracy and therefore brought the United States closer to having to directly confront another nuclear power. Thinking in these terms, American diplomats and policy makers magnified Ho Chi Minh's revolution far beyond its true geopolitical scale.

When the last French colonial stronghold fell at Dienbienphu in 1954, the fifteen-year-old debate about America's role in Southeast Asia took on a new urgency. The United States was already spending billions of dollars a year to help the French hold off Ho Chi Minh, who the new Eisenhower administration rightly believed to be backed by the Soviets and the Chinese. The following year, over the objections of Democratic senators such as Kennedy and Lyndon Johnson, President Dwight Eisenhower approved the deployment of military advisers in South Vietnam. They were to help an underdog army defeat the man who had just brought an end to over one hundred years of French colonial rule. Needless to say, among their biggest hurdles was Ho Chi Minh's widespread popularity.

Slowly but surely, the fight became America's. The advisers helped the United States' hand-picked leader for South Vietnam, Ngo Dinh Diem, orchestrate a ruthless but ultimately successful campaign to gain undisputed control of the south. The first U.S. casualties came in 1959, when anti-Diem South Korean guerrillas killed two military advisers. By 1963, the United States was working to shed itself of the repressive Diem regime. Then, in August 1964, came the incident in the Gulf of Tonkin. There, allegedly unprovoked North Vietnamese patrol boats fired on U.S. ships. The veracity of that allegation has since been hotly debated. But, true or not, it prompted Congress to nearly unanimously vote to unleash the American military. On August 7, Congress gave President Lyndon Johnson what amounted to a green light to prosecute war in Vietnam, without ever having to declare it as such. The U.S. commitment in Vietnam would quickly escalate, peaking in 1969 with over 540,000 troops deployed there. It was not America's most deadly war, but it was the country's longest, and certainly its least popular.

Early Enthusiasm and Dubious Victories

Things didn't start off so bad in Vietnam. The war effort, as with all previous ones, originally enjoyed the support of a nation convinced of the valor of standing against "Communist aggression." All but two members of Congress voted in support of the 1964 Gulf of Tonkin Resolution. Celebrities traveled to the country to register their support for the troops. And news organizations by and large reported on the military and diplomatic actions favorably.

Vietnam was the first American war since the Revolution to open with an integrated U.S. fighting force. And at the time, African Americans were flocking into the military. The armed forces had developed a national reputation as the standard bearer for an integrated society (excepting the state-run National Guards, some of which still excluded blacks from even enlisting). And the opportunities African Americans found there were miles beyond anything available in the civilian world and unparalleled in American history. So blacks continued to readily volunteer for service despite the Vietnam conflict. Many of the recruits must have calculated that ten thousand miles still wasn't far enough away from the racism and poverty of home. These young African Americans not only signed up in large numbers but also reenlisted at higher rates than whites. In 1965, over forty-five percent of black soldiers reenlisted, while only seventeen percent of whites chose to stay on. War or not, the military life was a relatively good one for black people.

The war effort enjoyed early popular support.

EXPANDING
THE TRUMAN ORDER

After the Department of Defense abolished the last segregated military unit in 1954, the services had set about debating and refining what else Truman's order meant when it called for "equality of treatment and opportunity for all persons." Some believed it simply meant integration. But others argued it meant much more and pushed the military on the matter. This led to successes such as the Defense Department's decision to desegregate schools on military bases—four months before the Supreme Court ordered all public schools integrated in *Brown v. Board of Education*. Given the time it took for the *Brown* decision to be implemented (in some states, such as Indiana, courts were still ordering changes as late as the 1970s), the decision meant black soldiers' children routinely enjoyed better educations than most African American kids.

The most controversial question in this debate over the scope of Truman's order asked what it meant for the military's interaction with the outside world. Was the military responsible for ensuring its black members equality of treatment and opportunity off base as well? Opinions ran the gamut. Civil rights groups, egged on by black troops, argued the military should intervene when black service members were discriminated against by the local communities in which they were stationed. In 1954, for instance, a large group of soldiers was arrested in Columbia, South Carolina, for refusing to sit in the rear of a public bus. Civil rights leaders petitioned Eisenhower to get involved, but Secretary of Defense Charles Wilson counseled otherwise. The administration's stance, in this case and throughout the 1950s, would be that it could not meddle in local affairs. EO

9981's reach stopped at the base's front door.

Some base commanders, however, argued the other extreme and disciplined black troops who ran afoul of local Jim Crow laws. In 1956, Secretary of the Air Force Harold Talbott recommended that his base commanders require their black airmen to respect local laws. Meanwhile, some African American troops asked to simply transfer from places where they experienced problems. A reasonable enough solution, except that it violated the spirit of Truman's order—assignments could not be made based on racial considerations. So the Defense Department declined such requests as a matter of policy. However, the army and air force both were willing to break this rule when it came to interracial marriages and did not assign soldiers in such unions to states where they were outlawed.

Off-base discrimination profoundly impacted black soldiers' lives. The disconnect between their worlds inside and outside of the camp gates proved emotionally difficult to manage for sure, but it also created significant practical problems. Housing and transportation presented the biggest hurdles, since on-base housing was limited and soldiers often had to find private residences in bitterly segregated communities. But the debate over the military's responsibilities in regard to local communities was also driven by broader politics. Civil rights advocates hoped to leverage their gains in the armed forces into advancements in society at large by expanding the reach of the military's groundbreaking policies.

While they made little progress in the 1950s, they found a new ally in President Kennedy. After initial reluctance, the administration embraced civil rights as a signature issue and started with the military. At his inauguration, Kennedy noticed that the Coast Guard's honor guard contained no African

Americans. He not only took the matter up with the Coast Guard but pointed it out at his first cabinet meeting as well. It was an indication that he planned to make an issue out of civil rights.

Taking a page out of both FDR's and Truman's books, the Kennedy administration created a committee ostensibly tasked with studying race relations in the services. Its real purpose was to develop and justify a policy for dealing with off-base discrimination, particularly in housing. The committee did not disappoint. Its June 1963 report declared off-base discrimination to be a leading downward pull on troop morale and recommended that the military take active part in preventing its impact on soldiers. Wherever local communities insisted upon segregation and discrimination, base commanders should make the offending businesses off limits to all personnel. When communities proved particularly recalcitrant, the Defense Department should relocate its facility to more hospitable locations. The administration stopped short of requiring such sanctions, or even empowering base commanders to employ them. But it did give the Department of Defense the power to do so, and for the first time explicitly stated that it had a responsibility to ensure that its troops found equality of treatment and opportunity both on and off base.

VIETNAM'S OPENING HOURS

By the end of 1965, the American commitment in Vietnam had grown from around eleven thousand advisers in 1962 to two hundred thousand troops. In October of that year, young Private First Class Milton Olive III earned the first of twenty Medals of Honor awarded to African Americans during the

conflict. Private First Class Olive's story perfectly illustrates the perspective many black troops held at the time. His unit, the army's 173rd Airborne Brigade, had been the first major combat group deployed in Vietnam, arriving in May 1963. Private First Class Olive, a native of Mississippi, had enlisted from his teenage home on the South Side of Chicago, Illinois, and joined the 173rd in Vietnam in June of 1965. He was an eager soldier and often volunteered to lead patrol. On October 22, his platoon was hit by heavy enemy fire in the jungles of Phu Cuong. The men repelled the Vietcong ambush, then pursued their fleeing attackers. Private First Class Olive and four others followed a group that had broken off from the main pack, and while giving chase, a grenade dropped into their midst. Private First Class Olive grabbed the explosive, tucked it into his midsection, and rolled away from the group. The grenade detonated, killing him but missing the others. His nineteenth birthday was just over two weeks away.

Private First Class Olive's selflessness was commonplace throughout the war, among both black and white troops. The story of the war's second black Medal of Honor recipient, also a member of the 173rd Airborne, offers another example. He was also the first black Medal of Honor recipient to survive the war. At thirty-seven years old, Medical Corpsman Lawrence Joel, Specialist Sixth Class, was old enough to remember the days when the army hadn't been so open to African Americans. A few weeks after Olive's death, Joel's company was brutally ambushed. Outnumbered and caught off guard, the company struggled to defend itself. Almost the entire lead squadron was killed. Wounded with a shot in the thigh, Joel worked his way through the company, crawling from man to man under a hailstorm of bul-

In the war's early years, African Americans still flocked to join the military and reenlisted at higher rates than whites.

lets to offer medical treatment and words of encouragement. He paused long enough to treat his own wound, self-administering morphine to stave off the pain. Even after he was again shot, Joel managed to treat thirteen additional men before running out of medical supplies. The battle dragged on for twenty-four hours and rearmed with new supplies, Joel continued crawling around and saving lives for the duration, despite his wounds. "His meticulous attention to duty," reads Joel's Medal of Honor citation, "saved a large number of lives and his unselfish, daring example under most adverse conditions was an inspiration to all."

But despite this sort of heroism, by the year's end the Vietnam conflict was already starting to show signs of becoming a protracted one. In November, in the Ia Drang Valley, the U.S. forces engaged their first major battle. Spanning four days, it was a bloody fight that should have indicated to American military planners that they were in for more than they bargained for. It instead duped commanding General William Westmoreland into believing that his strategy of "attrition" could be successful. Just over two hundred infantrymen were killed during the battle. The North Vietnamese Army had baited Westmoreland into the valley, then hit him with surprise attacks. It was here that the NVA troops showcased their strategy of striking in close-range ambushes, instigating nearly hand-to-hand combat in which the superior American airpower would be rendered useless. General Westmoreland, seeing that the NVA casualties far outnumbered his own, declared the Ia Drang debacle a victory. But America's two hundred deaths hurt a nation fighting for abstract concepts a lot more than North Vietnam's two thousand hurt a nation fighting for self-rule. After a couple of years of victories such

as these, the American public's original enthusiasm for the war effort decidedly turned, and the radical Black Panthers' demand that blacks be excluded from the draft no longer sounded quite so radical.

Colin Powell: The Early Years

The Army was living the democratic ideal ahead of the rest of America. Beginning in the fifties, less discrimination, a truer merit system, and leveler playing fields existed inside the gates of our military posts than in any Southern city hall or Northern corporation. The Army, therefore, made it easier for me to love my country, with all its flaws, and to serve her with all my heart.

This is how General Colin Powell explained the birth of his undying commitment to the United States Armed Forces in his 1995 best-selling memoir *My American Journey*. Growing up the son of Caribbean immigrants in the Bronx borough of New York City, Powell was a listless, unambitious young man until he joined the Reserve Officers Training Corps during his first year at the City College of New York. It was the first thing in his life that had ever sparked any real passion. "I was seventeen," he wrote. "I felt cut off and lonely [at college]. The uniform gave me a sense of belonging, and something I had never experienced all the while I was growing up; I felt distinctive." He graduated from CCNY a C-average student, but he was commissioned as an officer in the army. As he put it, the bachelor's degree was an incidental bonus to having been a Distinguished Military Graduate. He was on his way to a life in the services and would not look back.

Four years later, in 1962, Powell was off to South Vietnam to serve as a "counterinsurgency adviser." It was a plum assignment. It not only involved a promotion to captain but also indicated his status as a "comer"—someone the higher-ups had their eyes on, someone whom they expected great things from. It was the same year as the Cuban missile crisis, and the Cold War was at a zenith. The officers being selected to prosecute America's proxy wars were considered the best and the brightest, the leaders of tomorrow's military. Powell, who showed a natural ability at management and leadership, was among those visionaries. And, in no small part because he was African American, his career was moving on the fast track. Captain Powell was everything the integrationists in Washington dreamed of, and they were anxious to see him put to use.

But while Powell felt a sense of duty, and was certainly excited by the opportunity to prove himself on the battlefield, he was skeptical about America's involvement in Vietnam from the start. What exactly was the mission, he wondered? And what did this loose term "nation-building" mean in a practical sense?

Captain Powell's direct responsibility was to be the lead adviser for the Army of the Republic of Vietnam's Second Battalion, Third Infantry Regiment, Second Division. This four-hundred-man unit was stationed at A Shau, located in a dense rain forest near the Laotian border. It was one of four bases along the infamous Ho Chi Minh Trail that were tasked with blocking the flow of North Vietnamese supplies and troops that swept along this route and into South Vietnam. Captain Powell

learned quickly at A Shau that no one had thought much about the conflict beyond this level of planning. Upon his arrival, Powell questioned the base's positioning—in a vulnerable spot at the bottom of a large mountainside. His South Vietnamese counterpart, Captain Vo Cong Hieu, responded that the outpost was set up there in order to protect a nearby airfield. Asked why the airfield was there, Captain Hieu explained that it was needed to resupply the outpost. "I would spend nearly twenty years, one way or another, grappling with our experience in this country," Powell wrote when recounting the incident in his memoir. "And over all that time, Vietnam rarely made much more sense than Captain Hieu's circular reasoning on that January day in 1963. We're here because we're here, because we're . . ."

Powell was similarly disturbed by the modern military's reliance on cutting-edge management strategies. Secretary McNamara came to the job enamored with the business world's recent embrace of statistical analysis and with the newly developing science of management. But Captain Powell was one of those who cringed at having to "learn the latest strategic fashions concocted by Secretary of Defense Robert McNamara's whiz kids back at the Pentagon." One of the primary critiques of the American military's performance in Vietnam—both from soldiers who fought it and from scholars who have studied it—is that there developed a morbid and inefficient obsession with body counts. If companies and commanders could point to large numbers of dead North Vietnamese, they were considered successful. It reflected the Defense Department's hunger for data that could be crunched. Dissenters, such as Powell, believed this was a poor substitute for a defined mission with measurable goals.

And so, as with many of the military's future

leaders, Powell's experience in Vietnam profoundly impacted his views on later questions about when and how America's armed forces should be sent to war. Two of his bedrock principles grew out of these early days: Always have a clear mission, and always put more faith in ground-level experience and common sense than in "the latest strategic fashions."

But, at the time, Captain Powell kept his head down and stayed focused on his particular responsibilities. About six months into his tour he was injured by a device that caused all too many U.S. casualties and that epitomized the manner in which the North Vietnamese Army chased two better-equipped and better-trained armies out of the country: a punji trap. It's essentially a strong, sharp stick

A simple "punji" trap knocked Colin Powell out of combat in Vietnam.

or rod planted in a foot-deep hole and covered over with brush, and Powell stepped into one. The pole drove into Powell's sole, straight through his foot, and back out the boot top. When untreated, the injury easily fosters gangrene. But when treated, while excruciatingly painful, it's not a major injury. Nevertheless, since he was already more than halfway through his tour by the time he recovered, Captain Powell was transferred to division headquarters. The whole affair was one of his more frustrating experiences in Vietnam. "The infantry in the boondocks," Powell writes,

slogging back and forth over the same terrain, ambushed daily, taking casualties from an enemy who melts away, wonders, understandably, what good he is accomplishing. He seeks comfort in assuming that while he might not know, up there somewhere, wiser heads have the answer. My service on the headquarters staff exploded that assumption. We were the most sophisticated nation on earth. We were putting our superior technology in the service of the ARVN. Deep thinkers, like my intelligence officer behind the green door, were producing printouts, filing spreadsheets, crunching numbers, and coming out with blinding flashes of the obvious, while an enemy in black pajamas and Firestone flip-flops could put an officer out of the war with a piece of bamboo dipped in manure.

Soon Powell was again climbing the rungs. By August 1964 he was back in the States for Infantry Officers Advanced Course at Fort Benning—known as the "career course." He graduated the following year, now a major, and in 1966 joined the school's faculty. The school's staff was expanding because the Johnson administration had by now significantly escalated the U.S. commitment in Vietnam, to upward of three hundred thousand troops, and the army needed to start cranking out new officers to lead its rapidly growing infantry. In the spring of 1967, Major Powell was selected for the Army Command and General Staff College at Fort Leavenworth, Kansas. Fort Leavenworth separates the field officers from the general officers. Major Powell was clearly on a trajectory to the top.

In July 1968, Major Powell returned to Vietnam for a second tour. He found a very different infantry than the one he had left behind. By now, the war had deteriorated and morale had gone with it. The problems he saw in his first rotation seemed to be bearing fruit. And they were complicated by the fact that the new infantry was peopled with young men who had been unwillingly dragged into service rather than men who, like Powell and Medal of Honor winners Private First Class Olive and Specialist Sixth Class Joel, had eagerly embraced it. While this was true for troops from all backgrounds, this resentment was most profound among African Americans.

Times Change at Home

As Powell rose in ranks through an integrated and racially progressive military organization, the rest of the nation's racial divide became increasingly bitter. The civil rights movement had found receptive audiences in the corridors of Washington's government buildings and among the stark segregation of the Deep South. But it proved to be ill equipped for

dealing with the far more nuanced racial problems of the north's urban centers. There, young black men and women, trapped in ghettos where economic and educational opportunities were limited by institutional forces not so easily identifiable as those in places like Mississippi, began to move from frustration to anger. New political groups, such as the Black Panther Party and a radicalized Student Nonviolent Coordinating Committee, offered messages more resonant than those of the NAACP's work for gradual change within the system or Dr. King's nonviolent civil disobedience. For these leaders and their followers, America had been given enough time to change. And if the country still didn't want them, then they didn't want the country.

At the same time, as the fighting in Vietnam heated up, the peace movement similarly intensified. And it found engaged allies in the leaders of these frustrated urban black youth. But, while they were the first to join the movement, more established figures soon followed. From early in the war, a debate raged within Dr. King's Southern Christian Leadership Conference about whether he should speak out on the matter. The delicate consensus had been that he should stay out of it. His advisers felt that he had enough on his plate trying to find ways to connect with northern black communities, that there was no need to antagonize a friendly president, and that white college students who formed the peace movement's backbone couldn't necessarily be trusted. That consensus broke in April 1967, when Dr. King finally decided he could not avoid the issue any longer.

In his first major speech opposing the war, Dr. King articulated the reasons he believed the peace and civil rights movements necessarily coincided. The war, he complained, had derailed progress on domestic programs for social and economic equality. He could not work to stop the rioting plaguing black cities without also speaking against the violence the government unleashed in Vietnam. And increasing reports of the human rights abuses America committed as it prosecuted the war could not be overlooked. But, perhaps most compelling to the majority of blacks concerned about the war, there was the odd juxtaposition of poor black men being drafted and dying in such high numbers while their families remained in segregated, strangling ghettos, "paying the double price of smashed hopes at home and death and corruption in Vietnam," as King put it. "So we have been repeatedly faced with the cruel irony," he bemoaned,

of watching Negro and white boys on TV screens as they kill and die together for a nation that has been unable to seat them together in the same schools. So we watch them in brutal solidarity burning the huts of a poor village, but we realize that they would never live on the same block in Detroit. I could not be silent in the face of such cruel manipulation of the poor.

Questions about the inequity of the draft and subsequent casualty rate drove the black community's discontent with the war. Whereas twenty years earlier, African Americans were complaining about white-dominated draft boards blocking them from service in a popular war, they were now complaining about still-white-dominated draft boards enlisting them en masse for an unpopular one. By 1967, African Americans' percentage of America's battlefield deaths had finally begun to fall—down to the teens from the low twenties. But it was still much

higher than the eleven percent of society that black people represented.

The reasons for this overrepresentation were many and varied. Unquestionably, racist draft boards—in 1967, less than two percent of the nation's seventeen thousand draft board members were black—were more likely to deny blacks exemptions and grant them to whites. But Secretary McNamara, despite all of his support for civil rights and expanding Truman's order, had also created a system that clearly funneled poor blacks onto the front lines while weeding out middle-class whites. The primary mode of obtaining an unchallengeable deferment was to go to college or join the National Guard. Most blacks could not afford or gain entrance to the nation's colleges, and many state-run National Guards still either restricted or outright banned black enlistment. Meanwhile, as demand for troops continued to build throughout 1966, McNamara had to find a way to get more bodies in the army. He could have narrowed the exemption categories, or he could

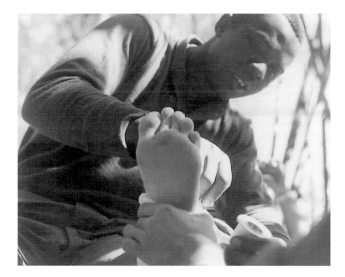

As the war dragged on and casualties mounted, morale at the front deteriorated.

have activated the National Guard. He chose instead to further lower the bar on the entrance exam so that fewer draftees would disqualify themselves. Couching the change as a program to help poor, uneducated blacks gain marketable skills in the military, McNamara promised that these troops would receive special training while in the service.

The combined effect of all these forces was dramatic: In 1967, sixty-four percent of eligible African Americans were drafted, while only thirty-one percent of eligible whites had to fight. Once in the service, black draftees also disproportionately drew infantry assignments—which account for the most deaths in any war, and certainly did in Vietnam. Assignments were made based on test scores, with those who score in the bottom two rungs assigned to ground combat roles and those at the top to technical jobs, such as electronics, that largely take place removed from the fighting. African American draftees, victims of substandard education systems in black communities, largely scored in the lower rungs.

So it was this sort of inequity that drove the Black Panther Party to include in its platform a demand that African Americans be exempted from military service. And it was this sort of inequity that motivated black America's most famous draft resister. In February 1967, the press got wind of the fact that boxing's heavyweight champion Muhammad Ali had come up for the draft. They hounded the Nation of Islam member about how he would respond. Being a Muslim, Ali declared himself a conscientious objector. But he made it clear that race was as much of an issue as religion, declaring at one point, "I am not going ten thousand miles to help murder and kill and burn other people simply to help continue the domination of the white slave masters over the dark people of the world." And he crafted one of his signature poems to serve as his stump response to inquiries about his drafting:

> **Keep asking me, no matter how long**
> **On the war in Vietnam, I sing this song**
> **I ain't got no quarrel with them Vietcong.**

The government rejected Ali's conscientious objector status and prosecuted him for draft evasion. He was convicted and stripped of both his title belt and his boxing license. Exiled from the world in which he made his living, Ali continued challenging the conviction until the Supreme Court overturned it in 1970. Black Americans, particularly young black men, were galvanized by his struggle. It was exactly the sort of protest thousands of young African Americans wished they could launch. But without the money and influence of Ali, they instead were forced to accept their assignments at the front line. They would bring the resentment born of their life experience with them.

Racial Turmoil at the Front

In 1968 the U.S. presence in Vietnam grew to 536,000 troops. The draft class of that year profoundly altered the makeup and nature of this force. Gone were the professional soldiers who had begun the fighting. Their replacements were young men, black and white, who wanted nothing less than to be fighting a war in the jungles of Southeast Asia. African Americans, who accounted for twenty percent of combat troops, brought with them the intensifying frustration of the ghetto. Poor whites, too often pitted against poor blacks in the competition for scarce economic resources back home, brought

Blacks accounted for a far higher percentage of battlefield deaths than their representation in society at large.

with them the prejudices they had learned as well. Rampant drug use, already prevalent on the streets of America, accompanied both populations, and local businesses that sold these troops drugs and sex blos-somed. Morale reached an all-time low in the American military, as the young men fought a losing war they didn't believe in alongside colleagues they didn't like or trust.

Vietnam veterans stress that, in battle, none of these tensions mattered. The jungle warfare was so hellish that it trumped all the pressures and prejudices that divided them, and they struggled through it as units irrelevant of race. But removed from the battles, those tensions reemerged. Bases in the United States were plagued by racially motivated violence, both on large and small scales. The marines' Camp Lejune, North Carolina, faced 160 such incidents in the first eight months of 1968 alone. The

The 1968 draft class brought with it the racial tensions of America's cities. Above, the aftermath of race rioting in Washington, D.C.

In 1967, sixty-four percent of eligible blacks were drafted while only thirty-one percent of eligible whites went to war.

Vets testify that, in battle, there was little time to think about race. Racial animosity occurred in camp and rear guard positions.

assassination of Dr. King in April pushed things beyond a manageable point. Black troops at rear guard posts gathered in angry and mournful protests; white troops responded by flying Confederate flags. From then forward, the hard-won integration of the

past two decades gave way to an unforgiving division. All of this took place as the fighting dragged into its fourth year, with U.S. forces not only making little progress in their war of attrition but also suffering increasingly unsustainable casualties themselves.

Major Powell described the scene he witnessed when he returned to Vietnam in 1968. Part of his duties included touring and inspecting outposts around the combat zone. What he found appalled him, not just because of the clear deterioration in upkeep of the posts—piles of rusted ammunition laying about, poor sanitation, soldiers with sloppy appearances—but because of the weathered attitude it reflected. His reaction perhaps best summarizes the changes that had occurred within the force. "These were good men," he explained,

the same kind of young Americans who had fought, bled and died winning victory after victory throughout our country's

"Both blacks and whites were resentful of the authority that kept them here for a dangerous and unclear purpose," said Powell.

history. They were no less brave or skilled, but by this time in the war, they lacked inspiration and a sense of purpose. Back home, the administration was trying to conduct the war with as little inconvenience to the country as possible. The reserves had not been called up. Taxes to finance the war had not been raised. Better off kids beat the draft with college deferments. The commander in chief, LBJ himself, was packing it in at the end of his term. Troops of the ally we had come to aid were deserting at a rate of over 100,000 a year. . . .

Both blacks and whites were resentful of the authority that kept them here for a

Black and white troops often fought a war they didn't believe in, alongside colleagues they didn't like or trust.

dangerous and unclear purpose. The number one goal was to do your time and get home alive. I was living in a large tent and I moved my cot every night, partly to thwart Viet Cong informants who might be tracking me, but also because I did not rule out attacks on authority from within the battalion itself.

But, despite Powell's assertion to the contrary, part of the problem was that this was in fact a different group of young men than had fought previous wars. Secretary McNamara's decision to lower the qualifications for entry in 1966 brought draft classes filled with young men more likely to be plagued by America's social ills—from bigotry to drug use. From the program's start until the summer of 1969, an additional 246,000 troops that would have previously been rejected joined the armed forces. Eighty percent of them had dropped out of high school. Over thirty percent never made it beyond basic training. They created severe discipline problems. Over a third were discharged early due to infractions or ultimately did not leave the forces with an honorable discharge.

About forty percent of these men were African Americans. Together with the black troops who may have qualified to enter the forces but wanted no more to be there, they banded together, forming units within units. They clashed with their white counterparts and openly protested the institutional racism that still existed in the military, regardless of how far ahead of the rest of society it had moved. The post-1968 black troops developed such a distinctive identity from the larger American forces that they gave themselves a name, Bloods. Wallace Terry, an African American war correspondent for *Time* magazine, was so moved by the perspectives of and challenges faced

Post-1968 black draftees banded together and dubbed themselves "Bloods."

Black vets, particularly officers, often felt they were considered traitors to the race for their participation in the war.

by these men during his reporting in Vietnam that he later published a collection of their oral histories. A best-seller, Terry's 1984 *Bloods* gave twenty black Vietnam vets an opportunity to recount their experiences in first person. Though published over ten years after America's pullout from Vietnam, the painful frustration of being forced to fight and die in a strange land for a cause they did not believe in was still palpable in their voices. The utter nightmare of jungle warfare had clearly lingered in their spirits. Specialist 4 Richard J. Ford III, who fought from June 1967 to July 1968, offered a chilling description of how the drug problem escalated:

> In the field most of the guys stayed high. Lot of them couldn't face it. In a sense, if you was high, it seemed like a game you was in. You didn't take it serious. It

stopped a lot of nervous breakdown.

See, the thing about the field that was so bad was this. If I'm working on the job with you stateside and you're my friend, if you get killed, there's a compassion. My boss say, "Well, you better take a couple of days off. Get yourself together." But in the field, we can be the best of friends and you get blown away. They put a poncho around you and send you back. They tell 'em keep moving.

We had a medic that give us a shot of morphine anytime you want one. I'm not talkin' about for wounded. I'm talkin' about when you want to just get high. So you can face it.

The Vietnam Veteran's Memorial on the National Mall in Washington, D.C. was erected in 1982.

For both black and white troops, these sorts of trials were worsened upon returning home. Rather than coming back to the sort of fanfare and ticker tape parades that greeted veterans of the World Wars, Vietnam soldiers, many of them physically and emotionally scarred for life, trickled back one at a time into a nation that saw them as villains rather than heroes. Atrocities such as the massacre at Mai Lai and the regular human rights abuses of Vietnamese civilians had created a vicious wing of the peace movement, one that not only denounced the war effort but also ostracized the young men whose government had forced them, by law, to carry

it out. At best, the troops met indifference upon their return. "It seemed nobody cared that you'd been to Vietnam," one vet told Terry. "As a matter of fact, everybody would be wondering where have you been for so long. They would say, how did you lose your leg? In a fight? A car wreck? Anything but Vietnam."

The sentiments engendered by the Black Power movement, which had largely usurped civil rights by the late sixties, added to this disregard by often leading black Americans to label black GI's traitors to the fight for equality, minions of a racist government who had traveled around the world to kill other people of color. Those African Americans who had found success in the armed forces, and rose to officer ranks, were particularly considered sellouts to the establishment.

America began trying to correct its embarrassing treatment of Vietnam war veterans with the 1982 erection of a Vietnam Veterans Memorial on the National Mall in Washington, D.C., located at the feet of the Mall's signature Lincoln Memorial. While workers poured the concrete for the Wall, on which the names of all 58,151 soldiers killed in action are inscribed, a navy officer tossed his brother's Purple Heart, awarded for death or injury in battle, into the molding. When the monument opened, vets and their families began to similarly leave belongings in front of the Wall, as though it were a gravestone. Park Service police picked up wreaths, dog tags, flags, stuffed animals, medals, and rations. Rather than throwing them out, the service kept the items in storage and began cataloging them. Black vet Duery Felton was among the volunteers who helped in the project, and in 1989 he became curator of the Vietnam Veterans Memorial Collection, housed at the Smithsonian Institute in Washington.

Prisoners of War

Coming partly in reaction to the disregard veterans met upon returning home, one of the most significant political movements to grow out of the Vietnam War was the veterans' lobby on behalf of those still missing in action. While the chaos of combat meant that too many of those who sacrificed their lives in the jungles of Southeast Asia died without being accounted for, veterans argued that many also remained in North Vietnamese prisons. In the 1980s, this POW-MIA movement became one of the most identifiable vestiges of America's four-decade foray into the Southeast Asian conflict. Its adherents argue, persuasively, that the nation's original lackluster effort to reclaim its lost soldiers and its subsequent refusal to at least attempt to concretely determine those troops' fates is but one more example of America's mistreatment of its Vietnam veterans.

The Vietnam War officially closed on January 27, 1973. The ceasefire agreement included provisions for a POW exchange, and 591 Americans emerged from North Vietnam's barbaric POW camps over the next few months. At least two thousand troops, however, remained unaccounted for. But both the beleaguered Nixon administration and the North Vietnamese government asserted that no American POWs remained in Vietnam. Subsequent investigations have raised considerable doubt about the truth of that claim. One investigation, which centered on the discovery of North Vietnamese documents in the Soviet archives, concluded that the NVA boasted to the Soviets that it held over one thousand American POWs as late as 1972. As the United States reestablished diplomatic relations with Vietnam in the mid-1990s, the Clinton administration highlighted the effort to shed light on the POW question as a primary goal of its rapprochement. But the U.S. government nevertheless continued to assert that if there were in fact unaccounted-for POWs, they were few in number and not likely still alive.

The most infamous of the NVA prison camps was the one located at Hoa Lo, which American GI's dubbed the Hanoi Hilton. In prisons such as this

POW Bobby Louis Johnson upon his release in 1973. He had been held captive since 1968.

POW Norman McDaniel upon
his arrival home in 1973. He
was captured in 1966.

Colonel Fred Cherry, the first black POW, upon his arrival home in 1973. He had been held since 1965.

with their families and the outside world, and required to subsist on the most meager diets—all in violation of the Geneva Convention that is supposed to mandate a minimum level of treatment for prisoners of war. The war's first black POW was housed at the Hanoi Hilton and stayed there throughout the war's duration. Like most prisoners of war, Virginia native Colonel Fred Cherry was an air force pilot, shot down on a bombing mission over the north, near Hanoi, in October 1965. He was the forty-third American taken captive and was not released until the prisoner exchange at the war's close in 1973.

A member of the Thirty-fifth Tactical Fighter Squadron based in Thailand, Colonel Cherry was already a veteran when the war began, having flown thirty-five bombing missions in Korea. He was flying one of the strong, fast F-105 bombers when he got hit. Electrical equipment in the plane was damaged by rifle fire from the ground, which reached Cherry's mount because he had been flying at extremely low altitudes, just above the treetops, in order to stay below the radar. It was his fiftieth mission in Vietnam, and he had moved from originally hitting supply trains on the Ho Chi Minh Trail to "open bombing" over the north. So when he went down it was in the heart of enemy territory. "I couldn't see whether I was upright, upside down, or what," he told Wallace Terry in recounting the crash. "I just pulled the nose up a few degrees to give me the best ejection altitude. I ejected instantly. At four hundred feet. And I prayed."

Colonel Cherry would need his prayers. The seven years he spent in captivity were perhaps more hellish than any combat tour in the jungle. His injuries required a series of operations, which his captors often purposely bungled or administered without anesthesia. When he wasn't recovering from these ordeals, he was being tortured twice a day for information. During these interrogations, the NVA operatives played upon race in the same way the Germans and Koreans had, citing Black Power leaders who argued that African Americans should not remain loyal to the United States in an effort to get him to officially denounce his government and its campaign in Vietnam. At one point, he spent fifty-three weeks in solitary confinement. As with most POWs, Cherry responded to all of this by holding fast and simply concocting one absurd lie after another to feed his interrogators misinformation.

Colonel Cherry described one of the most brutal tortures he underwent to Terry. It was during one of his several operations, on this particular occasion ostensibly meant to deal with a gangrene infection that had developed when prison guards denied him antibiotics following the last operation:

This time there was no anesthetic. They just took a scalpel and cut away the dead flesh, scraped at the infection on the bones. I knew about what they should have to do, so I knew they were makin' it

more painful than necessary, being very sadistic. I couldn't believe that a human being s'posed to be practicin' medicine was doing this.

Well, I knew they wanted me to cry out. Like a test of wills. We gon' break him.

Balls of perspiration was poppin' off me. Size of your fingertips. I was totally dehydrated. It was the worst straight pain I had yet known.

They had my face covered with a sheet. And they kept raising it to see if I'm going to beg for mercy, going to scream.

And each time they looked down at me, I would look at them and smile.

They kept at it for three hours. And I kept thinkin', I can take it.

When they gave up, I was still smilin'.

A New Military

Following the war and throughout the 1970s, the military circled its wagons and began the painful process of figuring out what had gone wrong. Never had it ranked so low in the American public's estimation. And never had it performed so haplessly in warfare.

The draft ended on the very same day as the war. The young Turks of Powell's generation, preparing to take the military's reigns in the 1980s, had

A 1968 crop of Women's Artillery Corps members in basic training.

learned some valuable lessons in Vietnam. Among those was that a functioning force would be a professional one. There should be no more forcing people to join an organization they resented, and no more of McNamara's lowered standards for entry. The armed forces should instead recruit from the nation's colleges and universities, offer attractive financial and

training incentives, and encourage recruits to choose the military as a career.

For African Americans this new reality presented a double-edged sword. Black enlistment remained high and, along with that of Latinos, continued to grow. The opportunities of a military career still outpaced those found in the civilian world. Even with all

By war's end, fourteen percent of women in the military were black.

of the turmoil of Vietnam, the military had continued its program of moving African Americans into higher ranks and more specialized positions. By 1973, there were fifteen black generals and one black navy admiral. The military academies created programs to actively recruit minority cadets, and the number of black graduates began to skyrocket as a result. Nineteen seventy-six saw thirty-six African Americans graduate from West Point, thirty-nine from Annapolis, and thirty-one from the new Air Force Academy at Colorado Springs.

Similarly, black women were benefiting from the armed forces' slow warming to the idea of

Colin Powell, with his wife Alma and their children, receiving the Legion of Merit in 1972.

employing female soldiers in its ranks. Women still could not enter combat, but in 1967 the Defense Department had lifted the enlistment cap and removed a number of assignment restrictions placed upon female recruits. In policy at least, black and white women were treated the same. By the war's end, over fourteen percent of the military's female charges were black and 431 of those 4,200 women were officers.

Nevertheless, a glass ceiling on advancement had replaced the explicit limitations of previous eras. While some individuals, such as Powell, rose quickly through the ranks, the vast majority remained on the bottom rungs. As the armed forces reorganized and reemerged in the 1980s, they would again provide a model for the direction of American race relations—both the positive and negative aspects. The military would boast a few surprisingly high-ranking African Americans. But, at the same time, far too many blacks would complain about ingrained, institutionalized racism that threw up barriers to their career advancement.

9

A NEW
BEGINNING

The Modern Military

It is impossible to overemphasize the significance of Colin Powell's role in the story of race in America. By the 2000 elections, a few African Americans had staged high-profile presidential campaigns. But no black candidate in American history had been judged to represent a viable threat. Yet in both 1996 and 2000, pundits around the nation discussed Colin Powell as a serious contender for the presidency. And he wasn't even running.

After Powell retired from his post as the country's highest-ranking uniformed military official, politicos on both sides of the isle fell over themselves trying to recruit him for a presidential run—or at least get him to join a ticket as the vice presidential candidate. Powell deflected the unwelcome attention. But, despite his clear statements of disinterest, the recruitment effort began anew in 2000. Repeating his distaste for campaign politics, Powell this time signaled his willingness to serve in an appointed post and ultimately became President George W. Bush's secretary of state. When Bush announced Powell's nomination, a Gallup News Service poll found that an unprecedented eighty-three percent of Americans had a "favorable" opinion of him. His popularity cut across political persuasion, with ninety percent of Republicans and eighty percent of both Democrats and Independents giving him high marks. The only secretary of state to win

It is inconceivable that another black public figure could draw adoration and respect from as broad a swath of America as Powell, pictured here with Dick Cheney and General Norman Schwarzkopf.

approval ratings rivaling Powell's was Henry Kissinger in 1973, whom eighty percent of respondents told Gallup they liked. It's inconceivable that another national black figure could command such respect from a similarly broad swath of the country.

But more than any public figure, Powell also embodies the paradoxes of the American twentieth century's tumultuous racial journey. In one sense, his triumphs provide irrefutable proof that we have slain the twin dragons of racial bigotry and discrimination. Certainly, his life seems to have made reality of an American ideal that black people once could only discuss as mythology—the son of black immigrants, born into a deeply segregated world, rising up on the back of public education to become one of the nation's most revered leaders. But Powell's success is also a bittersweet example of the manner in which America's racial caste system has managed to persevere, despite all of our efforts to dismantle it. He is a trophy flaunted by a nation eager to leave the difficult and often divisive work of conquering racism behind. He was chosen for that role early on and thereby given opportunities to showcase his undeniably impressive talents that the vast majority of African Americans still do not enjoy.

So Powell's legacy is a complex one. But, regardless of what light he is viewed in, there's no disputing the marvel of his achievements. And it is not coincidental that the first black person to rise to his stature did so through a life in the American military.

The All-Volunteer Force

When Major Powell's army limped out of Vietnam, half of its members were classified as Category Four—meaning they had just barely passed the entrance exam and struggled with basic life skills such as literacy. By the time Powell retired in 1993, only four percent of the army was in Category Four. The entire military had spent the previous two decades redesigning itself. The draft ended with Vietnam in 1973, and military leaders began building a volunteer force composed of people who either sought a career in the services or who intended to use their time to build skills and finance a college education. Ninety-eight percent of army soldiers in 1998 were high school graduates—a far higher percentage than that of the nation at large. The post-Vietnam military was no longer a place to dump people who had fallen through society's cracks; it was a place from which to begin rising through society's ranks.

The new military continued to tackle the sort of racial problems the rest of the nation could not. Military race relations may have hit their nadir in the early 1970s. Confrontations resulting from racial tensions, some violent, became commonplace on military installations around the world. So the leaders who intended to reform the services knew the first step would be learning to manage and eventually erase the black-white divide. In his memoir, Powell recalls being assigned to lead a battalion stationed in Korea in the early 1970s. He faced a starkly divided base, with hostility among both blacks and whites boiling over. He and his commanding general were forced to make bridging that gulf a top priority. Their efforts were reproduced on military posts everywhere and were actually part of a larger, systematic program emanating from Washington.

The Defense Department had committed itself to change. It mandated equal opportunity employment programs throughout its divisions and ranks, and it launched groundbreaking staff education programs. It finally decided to take a hard line on off-

Ninety-eight percent of army soldiers in today's military are high school graduates—a far higher percentage than in the nation at large.

post discrimination against black soldiers. And, following another of the recommendations President Kennedy's study board had offered a decade earlier, it began to include reports on race relations in evaluations of officers' performances. Moreover, for the first time, the forces began discussing civil rights in broader terms by considering the need for reforms surrounding women and Latinos as well. Meanwhile, in 1971, the Defense Department once again placed itself on the civil rights cutting edge by creating the Defense Race Relations Institute, which was tasked with training peer educators and developing curriculum on interracial relations. Subsequent civilian programs would draw heavily from the DRRI's experiences and the materials it produced. But perhaps most important, all of these changes were no longer viewed as political niceties offered to placate civil rights activists. Instead, they were driven by a conviction among the military's up-and-coming leaders that force effectiveness depended on the branches' ability to place black and white troops on equal grounds.

The armed forces also continued offering African Americans more opportunities than what could be found in the civilian sector. In 1975, Korea hero Daniel "Chappie" James Jr. became America's first black four-star general, and by 1984 there were thirty-three black general grade officers in the armed forces. Using its ROTC program, the army conducted aggressive outreach on black college campuses throughout the 1970s and 1980s. By the late 1990s, Junior ROTC programs were becoming popular in high schools with predominantly black and Latino students. As a result of this sort of openness, by the time of the American invasion of Grenada in 1983, thirty percent of the military was black. Twenty-six

Post-Vietnam efforts to improve race relations and ensure equal opportunity in the military were finally driven by an understanding of the positive impact they made on force effectiveness.

percent of the troops deployed in the Gulf War were black. And from Powell down, the Gulf force's leadership also contained unprecedented numbers of African Americans.

Problems, of course, have persisted in the new military, and as they arose they foreshadowed the troubles that would eventually plague the integrated civilian workforce. Black soldiers have complained about a glass ceiling. A few standouts, they have argued, skyrocket to the top, while most languish on the lower and middle rungs. At the inception of the All-Volunteer Force in 1973, almost three percent of the service's officers were black. By 1997, that number had risen only to 7.5 percent. And many observers note that these comparatively few African American officers do not often get the tactical operations assignments early in their careers that are necessary to later advance to the colonel and general ranks, keeping the real leadership still predominantly white.

President Jimmy Carter's Secretary of the Army, Clifford Alexander (left), refused to sign promotion lists that he believed excluded qualified minorities and women.

THE ARMY IN THE VANGUARD

If the American military has been the most racially progressive company in the country, the modern army has been that company's star division. The army remained the primary branch of service for African Americans in the All-Volunteer Force. And in recognition of this fact, in 1977 President Jimmy Carter appointed Washington lawyer Clifford Alexander to serve as his secretary of the army. Secretary Alexander was the first African American to lead a service branch and held the post throughout Carter's administration, until 1981. He came to the job with impressive civil rights credentials. He had been a special counsel on civil rights in the Johnson administration and chair of the U.S. Equal Employment Opportunity Commission from 1967 to 1969. A Howard University professor and a television commentator on race issues, he was a well-known voice in the rapidly changing world of black politics. And with the administration's blessing, he launched an unapologetic crusade to boost the number of minority and female officers in his army.

Powell's 1979 promotion from colonel to brigadier general under Secretary Alexander's watch has been a controversial issue, with both opponents and supporters of affirmative action trying to spin it in their favor. When the army review board responsible for nominating generals to the secretary submitted its first list to Alexander, he noted that no black names were on it. He directed the board to take another stab and see if they had overlooked any deserving African Americans. Suddenly, as Alexander put it, "Black people with sterling records emerged on those lists." Colonel Powell was one of them. Affirmative action's supporters, including President Bill Clinton, have held up this story and Powell's subsequent achievements as

proof of such programs' merit. Alexander, however, has argued that this was not an example of affirmative action, and critics of such programs have seized on his stance to aid their cause.

Either way, Alexander's refusal to sign a promotion list that contained no black names ensured that deserving African American officers like Powell would no longer be overlooked. During his tenure, the number of black generals in the army tripled. "My method was simple," Alexander later explained to *New Yorker* magazine writer and African American Studies scholar Henry Louis Gates Jr. "I just told everyone that I would not sign the goddamn list unless it was fair."

The army now boasts several high-command firsts for black officers. From 1977 to 1981, Lieutenant General Julius Becton Jr. commanded the army's VII Corps in Germany, America's largest combat-ready force. By 1982, the army had its first four-star general in Roscoe Robinson Jr.—who was only the second African American to earn four stars in any branch. He was among twenty-two active duty black generals in the army at the time. Having graduated from West Point in 1951, General Robinson's career saw him fight in Korea and lead a battalion in Vietnam. In 1976, he became the first commanding general of the famous Eighty-second Airborne Division, the army's first airborne group. In 1987, General Fred Gordon was appointed the first black Commandant of Cadets at West Point. He graduated from the academy himself in 1962, and went on to serve two tours in Vietnam and one in Korea following the war. His wife, Marcia Gordon, came from a rich black military lineage—her grandfather and father had been Buffalo Soldiers, with her grandfather fighting in the ninth Cavalry in the Philippines at the turn of the century.

General Fred Gordon was West Point's first black
commander, appointed in 1987.

BLACK WOMEN IN THE RANKS

The entire American military has struggled throughout recent decades with the issue of gender in much
the way it had with the issue of race. At its inception
in 1973, the All-Volunteer Force contained less than
two percent female service members, and women
accounted for six percent of its officer corps. By
1997, thirteen percent of military personnel was
female, as was fourteen percent of its officer corps. As
the number of female service members has grown,
the roles in which they are allowed to serve have
slowly expanded as well. In 1993 and 1994, the
Clinton administration's Defense Department finally

By the late 1990s, thirteen percent of military
personnel were female.

African Americans account for around thirty percent of military women.

removed restrictions on women serving on navy combat vessels and air force combat aircraft. The restriction on ground combat remained, which most impacts the army and marines. But the administration did lift the patronizing Risk Rule, which had prevented women from serving in combat support roles judged to be just as dangerous as fighting itself.

From the days of Major Charity Adams's World War II Six Triple Eight Battalion forward, black military women have had to face prejudice on two fronts. They have nevertheless continued to volunteer for service in remarkable numbers. By the late

Despite recent advancements, military policy continues to limit combat roles for women.

1990s, around thirty percent of the overall forces' female personnel were black—just over thirty percent of whom were enlisted and thirteen percent of whom were officers. As with all African American service members, the army has offered the most opportunities for black women. In 1996, nearly half of the army's enlisted women were African American and over twenty percent of its female officers were black—far larger percentages than seen in the other branches.

As with other African Americans and women in general, however, expanding opportunities have not included upper-level leadership roles. Throughout its history, the Army Nurse Corps served as the primary route of advancement for black women. The air force commissioned the military's first black female officers in 1951—Second Lieutenants Evelyn Brown, Fannie Jean Cotton, and Edwina Martin. But those to climb the highest have by and large been army nurses. In 1970, the Nurse Corps' Margaret Bailey became the first black woman to rise to the rank of a full colonel. In 1976, Clara Adams-Ender was the first black woman to graduate from the army's General Staff College at Fort Leavenworth—essentially the branch's graduate school. And three years later, during Secretary Alexander's tenure as the army's civilian head, Brigadier General Hazel Winifred Johnson became the first black woman to rise to flag rank. Not many would follow Brigadier General Johnson, however. By 2001, only five army women, including Brigadier General Adams-Ender, had risen to the flag officer rank. Only one, Brigadier General Von Richardson, remained on active duty. In 1995, however, Air Force Brigadier General Marcelite Harris became the first black woman promoted to major general.

In June of 1995, Brigadier General Johnson, by then retired, spoke at the dedication of the Women in Military Service for America Memorial, located at Arlington National Cemetery, just outside of Washington, D.C. She expressed concern that history would forget the sacrifices black women have made for the nation's defense, even while they faced prejudices from both their male and white colleagues. "Women," she declared, "particularly minority women, have always responded when there was a crisis or need."

NEW HEROES

Just before seven A.M. on a bitterly cold January morning in 1984, hundreds of reporters and citizens gathered at Andrews Air Force Base to greet the All-Volunteer Force's first war hero. Exactly one month earlier, on December 3, a young black navy pilot, Lieutenant Robert O. Goodman, had been shot down during a bombing mission over Lebanon. The Syrian forces that controlled the area took him captive, as the government of Syrian President Hafez Al-Assad thumbed its nose at the administration of President Ronald Reagan. The administration had

Hundreds gathered in pre-dawn hours to greet Lieutenant Robert Goodman, who Reverend Jesse Jackson had freed from Syrian captivity.

taken a hard line against Syria for its role in the Arab-Israeli conflict, and the fact that this rogue state managed to hold an American soldier hostage for a month shocked and appalled the nation. So when Reverend Jesse L. Jackson, having just inaugurated the first presidential campaign launched by an African American, traveled to Syria and won Lieutenant Goodman's release, America swooned. "We feel history is being made here," one woman told reporters at Andrews Air Force Base as she awaited Reverend Jackson and Lieutenant Goodman's arrival. "As black people, we have been a part of it and we feel it is our duty to be here."

The event was largely orchestrated by Jackson's campaign supporters. It nevertheless marked the opening hours of a national celebration in honor of Lieutenant Goodman. In a White House ceremony later that day, President Reagan—his trademark enthusiasm unfortunately tempered by the political embarrassment Jackson's mission handed him—declared, "Today is a homecoming celebration, and all of us are delighted to see Lieutenant Robert Goodman free, safe, and reunited with his family. This young naval officer was flying a mission of peace, and both during and after, he exemplified qualities of leadership and loyalty—qualities of so many fine men and women in our military that we're all proud of."

But this was not only Lieutenant Goodman's homecoming; it was part of a new welcoming for the entire armed forces. Ten years after Vietnam, with a president in office who had launched aggressive efforts to rebuild the military's image, America was finally beginning to forgive its armed services. And as the country reengaged the American military, it found a changed service, with minorities and women fully integrated throughout its ranks. No longer

would news coverage and popular depictions of military heroes erase African American contributions; black servicemen and women were simply unavoidable. They served on every American post from Europe to Georgia and in every role from steward to division commander. And soon, a Reagan administration golden boy would become America's most well known military hero since World War II.

America's Chairman

Throughout his career, Colin Powell moved fluidly between posts commanding troops in the field and positions back in Washington, where he not only managed the military's internal changes but also helped craft American foreign policy. Following his last tour in Vietnam, the military sent Powell to business school at George Washington University and then put him up for the new White House Fellowship program, in which up-and-comers from the academic, business, and military communities were offered an opportunity to learn the nuances of public policy up close and personal. Powell won the fellowship and spent the next year in the Nixon White House's Office of Management and Budget. Along with Congress, OMB controls America's purse strings, and as a result, almost nothing happens in Washington that doesn't involve the vital agency. So Powell learned invaluable lessons about the way things ran inside the Beltway during his year there.

Following Powell's brief tour in Korea the next spring, Lieutenant General Becton—his mentor and a trailblazing black graduate of all of the army's advanced officer training schools—nominated Powell to the National War College at Fort McNair,

Washington, D.C. Accepting 140 students a year, both from the military and from civilian foreign affairs agencies, the War College is the height of military education—as Powell calls it, the military's doctoral program. Upon graduation in 1977, now a full colonel, Powell reluctantly accepted the job that may have been the most significant in leading him down the path to where he is today. The Carter administration courted him to join its national security council staff, but he balked, hoping to avoid becoming overly associated with Washington politicking rather than field leadership. Eventually, however, he relented in part and reluctantly took a job as a special assistant to Deputy Secretary of Defense John Kester. The army brass didn't trust Kester, and they wanted Powell to watch over him.

Powell did not take to the Carter administration. He believed its leadership did not properly value the military and thus contributed to its decline rather than aiding those, like himself, who were committed to revitalizing the organization. (And it was Reagan's intense support for the military that won Powell's continued praise for a president many African Americans detest.) But while working in the Carter Defense Department he expanded the Beltway education he had begun during his White House fellowship, and his performance there convinced the army brass that he was even more valuable in D.C. than in the field. So when the Reagan administration began putting together its Pentagon team, Powell's name was high on the list of recruits. New Secretary of Defense Frank Carlucci hired him to be his right hand-man.

Powell, nervous about developing a reputation as a desk jockey that would limit his military career later, didn't stay long with Carlucci. The army gave him a reprieve and assigned him to training posts at Fort Carson and, later, Fort Leavenworth, where he was promoted to major general in 1982. He longed to command a division, but the army still wanted him in Washington, and in July 1983 incoming Army Chief of Staff John Wickham asked him to serve as the military assistant to Reagan's new secretary of defense, Casper Weinberger. Ever the soldier, Powell responded, "I'll serve wherever I'm sent."

IN THE REAGAN WHITE HOUSE

It was during his tenure serving Secretary Weinberger that Powell built the relationships that would keep him at the center of American foreign policy for the rest of his military and public service career. And he wasn't long in the post before he was knee-deep in his first major foreign policy crisis. In October 1983, a terrorist drove a truck laden with explosives into the marine barracks at the airport in Beirut, Lebanon. Two hundred and forty-one marines were murdered, and both Powell and Weinberger, himself a veteran, were incensed. But their anger turned inward as much as it did toward the terrorists. They had objected to the marines being stationed in Beirut in the first place. As was the case in Vietnam, Powell saw no clear mission beyond "the fuzzy idea of providing a 'presence.'" This was not the way things were supposed to run in the new military. And it reaffirmed for him the bedrock principle of what would become known as the Powell Doctrine: Don't put American troops in danger without a clear and measurable goal. "I was developing a strong distaste," Powell later wrote of his feelings after the Beirut bombing,

for the antiseptic phrases coined by State Department officials for foreign interven-

While working for Casper Weinberger (center), Powell built relationships that would keep him at the center of American foreign policy for years.

tions which usually had bloody consequences for the military, words like "presence," "symbol," "signal," "option on the table," "establishment of credibility." Their use was fine if beneath them lay a solid mission. But too often these words were used to give the appearance of clarity to mud. . . .

What I saw from my perch in the Pentagon was America sticking its hand into a thousand-year-old hornet's nest with the expectation that our mere presence might pacify the hornets. When ancient ethnic hatreds reignited in the former Yugoslavia in 1991 and well-meaning Americans thought we should "do something" in Bosnia, the shattered bodies of marines at the Beirut airport were never far from my mind in arguing for caution. There are times when American lives must be risked and lost. Foreign policy cannot be paralyzed by the prospect of casualties. But lives must not be risked until we can face a parent or a spouse or a child with a clear answer to the question of why a member of that family had to die. To provide a "symbol" or a "presence" is not good enough.

Powell was soon involved in two more high-profile military discussions at Weinberger's Defense Department. The first was America's 1983 invasion of Grenada. Powell characterizes himself as a "fly on the wall" during the planning process, but he says he witnessed another problem he would dedicate his later years to fixing. The military operation, he offers, was needlessly complicated by interbranch competition. Rather than working as a team, the service branches had developed an intense and, in Powell's estimation, unhealthy competition. Driven by each branch's need to prove its individual right to greater resources, Powell saw this competition as the primary problem plaguing the armed forces in the 1980s and 1990s.

He also characterizes himself as a passive witness to the dealings of the Iran-Contra scandal, in which the Reagan administration secretly transferred money to Nicaraguan rebels that it had earned from illegal arms sales to Iran. Powell and Weinberger both objected to aspects of the plan when it was floated early on, and argued that they had no knowledge of its details or full implementation later. Observers have since responded skeptically to this claim, charging that Powell and Weinberger at least had the responsibility of speaking up about the scandal.

In 1986, Powell received his third star and, to his great pleasure, was again sent to lead troops, this time as the commanding general of the prestigious V Corps in Germany. The other Europe-based army corps, the VII Corps, was also led by an African American three-star general at the time, General Andrew Chambers. But again Powell's rapidly moving career prevented him from remaining long in the field, and after only five months he was back in Washington to serve as Reagan's deputy national security adviser, working for his old boss Frank Carlucci. This time it took a personal request from the president himself to bring Powell back. Reagan asked Powell and Carlucci to clean things up in the wake of the Iran-Contra scandal, which was being pinned largely on the National Security Council's former leadership.

A year later, when Secretary Weinberger retired, Carlucci moved to the Defense Department and Powell rose to become the first black national security adviser. "I confess," he wrote in his memoir, "that I also felt along with the pride a certain burden to prove myself as the first African-American to hold the position." Powell's primary job as NSA was managing the administration's arms reduction negotiations with Soviet reformer Mikhail Gorbachev. The experience would prompt him to later speak as a leading American voice on the need to reshape America's military and strategic vision into one appropriate for a post–Cold War world. Many American hard-liners did not trust that the Soviet Union was no longer interested in fighting, but Powell's personal dealings with Gorbachev and his military planners convinced him that times had in fact changed, for good.

LEADING THE JOINT CHIEFS

In late 1988, following the presidential elections, General Powell returned to the army as head of Forces Command, or FORSCOM, which managed all of the army's U.S.-based forces. In his few months in this post, Powell began sketching out his vision of a military once again redesigned, this time shaped to deal with a world in which the Soviet Union was no longer America's primary threat. Powell's reforms turned on the intensely unpopular idea of "force reduction"—scaling back the massive buildup the military had enjoyed during the Reagan years. A year later, he would begin pushing his plan as the newly appointed chairman of the Joint Chiefs of Staff—the highest-ranking uniformed commander in the armed forces. He was the youngest officer, first ROTC graduate, and only African American (or nonwhite of any kind, for that matter) ever to hold the post.

Within twenty-four hours of assuming the chairmanship, General Powell faced the new Bush administration's first military crisis. President George Bush had despised Panamanian dictator and drug lord General Manuel Noriega while serving as vice president, and he longed for an opportunity to depose him as the Central American nation's de facto ruler (Noriega maintained a puppet president to offer the veneer of democracy). Reports of a potential coup to

overthrow Noriega began spilling out of Panama the first night Powell took office. This first coup was aborted, and the administration began preparing plans to aid any subsequent takeover that looked promising. Powell led the Joint Chiefs in putting together an invasion plan.

The plan led to Operation Just Cause, launched in December 1989. A group of marines stationed in Panama had been shot and killed by drunk soldiers in Noriega's corrupt army, and the Bush administration, at the urging of Powell and others, decided that was reason enough to strike. Powell placed great weight on the decision. It was to be America's first significant military action since its botched attempt to rescue hostages from Iran in 1979, and Powell knew they needed a decisive win. Just Cause was just that. The real fighting lasted a little more than a day, with

Powell was the youngest officer, first ROTC graduate, and first non-white person to serve as Chairman of the Joint Chiefs.

twenty-four Americans killed in battle. Noriega and his Panamanian Defense Forces were driven out, and the elected president, whom Noriega had by now driven into exile, was sworn into power.

The mission was clean and decisive—depose Noriega, restore the president—just as the Powell doctrine called for. And it was during his televised media briefings on the action in Panama that America first fell in love with Colin Powell. He was a born communicator. His presence and tone were confident, and his down-to-earth personality translated perfectly over the airwaves. He was soon being compared to Eisenhower, previously America's most beloved military figure—and the same man who, during World War II, refused to sign commendations for soldiers like Powell.

Powell wasn't long in office before launching an invasion of Panama.

The Panama invasion was the first test of the so-called Powell Doctrine.

DOWNSIZING: POWELL'S "BASE FORCE"

General Powell moved from Panama straight to the unpopular business of downsizing the military. He believed that the country needed to establish what he called a "base force"—essentially, the minimum necessary to fight in one or two areas of the world determined to be likely hot spots (Korea and the Persian Gulf) and to move into emergency situations such as that in Panama. This meant massively scaling back the Europe-based forces and, in his mind, making budget cuts as deep as twenty-five percent.

Powell's base force idea not only faced criticism within the military and from congressional conservatives, it also faced strong opposition from minority community leaders, in particular African Americans. By now, it was abundantly clear that the military had offered and would continue to offer young blacks more chances to build skills, finance an education, and take leadership roles than would any organization in American history. Many black leaders reacted to the idea of cutting the number of jobs available there with more vigor than they would for nearly any other economic issue. Critics especially worried about the fate of minority and women officers—fearing the most junior people, where minorities and women were clumped, would be the first to go.

These worries, however, proved unfounded. Between 1987 and 1997, the period spanned by the military downsizing, the percentage of black officers rose from 6.5 to 7.5, while white officers dropped from eighty-nine percent to eighty-two percent of the total. Similarly, male officers dropped from eighty-nine percent to eighty-five percent, while women rose from eleven percent to fourteen percent of the total number. Overall minority representation in the officer corps climbed from 2.6 percent to 4.7 percent

Powell's media briefings during Panama inaugurated America's love affair with the telegenic general.

Powell, pictured here with troops in Honduras, argued America needed only a force large enough to fight simultaneously in what he saw as the world's two hot spots: Korea and the Persian Gulf.

Perhaps this sluggish growth would have proceeded at a more advanced pace had the downsizing not occurred, but there is no evidence that the military's shrinking disproportionately impacted minorities and women.

Operation Desert Storm

Much of Colin Powell's popularity stems from his leadership during what turned out to be America's most popular war since it joined the fray in Europe. On the evening of July 31, 1990, the Iraqi Republican Guard—despotic President Saddam Hussein's elite special forces unit—stormed across the Kuwaiti border, claiming that it was acting in defense of its oil fields, from which Kuwait had allegedly been siphoning. Powell had just declared

the Persian Gulf to be the future's hot spot, and now his predictions were confirmed. The Iraqis made quick work of their neighbor and continued south, appearing to head for Saudi Arabia, where their success would have left them in control of a fifth of the world's oil supply. After a robust internal debate, the Bush administration decided, in President Bush's famous words, that "This will not stand." And on the evening of January 16 (it was three A.M. in Iraq), American warplanes and attack helicopters began bombing Baghdad.

Operation Desert Storm, as the offensive was termed, declared its goal to be threefold: Drive Iraq out of Kuwait, restore the local government, and reduce if not eliminate President Hussein's military capabilities for future attacks. Vietnam had been the first war to receive intense and critical press coverage from the battlefield; the Gulf War was the first to be

Lieutenant General Calvin Waller served as Schwarzkopf's second in command during the Gulf War.

broadcast live on television. With twenty-four-hour cable news becoming a staple of American life, the military campaign became a television event. And its star was the trustworthy, firm yet mild-mannered, and utterly likable chairman of the Joint Chiefs of Staff. For the time being, at least, the fact that he was African American seemed almost a side note.

But while Powell was the most high profile black soldier involved, the Gulf War force contained more African Americans, in higher and broader positions, than had any previous military campaign. Twenty-six percent of the men and women mobilized in the Gulf were African American. (And sixteen percent of the force was female.) One hundred and eighty-two Americans died during the war's forty-three days of bombing and one hundred hours of ground combat. Fifteen percent of those men and women were African American. And while Powell joined Secretary of Defense Dick Cheney in directing the operations from Washington, another black general helped lead the mission from the ground in the Gulf. Lieutenant General Calvin Waller was the operation's deputy commander, serving under General "Stormin' " Norman Schwarzkopf.

Perhaps Lieutenant General Waller's most important role was to act as a buffer between General Schwarzkopf and the rest of the officer staff. Schwarzkopf, somewhat of a Vince Lombardi of military management, was famous for his short temper and unforgiving posture toward his subordinate officers. Enlisted troops loved him; junior officers were all but paralyzed by their fear of him. Waller stepped in the middle, propping the young officers back up after Schwarzkopf tore them down and helping them to get things right the next time. The two men had served together in varied capacities for years—as had Waller and Powell. They studied together at Fort

Leavenworth, and Waller had been Schwarzkopf's chief of staff throughout the 1980s. Lieutenant General Waller explained to PBS's program *Frontline* the state of affairs he found when he arrived at the Operation Desert Storm headquarters in Riyadh, Saudi Arabia:

> **The staff officers appeared to be timid, a little bit like walking around on eggshells. They were very reluctant to give bad news to General Schwarzkopf, for fear that they would cause some minor eruption. And therein was a problem, to make sure that staff officers did not fear saying what needed to be said so that we could get to the bottom of all those issues.**

Many observers have argued that Powell and Cheney sent Lieutenant General Waller to the Gulf specifically to fix this problem. Waller, however, denies that fact. Again, he explained to *Frontline* :

> **You know, a lot of people have said that the reason why General Cal Waller was sent to Saudi Arabia was to keep General Schwarzkopf at peace with the staff and with the commanders. You know, if that is the truth, no one ever instructed me that that's the reason why I was being sent to Saudi Arabia or to Riyadh. I was told by General Powell, as well as by the Army Chief of Staff, that I was going to Saudi Arabia because of my experience as a ground combat commander and that I was going there to assist General Schwarzkopf with the combat operation. . . . Now, it just so happened that that was**

my fourth time working for General Schwarzkopf, and we were friends and had known each other for years, and I certainly understood what was required in working with Norman Schwarzkopf.

Lieutenant General Waller caused some public fuss of his own with an interview he gave a month before the fighting began. He and Schwarzkopf were managing a Herculean task throughout the weeks leading up to Desert Storm's launch. Bush and the United Nations had set January 15 as the deadline for Iraq to pull out of Kuwait—or else. The air war plan had been drawn up and was ready to go well in advance, but the ground attack was another matter. Schwarzkopf wanted to make sure he had enough troops to do the job, and Powell agreed. So, in an historic step, they moved the army's massive VII Corps from Europe to the Gulf. With over 130,000 troops, the VII Corps was the world's largest combat-ready

Over a quarter of the troops deployed in the Gulf War were black.

Powell managed tensions between hawks in the White House and Schwarzkopf over the timing of the Gulf War's start.

force, conceived as America's first weapon in World War III. As Lieutenant General Waller put it, moving them was akin to relocating a small U.S. city. Under this stress, Schwarzkopf and Waller found themselves fending off an impatient White House and press corps, both of which were ready to see the action start. Bush didn't believe he had much political breathing room and did not wish to prolong the waiting period between issuing a threat and acting. The media, meanwhile, had begun asking tough questions about how and when the war would unfold. Responding to questions of that sort, Waller told the press that it would be February at the earliest before the team could launch a ground attack. Bush's critics erupted. What about the deadline? Was this president, already labeled a "wimp," scared to carry out his ultimatum? Why was the White House saying one thing about readiness while the generals on the ground were saying another?

Underlying this tension was a difficult, and heated, dispute between the White House and Schwarzkopf. Hawks within the administration, led by National Security Adviser Brent Scowcroft,

believed that General Schwarzkopf was reluctant to pull the proverbial trigger, and that he would never be satisfied with his readiness, no matter how many troops the White House committed and no matter how much time they gave him to put those soldiers in place. Schwarzkopf knew that he simply didn't have the bodies to fight a ground war against an army estimated to be half a million strong (it turns out this estimate was extremely high). General Powell, now adept at managing the usual gap between Beltway policy makers and military leaders, placed himself between the two sides, massaging each into cooperation with the other. He got Schwarzkopf his troops and delayed the ground war until they were ready. But he made Schwarzkopf and Waller operate the air war in step with the political timeline.

Desert Storm opened with the air force unleashing what would be five weeks of history's most intense bombing on Iraq. President Hussein responded with Scud missiles—old Soviet weapons with little range and less accuracy. Outdated though they may have been, the Scuds proved a thorn in the Desert Storm forces' side when Iraq began launching them at Israeli cities. It was a brilliant move, as it predictably goaded the Israelis into demanding the right to fight back. Allowing them to do so would have completely destroyed the war's remarkable international coalition, which included most of the Arab world. Stopping Scud attacks therefore quickly became a priority, and that effort eventually produced one of the war's first heroes—a black woman.

On the night of January 21, Iraq launched a substantial Scud attack on Riyadh. First Lieutenant Phoebe Jeter led a platoon of fifteen men at a Patriot missile control center in Riyadh (the U.S. used the Patriots to shoot down incoming Scuds). Her job was to monitor incoming missiles and direct her men to

POW Melissa Rathbun-Healy (left) began deflecting intense media attention after she received hate mail for marrying a black man.

destroy them as needed. That night, she told *People* magazine, her monitoring screen "looked like popcorn." She nevertheless successfully led the city's defense and earned an Army Commendation Medal for her work. Future Iraqi Scud attacks would be devastatingly successful, however. On February 25, Scud missiles struck the U.S. barracks at Al-Khobar, killing twenty-eight Americans, including a black woman, twenty-eight-year-old Private Adrienne Mitchell.

First Lieutenant Jeter was among a number of female Desert Storm heroes. Another was twenty-year-old Specialist Melissa Rathbun-Healy, who was the first American female prisoner of war since World War II. She was captured along with another member of her unit while moving heavy equipment vehicles through Saudi Arabia near the contested border area and held for over a month. Specialist Rathbun-Healy, who was white, became a media darling until, after finally being released and coming home, she married a black man. She then began receiving so

much hate mail from her Grand Rapids, Michigan, hometown that she stopped granting interviews.

CRITICISM AND SECOND GUESSES

In Desert Storm's opening hours, and even before it began, some of the most vocal criticism came from the black community. Part of this was party politics—most black congresspeople were Democrats, and they dutifully took shots at an unsure Republican administration facing difficult political decisions. But part of it reflected a lingering ambiguity about military service among the African American community's political leadership.

Vietnam's scars had not healed as easily in the black community as they had in the rest of the nation. To a large degree, this was due to the horrid conditions in which too many black veterans lived.

They were three times as likely to be unemployed as their white counterparts and represented as much as thirty percent of homeless vets in some cities. But it also reflected the general intellectual chaos of black politics in the late 1980s. After a decade of fighting Ronald Reagan's aggressively conservative social agenda, the breadth of problems beyond basic civil rights concerns that threatened the black community was immense, and there was little agreement about which issues were most important or how they should be addressed. On military matters, the pre-Vietnam goals of further prying open the service's doors and leveraging those gains in civil society had never reconciled with the Vietnam-era goals of stopping the massive flow of young blacks to a hellish war zone.

The buildup to the Gulf War placed this unresolved tension under a spotlight, as blacks once again made up a disproportionate share of the fighting force. Some black congressional members declared that the nation was about to repeat the pattern it had seen in Vietnam. Poverty had replaced the draft, they said, driving poor black youth into the military to

find economic opportunities denied them in civil society. Poor black families, they warned, would again carry the burden of America's grief. A *New York Times*/CBS poll found that only fifty percent of African Americans supported the Gulf War, while eighty percent of whites approved. So during a congressional oversight hearing, Democratic Representative Julian Dixon raised the matter with General Powell and Secretary Cheney. The general, who testily recounts the discussion in his memoir, came to the defense of the organization that had taken him so far. "I said that I regretted that any American, black or white, might die in combat," Powell recalled in his memoir.

But black fighting men and women, particularly in an all-volunteer force, would be offended to think that when duty called, they would be excluded on the basis of color. Go into the NCO club at Fort Bragg, I said. Tell the black sergeants that we have too many of them in the Army. Tell them that they will have to stay behind while their white buddies go off to do the fighting. See what reaction you get.

The military had given African-Americans more equal opportunity than any other institution in American society, I pointed out. Naturally, they flocked to the armed forces. When we come before Congress saying we have to cut the forces, you complain that we're reducing opportunities for blacks, I said. Now you're saying, yes, opportunities to get killed. But as soon as this crisis passes, you'll be back, worried about our cutting the force and closing off

Powell's Gulf War media briefings reinforced his star status.

one of the best career fields for African-Americans. . . . There was only one way to reduce the proportion of blacks in the military: let the rest of American society open its doors to African-Americans and give them the opportunities they now enjoyed in the armed forces.

Powell perhaps chose to overlook the charge that the Reagan and Bush administrations had helped to close off opportunities in civil society for African Americans by fighting affirmative action and slashing

funding for social programs developed during the Johnson years. But he nonetheless deftly articulated the paradox of African American politics on military matters. And black community leaders' enthusiasm for the military's outreach to young African Americans remained mixed heading into the twenty-first century.

All the criticism didn't come from the black community, however. Both during the war and for years afterward, hawkish observers would argue that, led by the "reluctant warrior" Powell, Bush had fought a timid war. Why had he not pursued the

Images of the "Highway of Death" helped convince Powell and Bush to pull up their drive to Baghdad.

retreating Republican Guard into Iraq in the war's closing days? Why had he not taken out Saddam Hussein while he had the chance? Powell and Bush have steadfastly defended their decision to pull up after driving Iraq out of Kuwait. Powell stresses that this was the limit of the military mission—kick Iraq out, restore Kuwaiti sovereignty, and destroy the Republican Guard—and with that accomplished it was time to send the troops home. Bush stresses that diplomatic support for expanding the war simply did not exist. And both men note that the world would have only stomached so much more of the relentless bombing of retreating Iraqi forces on what became known as the "highway of death."

But what was remarkable about the Gulf War is that none of the criticism extended to the soldiers in the way it had during Vietnam. Americans of all political persuasions rallied around the men and women who fought Operation Desert Storm and remained strong supporters of the military as an institution as well. Things had certainly changed in the past seventeen years, and this was no coincidence. Buoyed by the massive funding increases of the Reagan years, a new generation of military leaders had orchestrated the organization's return to favor. Vietnam veterans came home to protests; Gulf War troops returned to ticker tape parades reminiscent of World War II.

Keeping the Peace

When the Gulf War ended, the Bush administration returned to the job of scaling America's oversized military back to an appropriate size for the post–Cold War world. Colin Powell's base force became a reality, as first Bush and then President Bill Clinton slashed the armed forces' size. It was supposed to be a leaner, more versatile fighting machine that could respond to emergencies around the world while simultaneously containing Iraq and maintaining readiness in Korea. Powell had understood that America had new enemies. But neither he nor any of the nation's other leaders had fully grasped the changes, both military and diplomatic, that those new enemies necessitated. As a result, America's military and foreign policy apparatus was well positioned to handle the traditional conflicts it found in the Persian Gulf and the Korean Peninsula. But it was ill prepared for the two tasks that would loom largest in the coming millennium: peacekeeping and fighting terrorism.

Bush had been charged with facing down Iraq and reshaping the armed forces. The Clinton administration would confront the unenviable task of managing America's foreign policy through the unknown early years of the world for which Powell was preparing his military. In this new era, television beamed the unimaginable suffering that brutal wars around the world spawned into Americans' homes. As a nation that had always justified its military actions as at least in part humanitarian missions, what responsibility did the United States have in stopping these new atrocities? Where did the country's national interest begin and end? There were, of course, no easy answers to these questions. Some on both the left and the right called for an expansive definition of national interest. Powell urged caution, drawing the ire of both human rights advocates and those in favor of an expanded and more active military.

In Somalia, American troops first deployed with the intent of protecting and aiding humanitarian assistance efforts for civilians were caught in the middle of brutal clashes between rival warlords. But the mission, dubbed Operation Restore Hope, became the premier example of how the American military should not be used in the new era. Troops faced myriad and often conflicting orders about when and how they could engage the enemy, and even about who the enemy was. And the humanitarian mission slowly crept into something more akin to the Panama invasion, but without the clear goals and accompanying force necessary to succeed. The ensuing effort to capture Somali warlord Mohammed Farah Aidid therefore ended in disaster.

The mission had begun in the waning days of the Bush administration, but it had expanded during Clinton's first year. Just as the United States was beginning to pull out in June 1993, the Clinton administration gave in to United Nations pressure to

American helicopters dropped leaflets depicting themselves as friends to the Somali people.

The Somalia campaign started off as humanitarian relief.

In response to United Nations requests, Powell mobilized the Special Forces to hunt down Aidid.

help track down Aidid. So Powell mobilized the Army Rangers and the special operations unit Delta Force, designed as an elite counterterrorism troupe. That fall, those units engaged in a firefight with Aidid's clan, and eighteen soldiers ended up dead. Aidid's supporters dragged one of their bodies through the streets of the Somali capital, Mogadishu, and CNN broadcast the image worldwide.

From Haiti to the Balkans to conflicts throughout Africa, the Clinton administration would struggle to find the balance between honoring America's responsibility on the global stage and avoiding the

A Somali man greets a marine posted near his home.

Marines raided storage facilities for Aidid's weapons in an effort limit his ability to make war.

mistakes of Somalia. Meanwhile, it would begin to confront a completely new sort of enemy in terrorism. Rarely tied directly to a state, terrorist organizations throughout the world began targeting U.S. installations in efforts to undermine American support for local regimes that they opposed. Following the Gulf War, the United States had maintained a military presence in Saudi Arabia. Muslim extremists who had long opposed the secular Saudi government took particular offense to the existence of American

An army photographer trades insignia with Ukraine soldiers in Bosnia.

An operations specialist on board the USS *Gonzales*, which supported the mission Kosovo.

military posts on Saudi soil and vowed to drive the intruders out. In June 1996, a truck laden with five thousand pounds of explosives drove up to the front of the Al-Khobar Towers military housing facility on Saudi Arabia's King Abdul Aziz Air Force Base and detonated. The blast collapsed the entire front side of the building and killed nineteen American troops, injuring scores more. It was the first major terrorist attack against the United States since the 1983 marine barracks bombing in Beirut. And it marked the beginning of America's war with global terrorism.

Powell, who had retired in late 1993, returned to public service in 2001 to serve as secretary of state in the new Bush administration. He again found himself in the spotlight, as America turned to a familiar face for reassurance in what suddenly became an urgent war against terrorism. Nine months into his tenure, on September 11, terrorists flew three hijacked commercial airplanes into the World Trade Center in New York City and the

Pentagon in Washington, D.C. The administration struck back by invading the Central Asian nation of Afghanistan, where the terrorist organization al-Qaeda was believed to be based. It was fitting that Powell would lead this fight, as it was in many ways an extension of the Gulf War he had prosecuted. Al-Qaeda's original home was Saudi Arabia, and its core members were motivated, in part, by a desire to expel the American military presence from their country.

The breadth and depth of America's affinity for Colin Powell would be remarkable even if he were white. It would be inconceivable for an African American but for the fact that he is a military man. Powell's story is proof that the U.S. armed forces have been the site of America's most triumphant civil rights success. Powell regularly declares himself the product of that success and stresses that he stands on the shoulders of pioneering black soldiers before him. Indeed, while the rest of America at best condoned

A terrorist's 1996 truck bomb destroyed the Al-Khobar Towers, a U.S. military housing facility in Saudi Arabia, killing nineteen troops.

the enslavement of African Americans, the Revolutionary War–era military opened its ranks to the likes of soldiers such as Peter Salem. The armed forces have been far from immune to the bigotry of American society at large, but at every turn they have nevertheless advanced relations between black and white Americans ahead of the rest of the nation. This is due in no small part to the fact that both the abolitionist and civil rights movements targeted the armed forces, declaring them to be at the front line of America's race wars. Movement leaders believed that the nation's general embrace of its defenders would extend to even black soldiers and thereby eventually leave bigotry in society at large vulnerable to attack. Generations of black men and women would first have to sacrifice their lives in defense of a country that did not value their contributions, but Colin Powell stands as proof that the movement activists were ultimately correct.

BIBLIOGRAPHY

Books

Adams, Virginia Matzke. On the Altar of Freedom: A Black Soldier's Civil War Letters from the Front. Amherst: University of Massachusetts Press, 1991.

Appiah, Kwame Anthony, and Henry Louis Gates Jr. Africana: The Encyclopedia of the African American Experience. New York: Basic Civitas Books, 1999.

Aptheker, Herbert. American Negro Slave Revolts. New York: International Publishers, 1974.

Astor, Gerald. The Right to Fight: A History of African Americans in the Military. New York: Presidio Press, 1988.

Bell, William Gardner. Secretaries of War and Secretaries of the Army. Washington, D.C.: Center of Military History, United States Army, 1992.

Blakeley, Phyllis R. Boston King. Toronto: Dundurn Press, 1977.

Blakeley, Phyllis R., and John N. Grant. Eleven Exiles: Accounts of Loyalists of the American Revolution. Toronto: Dundurn Press, 1982.

Blassingame, John W. The Frederick Douglass Papers. Vol. 3. New Haven: Yale University Press, 1985.

Buckley, Gail. American Patriots: The Story of Blacks in the Military from the Revolution to Desert Storm. New York: Random House, 2001.

Carroll, Joseph Cephas. Slave Insurrections in the United States, 1800–1865. New York: Negro Universities Press, 1938.

Cooley, Timothy Matthew. Sketches of the life and character of Rev. Lemuel Haynes. 1837. Reprint, New York: Negro Universities Press, 1969.

Drotning, Phillip T. Black Heroes in Our Nation's History. New York: Cowles Book Company, 1969.

Flipper, Henry Ossian. The Colored Cadet at West Point. 1878. Reprint, New York: Arno Press, 1969.

Foner, Philip S. The Black Panthers Speak. New York: Da Capo Press, 1995.

Frankel, Noralee. The Young Oxford History of African Americans. Vol. 5, Break Those Chains at Last, African Americans 1860–1880. New York: Oxford University Press, 1996.

Graf, LeRoy P., and Ralph W. Haskins. The Papers of Andrew Johnson. Vol. 6. Knoxville: University of Tennessee Press, 1967.

——. The Papers of Andrew Johnson. Vol. 7. Knoxville: University of Tennessee Press, 1967.

Gray, Thomas. The Confessions of Nat Turner, the Leader of the Late Insurrection in South Hampton. Richmond: T. R. Gray, 1832.

Ham, Debra Newman. The African American Mosaic: A Library of Congress Resource Guide for the Study of Black History and Culture. Washington, D.C.: Library of Congress, 1993.

Huggins, Nathan. DuBois: Writings. New York: Library of America, 1986.

Johnson, Charles, and Patricia Smith. Africans in America: America's Journey Through Slavery. New York: Harcourt Brace, 1998.

Kaplan, Sidney, and Emma Kaplan-Norgrady. The Black Presence in the Era of the American Revolution. Amherst: University of Massachusetts Press, 1989.

Katz, William Loren. The Black West: A Documentary and Pictorial History of the African American Role in the Westward Expansion of the United States. New York: Simon & Schuster, 1996.

Kennedy, Lionel H., and Thomas Parker. The Trial Record of Denmark Vesey. 1822. Reprint, Boston: Beacon Press, 1970.

Lanning, Michael Lee. Defenders of Liberty: African Americans in the Revolutionary War. New York: Citadel Press, 2000.

—— The African American Soldier: From Crispus Attucks to Colin Powell. New Jersey: Birch Lane Press, 1997.

Lee, Irvin H. Negro Medal of Honor Men. New York: Dodd, Mead, 1969.

MacGregor, Morris J. Jr. Integration of the Armed Forces, 1940–1965. Washington, D.C.: Center of Military History, United States Army, 1985.

Nalty, Bernard C. Strength for the Fight: A History of Black Americans in the Military. New York: The Free Press, 1986.

Nell, William C. The Colored Patriots of the American Revolution. 1855. Reprint, New York: Arno Press, 1968.

Office of the Deputy Assistant Secretary of Defense for Civilian Personnel Policy, Equal Opportunity. Black Americans in Our Nation's Defense. Washington, D.C.: Government Printing Office, 1991.

Powell, Colin. My American Journey. New York: Random House, 1995.

President's Committee on Civil Rights. To Secure These Rights: The Report of the President's Committee on Civil Rights. New York: Simon & Schuster, 1947.

Quarles, Benjamin. The Negro in the American Revolution. Chapel Hill: University of North Carolina Press, 1996.

Rollin, Frank A. The Life and Public Services of Martin R. Delany. Boston: Lee and Shepard, 1883.

Schubert, Frank N., and Theresa L. Kraus. The Whirlwind War: The United States Army in Operations Desert Shield and Desert Storm. Washington, D.C.: Center of Military History, United States Army, 1995.

Scott, Emmett J. Scott's Official History of the American Negro in the World War. New York: Arno Press, 1969.

Skinner, Charles M. Myths and Legends of Our Own Land. Philadelphia: Lippincott, 1896.

Taylor, Susie King. Reminiscences of My Life in Camp. 1902. Reprint, New York: Arno Press, 1968.

Terry, Wallace. Bloods: An Oral History of the Vietnam War by Black Veterans. New York: Ballantine Books, 1984.

Wood, Peter. Black Majority: Negroes in Colonial South Carolina from 1670 Through the Stono Rebellion. New York: Alfred A. Knopf, 1974.

Wright, Kai. The African American Archive: The History of the Black Experience Through Documents. New York: Black Dog & Leventhal Publishers, 2001.

Zobel, Hiller B. The Boston Massacre. Connecticut: Easton Press, 1987.

Additional Sources

DuBois, W. E. B. "An Essay Toward a History of the Black Man in the Great War." The Crisis, June 1919.

Gates, Henry Louis Jr. "Powell and the Black Elite." The New Yorker, 25 September 1995.

Matthews, Eamonn, and Ben Loeterman. "The Gulf War: An In-Depth Examination of the 1990–1991 Persian Gulf Crisis." Frontline, 9 January 1996.

Neely, Mark E. Jr. and Harold Holzer. "The Picture of Bravery." American Legacy, Fall 2000.

Ochs, Stephen J. "American Spartacus." American Legacy, Fall 2001.

Office of the Undersecretary of Defense, Personnel and Readiness. "Career Progression of Minority and Women Officers."

Patrick, Bethanne Kelly. "Pfc. Milton Lee Olive III: With One Selfless Act, Young Combat Veteran Became a Battlefield Legend." Military.com biography.

——. "Gen. Roscoe Robinson Jr.: Army's First Black Four-Star Remembered as Exemplar of Combat Arms Officer." Military.com biography.

Reagan, Ronald. Remarks to Reporters Following a Meeting with Navy Lieutenant Robert O. Goodman Jr. 4 January 1984. Public Papers of President Ronald W. Reagan, The Ronald Reagan Library.

Senior Surviving Officer. USS West Virginia to Commander-in-Chief, United States Pacific Fleet. Report of Action of 7 December 1941. Dated 11 December 1941.

Slacum, Marcia A. "The Homecoming: Early Risers Cheer Jackson, Goodman at Andrews." Washington Post, 5 January 1984.

Tovares, Joseph. "Vietnam Online." The American Experience, PBS Online, 1997. Companion to PBS affiliate WGBH Boston's documentary, Vietnam: A Television History.

PHOTO CREDITS

INDEX